The Legal Aspects *of* Public Procurement

SECOND EDITION, REVISED 2010

Michael Flynn, Esq.
and
Kirk W. Buffington, CPPO, C.P.M., MBA

NIGP: The Institute for Public Procurement.
All rights are conveyed to NIGP upon completion of this book.

The Legal Aspects of Public Procurement

Information in this book is accurate as of the time of publication and consistent with generally accepted public purchasing principles. However, as research and practice advance, standards may change. For this reason, it is recommended that readers evaluate the applicability of any recommendation in light of particular situations and changing standards.

National Institute of Governmental Purchasing, Inc. (NIGP)
151 Spring Street
Herndon, VA 20170
Phone: 703-736-8900; 800-367-6447
Fax: 703-736-9639 Email: education@nigp.org

This book is available at a special discount when ordered in bulk quantities. For information, contact NIGP at 800-367-6447. A complete catalog of titles is available on the NIGP website at www.nigp.org.

ISBN number 1-932315-01-2
ISBN number 978-1-932315-01-1

This book set in Berkeley Oldstyle.
Design & production by Vizual, Inc. – www.vizual.com.
Printed & bound by HBP.

Acknowledgments

I cannot begin to thank all of the people who have guided, supported and inspired me in the writing of my portion of this book. As a litigator and trial lawyer turned law professor, I did not envision that I would ever actually write a book. I first must acknowledge Professor Robert Whaley of The Ohio State University Law School. Professor Whaley is, in my estimation, the preeminent educator and textbook author concerning the Uniform Commercial Code. I hope that my modeling of this book in part on his work is a tribute. I also cannot leave out Professor Thomas Crandall, who taught me the Uniform Commercial Code at the Gonzaga University School of Law. Professor Crandall was a treat to have as a teacher!

I want to thank NIGP for allowing me to contribute to this book and to all of the NIGP staff for their patience. I especially thank my co-author, Kirk Buffington, a good guy.

I also thank my support group at the Nova Southeastern University Shepard Broad Law Center, including Janet Corso, my secretary who is much more than a typist and editor; Venus Zilierus, my research assistant and editor; and to my "West Wing" colleagues, Professors Mike Dale, Anthony ("Tony") Chase, Joel Mintz, Cathy Arcabascio, and Kathy Cerminara. They not only represent the standard of excellence for law teachers and scholars but also make coming to work fun (and they did not laugh too loud when I said that I was going to write this book!).

I also want to thank my wife RoseAnn Flynn, a better lawyer and person than I, my daughter Kelsey Flynn for being who she is and for knowing a lot about computers, and my daughter Mallory for being so smart and cute.

I know I have left out people to thank, and I thank them all now. (I may never have a chance to write this kind of acknowledgement again!). It almost goes without saying that any mistakes or inaccuracies in this book should be blamed on me, and anything that is good about this book is a credit to others.

Mike Flynn

The decision to assist in this portion of the LEAP Text Writing Project was not taken lightly when I was first approached by NIGP. But, even so, I had no idea of the amount of work, time and effort that would ultimately be expended in completing this text. As a full-time working professional with more than 15 years into his working life, I would never have thought I would actually write a textbook. Completing this project has been a true exercise in realizing the potential that is in all of us.

I must first thank the staff of NIGP and especially Carol Hodes who first approached me and believed in me enough to think I could complete this task. Carol became a true sounding board throughout this project. Her humor and good sense kept me going, when I thought I couldn't. I must also thank and acknowledge the contribution of my co-author, Michael

Flynn, who stepped in at the last minute and said, "Yes, we can do this." Without his encouragement and very competent editing, this book would not have begun, much less been completed.

I must also acknowledge the support of both my employer, the City of Fort Lauderdale, and the staff of the Procurement Division, including Patty Oliveira, who assisted in typing and support of my efforts; Leroy Harvey, my research assistant and contributor of one of our chapters; and, of course, the rest of the staff: Linda Wilson, who always told me what she thought; James Hemphill, my able number two, who provided assistance at work; Carrie LeBlanc, Frankie Faison, Richard Ewell, Marsha Perri Bennett, and David Nash, all of whom never thought I was crazy for this endeavor, or at least didn't tell me so to my face. They all made it possible for me to complete this project. In addition, I must acknowledge the support and patience of Mr. Bruce Larkin, my Director, who encouraged me and has mentored me throughout my career at the City.

This book and many other projects would not be possible without the support and patience of my partner and companion Glenn Voeltner. His belief in my abilities was greater than my own.

Obviously, I have left out some who contributed to the completion of this text. I must agree with my co-author that all inaccuracies and mistakes are my responsibility, and what is good about this book is a credit to those mentioned above and to many others in my life.

My thanks to all.

Kirk W. Buffington, CPPO, C.P.M., MBA

Contents

Preface

There can be a no more daunting task than trying to assimilate and explain the legal aspects of public procurement in a comprehensive manner in this text. Yet, that is the purpose of this book, which contains an amalgam of instructional text, statutory provisions, and relevant case studies—real and hypothetical.

The vast amount of law available and applicable to procurement contracts requires that the book focus on some of the most critical and used portions of the law of contracts. However, by picking and choosing the focus of the book, comprehensive coverage of the basics and the nuances of public procurement contracts are not sacrificed.

Chapter 1 contains the essential principles and structure of the United States legal system. It includes the foundations of statutory, common, and administrative law. It also provides a brief, but relevant, history of statutory law affecting public procurement, including a review of legal precedents affecting the protection of market competition. The chapter also includes a short presentation on laws governing intellectual property rights, including patents, copyrights, and trademarks. Finally, this chapter provides an overview of the United States judicial structure and suggested guidelines for performing legal research.

Chapter 2 discusses the legal framework for procurement law and highlights the sources and types of contract and public law. Within the framework of public procurement, the chapter reviews the general principles for applying and interpreting public contract law and describes its relationship to civil and public law, criminal law, and tort law. Of particular importance to the public procurement official, this chapter also discusses the government's authority to contract, the provisions of the law of agency, and the relationship between the principal (typically, the government) and its agents (typically, the public procurement official). As a result, the reader should be able to distinguish between express, implied, and apparent authority. And since statutory law defines the operational parameters of public procurement, this chapter also discusses the framework and key concepts of ABA's *Model Procurement Code for State and Local Governments* in detail as well as other statutes, such as budgetary or federal laws, that impact the public procurement function. At the end of the chapter, the value of developing enabling legislation is emphasized.

Chapter 3 focuses on the basic components of contracting, including the six essential elements needed to form a legal contract. In several cases, these contractual elements are paralleled to the Uniform Commercial Code and public procurement practices. The chapter addresses conditions that could lead to a voidable contract, including mistakes, misrepresentations, trade constraints, and disputes. The chapter reviews the conditions for oral and written contracts and contrasts some of the differences between private and public contracting.

Chapter 4 provides a comprehensive review of Article 2 of the Uniform Commercial Code, which serves as the template of laws governing the sale of goods. Within the chapter, the reader will learn about the range of contract warranties, from warranty of title and express warranties to two essential types of implied warranties. The chapter also offers a good understanding of contractual performance requirements under the Code, which include both the buyer's and seller's rights when performance is not consistent with contractual provisions, the concepts of acceptance and rejection of goods, and the remedies that are available if one of the parties breaches the contract. The chapter addresses special remedies, such as liquidated damages as well as incidental and consequential damages. Finally, the chapter highlights four key concepts within Article 2 of the Code: the statute of frauds, the parol evidence rule, assessing conflicts on the use of different contract forms, and the principle of unconscionability.

Chapter 5 emphasizes the importance of legal terms and conditions when developing formal bids and solicitations. To some degree, the concepts in this chapter are cross-referenced with two other texts produced by the National Institute of Governmental Purchasing, Inc. (NIGP): *Sourcing in the Public Sector*, which provides, in great detail, the framework for developing specifications into a sourcing document; and *Contract Administration*, which emphasizes the critical nature of developing a solid sourcing document as an essential component for minimizing risks during the contract administration phase. The public procurement official is strongly encouraged to read these texts as well because this text is primarily focused on the legal aspects of public procurement and its inter-dependent relationship with sourcing and contract administration.

With permission from Mr. Leroy Harvey, a doctoral candidate at Florida Atlantic University, Chapter 6 provides an excellent dissertation written by Mr. Harvey on the concept of ethics and professionalism in public procurement. The chapter focuses on the origin of ethics and its differentiation as a code of behavior rather than a legal structure. Mr. Harvey offers the perspective of several contributors on the characteristics of a profession and its role in advocating ethical doctrine. Finally, the chapter discusses ethics within public procurement with respect to obligations to employers, suppliers, the profession, the field of public administration, and the general public. The Code of Ethics prescribed by the National Institute of Governmental Purchasing is included as Appendix A and the Code of Ethics prescribed by the Universal Public Purchasing Certification Council is included as Appendix B.

With the phenomenal growth and impact of technology on the public sector, Chapter 7 provides an opportunity to explore the nuances of legal contracting with software providers. The chapter also provides a good framework for understanding the "small print" in contracts and offers eight issues to consider when negotiating software licenses. Legal issues surrounding licensing are discussed, and a detailed checklist is provided to the public procurement official to refer to when executing software licenses.

Chapter 8 concludes the text by providing both actual case law and hypothetical situations for consideration. The case law explores actual legal decisions on the acceptance and rejection of goods and cases involving the rights of both parties in bid awards. The hypothetical studies parallel issues related to Article 2 of the Uniform Commercial Code with respect to liquidated damages, the application of indefiniteness contracts, the unenforceable terms of a purchase order, applying implied warranties to a contract breach, the implications of law of agency, and volume purchase commitments.

Finally, this text provides a good glossary of legal terms, found in Appendix C, that are relevant to the public procurement profession.

The book covers a lot of legal ground, and yet it provides only a glimpse of the legal framework that governs public contracting. Hopefully, the reader will gain a true appreciation and understanding of the breadth and depth of the legal aspects of public procurement.

Chapter 1

The Essential Principles and Structure of the United States Legal System

The center of every public procurement official's responsibility is a contract — that document that creates a legally binding obligation for the seller to deliver the goods or services and for the buyer to pay for them. Whether you call this agreement a purchase order, a letter agreement, a procurement contract or any other name, the contract is the procurement agent's responsibility.

Within this area of responsibility, the public procurement official must know and understand the law of contracts within the context of public procurement. Though not expected to be a lawyer, it is imperative that the procurement agent has a sense about the principles of contract law and the legal consequences of a procurement official's actions. Additionally, being able to talk intelligently with legal counsel regarding strategy, methods, and legal justifications will go a long way in giving the public procurement official greater credibility. There may be times that the public procurement official finds a specific court case regarding a procurement issue that applies to a specific contract of which legal counsel may not be aware.

This chapter focuses on the essential principles and structure of the United States legal system. The reader will begin with the underpinnings of statutory, common and administrative law. The chapter then provides a brief but relevant history of statutory law affecting public procurement, including the Sherman and Clayton Anti-Trust Acts and their affect on the protection of market competition. It also includes a short presentation on laws governing intellectual property rights including patents, copyrights, and trademarks. The chapter concludes with an overview of the United States judicial structure and suggested guidelines for performing legal research.

The Foundation of Law

The American legal system is founded upon English tradition with a singularly American twist. The American legal system looks to statutory law, common law, and administrative law for its guidance.

Statutory law includes the Constitution of the United States and the constitution of the various states and the charters of local government entities. Statutory law also includes the legislative enactments by the U.S. Congress, the various states' legislative bodies, and the legislative actions of local government entities. It also includes the rules, regulations, and guidelines promulgated by federal, state and local government agencies. While the public procurement officer will encounter just a small piece of these different kinds of statutory law dealing with public procurement, this small portion still amounts to volumes of legal rules that a public procurement official must live by.

In contrast to statutory law, **common law** is created by judicial decisions through the court systems. The collection of judicial opinions from both the Federal Court System and the various state court systems makes up the common law. This common law is the court's binding opinion interpreting the statutory law and the conduct of the parties to a lawsuit. Therefore, judicial opinions represent the case law that is aggregated into the common law. This case law has value because it sets a precedent for what a public procurement official should and should not do in particular circumstances.

All of these judicial opinions are collected and published in volumes of books and on Internet sites. These volumes contain judicial opinions from the Federal District Courts, the trial courts, the Federal Courts of Appeals and the Supreme Court of the United States. A separate set of volumes contains the judicial opinions from the trial courts, appellate courts, and the equivalent of the Supreme Court for each state. The various federal and state administrative agency legal rulings are also collected in another set of volumes.

It is important to keep in mind that judicial opinions are added to these volumes frequently. This "common law" consists of an overwhelming amount of legal precedent; however, it is important for the public procurement official to have sufficient knowledge regarding applicable common law precedent to do the job of public procurement efficiently and effectively. One note of caution is that the State of Louisiana, based on its French heritage, eschews the common law and relies almost exclusively on statutory law.

A third type of law is **administrative law** that includes those rules or regulations and orders or directives issued by administrative agencies under the quasi-legislative and quasi-judicial authority. A separate chapter within this text will provide greater detail on the importance of creating administrative law that enables the public procurement official to maximize the efficiency, effectiveness, and economy of the procurement function.

History of Statutory Law Affecting Public Procurement

P*ublic Purchasing and Materials Management*, written by Page (1989) and published by the National Institute of Governmental Purchasing, Inc. (NIGP), contains a good description of the history of statutory law affecting public procurement. The description that follows is a shorter version of his discussion.

The first purchasing-related action for the new American nation occurred in 1778, when the Continental Congress approved the appointment of purchasing commissaries. They were paid 2% of the value of their disbursements in support of the Continental Army. However, it was not until 1792 that the U.S. Congress passed its first statute addressing purchasing. That statute authorized the Departments of War and Treasury to contract on the nation's behalf. The first large acquisition was of six frigates for the Navy. Page (1989) reports the Department of War, under political pressure, awarded contracts for the ships to six different contractors in six different states. Congress later canceled three of the contracts due to delays and cost overruns. Two of the ships built were the U.S.S. Constellation and the U.S.S. Constitution.

The Purveyor of Public Supplies Act, which Congress passed in 1795, was the first comprehensive legislation dealing with procurement. Procurement abuses led Congress to pass the Procurement Act in 1809, which established a general requirement to conduct purchases through the use of formal advertising. It also permitted other procurement options, such as open purchases and advertising for proposals.

The Civil Sundry Appropriations Act, passed in 1861, was the first law to create a statutory preference for formal advertising — that is, competitive bidding. It mandated the use of that selection method except for the purchase of personal services and procurements to meet public exigencies.

During World War II, Congress suspended that 1861 Act and, by executive order, President Franklin Roosevelt created the War Production Board. The executive order gave the board extraordinary powers over procurement. Congress reinstated the 1861 Act after the end of the war.

The 1861 Act governed federal procurement until the passage of the Armed Services Procurement Act in 1947 and the Federal Property and Administrative Services Act in 1949. Those laws applied generally to military and civilian agencies, respectively, and maintained a preference for formal advertising.

In the meantime, the Council of State Governments commissioned a study in 1975 of procurement practices at the state and local levels. That study, entitled *State and Local Government Purchasing*, is updated and republished periodically by the National Association of State Procurement Officials (NASPO) (NASPO, 1997). The study became the foundation of a groundbreaking project undertaken by the American Bar Association, funded in large part by the U.S. Department of Justice, to draft model procurement legislation for state and local governments. The result of the project was the creation of the *Model Procurement Code for State and Local Governments*, approved by the American Bar Association's (ABA) House of Delegates in 1979. Refer to the chapter on statutory and administrative law in this text for a detailed explanation of the Model Procurement Code (ABA, 2000).

The Federal

Acquisition Reform

Act of 1995 ...

simplified ...

the purchase of

commercial items ...

Congress, in 1984, passed the Competition in Contracting Act that made major changes in the manner in which the Federal Government conducted its procurements. That Act amended the Armed Services Procurement Act and the Federal Property and Administrative Services Act. Among the most important changes were the abolishment of the traditional bias toward formal advertising and the authorization of the use of a variety of competitive procurement procedures.

More recently, Congress passed other major reforms of the federal procurement system. The Federal Acquisition Streamlining Act of 1994, among other things, eased the procedures for buying commercial products, raised the small-dollar-purchasing limit to $100,000, required electronic procurement by the year 2000, and encouraged consideration of past performance in selecting contractors. The Federal Acquisition Reform Act of 1995 further refined the procurement process. The changes it made included further simplifying the purchase of commercial items between $100,000 and $5 million and authorizing certain design-build selection procedures.

Statutory Law Affecting Market Competition

Federal and state antitrust laws and federal and state unfair and deceptive trade practice laws seek to control commercial behavior by prohibiting unfair competition, preventing the concentration of economic power, and proscribing deceptive and unfair business practices. A comprehensive discussion of the various federal and state antitrust and unfair and deceptive trade practice statutes is beyond the scope of this text; however, public procurement officials need to be familiar with key laws in order to recognize and report potential violations to legal counsel.

The Sherman Antitrust Act

The U.S. Congress enacted the Sherman Antitrust Act in 1890, which makes antitrust violations a crime. Section 1 of the statute prohibits any contract or combination or conspiracy that results in a restraint of trade that effects interstate commerce. The key to a Section 1 violation of the Sherman Antitrust Act is proof of collective action by two or more entities. Section 2 of the statute prohibits every person from monopolizing any part of interstate trade or commerce. In contrast to a Section 1 violation, a Section 2 violation of the Sherman Antitrust Act is primarily concerned with unilateral conduct and requires a threshold finding of monopoly power.

Section 1 violations of the Sherman Antitrust Act can be categorized into horizontal restraints of trade and vertical restraints of trade. Horizontal restraints of trade in violation of Section 1 of the Sherman Antitrust Act concern agreements among rival competitors to restrict output, fix prices, divide markets and exclude other competitors. For example, when all of the manufacturers or all of the wholesalers or all of the retailers of a product agree to raise the price of the product, then such action by the manufacturers or the wholesalers or the retailers would violate Section 1 of the Sherman Antitrust Act. Perhaps one of the best examples of this kind of violation can be found in an examination of the oil companies and the price of gas. The crucial proof problem in this kind of antitrust case is proof of an agreement among competitors. Although proof of an actual written or oral agreement between competitors is possible, an agreement in violation of Section 1 of the Sherman Act can also be proven by circumstantial evidence. For example, proof that on a particular day every month for a certain period of time, the price of gas sold to gas stations went up by $.02 per gallon is some proof that the oil companies may have an agreement to fix the price of gas.

Another customary practice that may result in a violation of Section 1 of the Sherman Act occurs when two or more competitors agree to allocate geographic markets. For example, if one group of onion growers agree with another group of onion growers to only sell onions in a particular number of states in the western part of the United States and the other onion growers agree to only sell onions in other particular states in the western part of the United States, then this kind of "horizontal" agreement to divide market territories would be illegal.

Finally, another kind of Section 1 violation involves a group boycott by rival competitors. For example, when a group of dentists in Indiana collectively refused to provide x-rays of patients to insurance companies who wanted to use the x-rays to reassess the dentists' charges for services and implement cost containment measures, such an agreement violates the prohibitions of Section 1 of the Sherman Antitrust Act.

From the perspective of the public procurement official, one of the most common violations of Section 1 of the Sherman Antitrust Act is *bid* rigging — an agreement by two competitors to not bid against each other for a public works job. Some of the signs that bid rigging may be involved in a project include the following:

- Bids seem to be awarded on a rotating basis to the same limited group of contractors;

- The same business is the low bidder for certain kinds of contracts;

- Few, if any, companies submit bids for a project; and

- There are noticeable changes in the price of goods or work among all businesses that bid on a contract.

One need only look at the ongoing saga of bid-rigging among milk suppliers. For example, let's say that a single school district solicits bids to provide individual milk cartons for school lunches. In response to this solicitation, the six major suppliers of milk in the region of the school district agree which milk supplier will be the lower bidder to supply milk cartons to this school district. In return, the designated winner of the school district bid submits a bid to supply the milk cartons for the school district for one year at an inflated market price. The other five milk suppliers in the region either do not bid on the contract or submit a bid that is much higher than the designated milk supplier's bid. The school district, in evaluating the bids in response to its solicitation, with all of the terms and conditions of the bids and bidders being the same, chooses the designated milk supplier as the bid winner. This kind of agreement to fix an inflated price to supply milk to the school district by "rigging" the bidding process for the contract is a classic example of a horizontal restraint of trade in violation of Section 1 of the Sherman Antitrust Act.

Aside from horizontal restraints of trade, Section 1 of the Sherman Act also prohibits vertical restraints of trade, that is, for example, an agreement between a manufacturer of a product and its wholesale sellers of the product that sets the minimum price at which the product may be sold. This kind of "vertical" agreement is labeled resale price maintenance. Such agreements imposed by a manufacturer on a wholesaler or by a wholesaler on a retailer have occurred in many industries. For example, when the manufacturer of automobile parts and the wholesaler of those automobile parts agree not to sell the parts for less than a certain dollar amount to a car dealership or parts store, then the price of the parts may be inflated above the market value of the part. This kind of agreement insures an inflated profit for both the parts manufacturer and wholesaler and inflates the cost of the automobile parts to the consumer.

Another example of a vertical restraint of trade in violation of Section 1 of the Sherman Antitrust Act, is a tying arrangement. In this scenario, a seller of a good or product requires a buyer to agree to purchase one particular item in order to purchase another particular item. For example, if the seller or lessor of mobile home park land for placement of a mobile home conditions the purchase or lease of such land to the purchase of a mobile home from that same seller or another designated seller of mobile homes, this kind of "conditioned" agreement is an illegal tying arrangement. This kind of anti-competitive conduct requires a showing that the seller who is "tying" the sale of one product to the sale of another product has substantial market power. Perhaps, an interesting example of this kind of tying arrangement can be seen in the aftermath and re-housing of many of the citizens of New Orleans after Hurricane Katrina.

Although this review of Sherman Antitrust Act violations is by no means comprehensive, the public procurement official needs to be aware of the application of the principles and concepts contained in the prohibitions of the Act that will apply to public works and other projects.

The Clayton Antitrust Act and the Robinson-Patman Act

The U.S. Congress enacted the Clayton Antitrust Act in 1914 to strengthen and expand the prohibitions contained in the Sherman Antitrust Act. The key differences between a violation of the Sherman Antitrust Act and the Clayton Antitrust Act are:

1) A violation of the Clayton Antitrust Act does not require proof of an agreement or conspiracy or concerted action among commercial entities to make out a violation;

2) The penalties under the Clayton Antitrust Act include a civil remedy, which means that private citizens do have the right to initiate a lawsuit and recover money damages for a violation;

3) The activities complained of as a violation must be in, not just effect, interstate commerce.

The Clayton Antitrust Act and its amendments contained in the Robinson-Patman Act prohibit price discrimination, certain kinds of mergers, interlocking directorships between competing companies, certain kinds of exclusive dealing, and refusal to deal arrangements that substantially lessen competition.

The courts and legal scholars have struggled with the application of both the Clayton Antitrust Act and most notably the Robinson Patman Act. The legal nuances in applying these statutory provisions stem from the varying economic perspectives that a court may adopt. However, the purpose behind both of these statutory provisions is to protect small businesses and consumers from the predatory practices of other larger businesses who wield monopoly power.

Perhaps, the best way to understand the thrust of both the Clayton Antitrust Act and the Robinson Patman is through case studies. For example, let's say that one manufacturer of pre-packaged pies controls over three-fourths of the pre-packaged pie market in a particular state and makes a high profit on its sales. A national manufacturer of pre-packaged pies notes the high profit margin of this other essentially local and state confined pre-packaged pie manufacturer and is attracted to enter that market. In entering this market, the national pre-packaged pie maker offers its product at a price well below the existing supplier of the product. In fact, the national pre-packaged pie supplier offers to sell its pies below its actual cost to produce the pies and well below the price it offers its pies in any other state. The thinking and planning of the national pre-packaged pie supplier is that because of its market power it can offer its pies below cost in one particular state and make up for its loss in the volume of sales of its pies in other states. Further, the national pre-packaged pie manufacturer figures that such "below cost" pricing will eventually force the local, pre-packaged pie supplier to go out of business. Once this occurs, and the national pre-packaged pie supplier can afford to be patient, then the national pre-packaged pie supplier can raise prices above the market price level to recoup if not exceed its temporary loss from selling below cost. This kind of "predatory pricing" amounts to geographic price discrimination in violation of the Robinson-Patman Act.

From this example one can see that the key to prohibitions contained in the Clayton Antitrust Act and the Robinson-Patman Act is proof of market power in the offending business. This is precisely the intended effect of the Clayton Act, namely, to prevent monopolies and the use of monopoly power to lessen competition and injure consumers. The controversy surrounding the enforcement of these Acts centers on the notion that some kinds of monopolies may actually be more economically efficient and benefit consumers. This debate is still ongoing and will be the subject of more extensive academic, judicial and political discussion.

From the perspective of the public procurement official, the prohibitions of the Clayton and Robinson-Patman Act apply equally to public works and other contracts and are additional enforcement tools available for use.

The Federal Trade Commission Act

The U.S. Congress passed the Federal Trade Commission Act in 1914. This established the Federal Trade Commission as an independent regulatory agency of the Federal Government empowered to enforce the Clayton Antitrust Act and the Robinson-Patman Act. In addition, with the passage of the Wheeler-Lea Amendment to the Federal Trade Commission Act in 1938, the Federal Trade Commission's power was extended to cover any business practice that results in unfair competition and any deceptive and unfair business practice.

State Antitrust Laws

State antitrust laws mirror the prohibitions contained in the Sherman and Clayton Antitrust statutes and provide for private and public, civil, and criminal enforcement. In addition, state unfair and deceptive trade practice statutes borrow the proscriptions of the Federal Trade Commission Act; however, unlike its federal counterpart, state unfair and deceptive trade practice statutes permit private enforcement.

State and Federal False Claim Statutes

These statutes prohibit filing a false claim or statement with the government. In the context of procurement, these statutes prohibit a vendor or other provider of goods or services from falsifying or inflating in any way a request for payment. These statutes provide for both public and private enforcement and civil and criminal penalties. These statutes also contain generous "whistleblower" provisions. In this situation, if the government is successful in a subsequent lawsuit involving a person who reports a false claim to the government, that person reporting the violation will receive a percentage of the money recovered in the lawsuit.

Statutory Law Governing Public Records

At the federal, state, and local government levels, there are a variety of public record, open meeting and Freedom of Information Act statutes. These statutes provide the guidelines under which the public is entitled to review the work and records of government. This means that bidding files and other records as well as meetings where procurement and other kinds of purchasing contracts are discussed may be accessible to the public.

The statutes vary by locality and jurisdiction, so it is impossible to discuss the various scenarios within the context of this text. Nevertheless, it is absolutely critical for the public procurement official to clearly understand and operate under these statutory laws. It is also critical to understand the breadth of the applicable law in terms of the inclusion or exclusion of working documents, handwritten notes, e-mails, and drafts. For example, in some jurisdictions, a proposal submitted by a firm in response to a Request for Proposal (RFP) is subject to the public records laws; while, in other jurisdictions, the submittal is considered a working or draft document and is, therefore, not subject to the public records laws until such time as the proposal is negotiated and finalized via a contract.

...the public procurement official must have a full understanding of the conditions for which a potential supplier submits proprietary and trade information...

Finally, within the context of public records, the public procurement official must have a full understanding of the conditions for which a potential supplier submits proprietary and trade information to the public entity for evaluative purposes. Typically, this information is submitted as a confidential document by the potential supplier and must be returned upon completion of the evaluation process. However, the public procurement official must be clear and consistent in treating confidential and proprietary information within the parameters established by the jurisdiction's open records law.

Statutory Law Governing Intellectual Property Rights

Intellectual Property Rights refers to the right of a holder of a patent, copyright, or trademark to be protected from the unauthorized use of the patented, copyrighted, or trademarked items. The nuances of patent law, copyright law, and trademark law are well beyond the reach of public procurement officers; however, public procurement officers should be generally aware of the parameters of the protections afforded to the holders of such rights.

Patent Law

Patent law is designed to protect the original inventor's rights in a product or process. Patents must be registered with the U.S. Patent Office. Upon submitting an application for a patent, the patent holder is entitled to protection for a period of 20 years.

While ideas are not subject to patent protection, the end product or process generated as a result of an idea may be patented. For example, the idea of intermittent automobile window wipers cannot be patented; however, the design for and the actual physical components of intermittent automobile window wipers can be patented. In addition, a process may be patented. For example, the chemical process used to produce a particular drug as well as the drug itself can be patented both as a process and a product.

Yet, not all products and processes can be patented. The product or process must be "new"; that is, the product or process must be novel or at least a new and improved version of an existing product or process. For example, a company that creates a "new and better" mousetrap can seek the protection of patent law.

The purpose of obtaining a patent is to prevent the use of a patented product or process without the holder's permission. The unauthorized use of a patented product or process would constitute patent infringement and subject the violator to legal liability, including money damages. These money damages can be substantial and include lost profits, payment of a fee for the past, present and future use of the patented item, and an injunction prohibiting the violator from using the patented item without permission.

Copyright Law

Copyright protection is granted in favor of an author of any original work that is produced in a medium from which the work can be reproduced. What is not protected by copyright is the actual content of the original work. Consequently, an oral presentation or speech cannot be copyrighted because it is not reduced to a tangible medium; however, the tape recording or printed pages of a speech can be copyrighted. Likewise, a compact disc of music can be copyrighted, but actual music notes that make up the music cannot be copyrighted.

Copyright protection is provided for the life of the author plus 70 years. The employer, absent some kind of contrary agreement, owns the copyright of works produced by an employee. So, too, are works "made for hire" — that is, works produced by independent contractors at the request of another. In this instance, the copyright protection is provided for 120 years from the date of creation or 95 years from the date of publication of the work, whichever is shorter.

The major exception to copyright protection is fair use. The fair use doctrine permits the reproduction and use of copyrighted material for the purpose of teaching, scholarship, research, reporting, comment, and criticism. For example, this exception permits a literary critic for a newspaper to reprint excerpts from a copyrighted book in a book review. However, the fair use doctrine has limits based on the amount of copyrighted material that is being "fairly used" and whether the "fair use" of the copyrighted material is for profit. Additionally, the type of work that is copyrighted and the market effect of the "fair use" are all factors that limit the application of the fair use doctrine. For example, the fair use doctrine exception to copyright protection would not apply to a teacher who photocopies a 500-page book for the students and then sells the photocopied book at a profit.

For the public procurement official, the copyright protection of computer software is a good case study and an important issue. Most, if not all, software is copyrighted. Consequently, the holder of the copyright has the authority to limit the use of the copyrighted material. On the other hand, the copyright holder may also permit the use of copyrighted material. In the context of software, the holder of the copyright may enter into a contract that grants a prospective user a license to use the software. These software licenses come in many shapes and forms.

An individual software license would permit one person to load and use software on one computer. Copying or loading the software into another computer would constitute a copyright violation. A "machine" software license would permit the software to be used on a specific computer. This would require the purchase of a license for every computer that uses the software.

A "site" software license usually permits the software to be used at a single location on a specified maximum number of computers and/or provides for a discounted price on multiple copies of software. The various terms and conditions in these kinds of software licenses differ from the particular needs and circumstances of both the copyright holder and the licensee. However, a "site" software license is usually restricted to a specific organization, a single geographic area, a specific department within a location, or a particular school. For example, the latest version of accounting software may be covered by a site license that is restricted to the business office of a corporation.

The "enterprise" software license is similar to the site license, but it permits the standardized use of a software program for an entire organization. This type of license usually runs for a limited time and may be subject to renewal. The most visible example of this type of enterprise license is a multinational corporation's license to use Microsoft Word.

A "suite" license allows a single user to purchase permission to use a group of many applications of the software. The license to use a "suite" of software applications is sold as one unit, and the various applications of the software covered by this license cannot be separated and given to other users. In short, a suite license permits a software package that has a number of different applications to be loaded into a single computer. For example, an in-home educational software package may require a suite license.

Finally, a "concurrent" license permits a maximum number of users to simultaneously connect to a software application within a network. For example, if the concurrent license allows 10 simultaneous applications for an agency staff of 25 employees, up to 10 of the 25 employees can connect to that particular software program at the same time. The concurrent licensee in this example would need a license for 10, not 25, copies of the software program.

The unauthorized use of copyrighted software or any other type of copyrighted material would amount to copyright infringement.

The unauthorized use of copyrighted software or any other type of copyrighted material would amount to copyright infringement. The penalties for copyright infringement can be severe. In some instances, copyright infringement has led to criminal prosecution of the violators. Regardless, every person who participates in copyright infringement is subject to legal liability. This means that any individual as well as any organization and its employees involved in copyright infringement will be liable for the violation. The legal remedy afforded a copyright holder includes money damages for lost profits, injury to reputation, lost business opportunities, payment of a copyright fee for past, present and future use of the copyright material, and an injunction prohibiting the use of the copyrighted material by the violator without permission.

Trademark Law

Trademark law protects distinctive marks or other symbols by which an author seeks to specially identify a product, good, or service. The original purpose of trademark protection was not only to protect the trademark holder's rights to a distinctive mark or symbol but also to prevent consumer confusion or deception regarding similar products, goods, or services. For example, the Nike "swoosh" is a trademark as was the RCA gramophone with the perched dog. Trademarks should, but are not required, to be registered with the Federal Government. Some of the advantages of registering a trademark include:

    a. a presumption that the trademark belongs to the person or entity that registered the mark;

    b. notice to other persons of the mark and

    c. ease in registering the mark in foreign countries,

A trademark's registration extends for ten years and may be renewed.

The penalty for trademark infringement is substantial. The violator of a trademark will be subject to an injunction that will prohibit the violator from using a mark or symbol. In addition, a violator may be liable to pay for the trademark holder's attorney's fees and lost profits including treble damages.

An Overview of the United States Judicial Structure

The United States has one of the most complex yet simple legal systems in the world. Most geographically large nations with a federal system have only a few regional courts from which cases may be appealed to one national court. In the United States, each of the 50 states has a separate court system composed of trial, intermediate appellate, and supreme courts. There is some variation across states in how courts are structured and named (Council of State Governments [CSG], 1988, pp. 157-160). In Florida, for example, there is a county court in each of Florida's 67 counties and a circuit court in each of Florida's 20 judicial circuits and a district court of appeals in each of Florida's five appellate districts and one Florida Supreme Court.

In addition, the United States has a Federal Court System consisting of trial courts, intermediate appellate courts, and the Supreme Court. There are presently almost 100 federal trial courts (called District Courts) with at least one in every state, the District of Columbia (DC), and the territories of Guam, Puerto Rico, the Northern Marianas, and the U.S. Virgin Islands. There are presently 12 federal intermediate appellate courts called the Circuit Courts of Appeal. One of the Courts of Appeal is located in Washington, DC, and the others are spread regionally across the 50 states. In 1982, the U.S. Congress also created a Court of Appeals for the Federal Circuit that has nationwide original and appellate jurisdiction over specific kinds of lawsuits.

Both state and federal court systems also have specialized courts of limited jurisdiction. At the state level, examples include juvenile, probate, small claims, and traffic courts. At the federal level, examples include international trade, military appeals, and tax courts.

Courts at the same level in either the federal or state court structure perform basically the same function. *Trial courts* are where most criminal and civil cases begin. There are two parties to each trial court case: (1) the *plaintiff* (the individual or government that brings a civil complaint) or the *prosecution* (the government that brings a criminal charge), and (2) the *defendant* (against whom the complaint or charge is brought).

As mentioned earlier in this text, case law creates judicial precedent. For example, when the Fourth District Court of Appeals in Florida decided *Port Everglades Authority v. International Longshoremen's Association, Local No. 1922-1*, it became binding on all public agencies within that jurisdiction (the Fourth District); however, it was not binding outside that jurisdiction. Had a similar case come up in another part of Florida, however, either side in the suit could have cited this case as persuasive precedent. As this case involved state statue, the "court of last appeal" would have been the Florida Supreme Court.

The title of most trial court cases takes the form of plaintiff or prosecution v. defendant. Hence, Smith v. Jones would be a civil case in which Smith brought a complaint against Jones. North Carolina v. Smith or United States v. Jones could be either civil or criminal cases; but, in both cases, the individual is the defendant. However, not all court cases involve adversarial parties (e.g., bankruptcy, probate, or guardianship cases). The title of such cases takes the form, *In re* Smith, meaning in the matter of or concerning Smith.

Trial court judges (and often, but not always, juries) listen to witnesses, see evidence presented, and consider legal arguments before reaching a verdict. It is at the trial court level that verdicts are handed down and sentences imposed. Most legal disputes end at the trial court level.

Appellate courts exist in both state and federal court systems to hear appeals of trial court decisions. Either or both a plaintiff and defendant may appeal a civil trial court decision. An appellate court case involving adversarial parties first lists the name of the party appealing the adverse judgment of the lower court (called the *petitioner* or *appellant*) followed by the name of the party against whom the appeal is taken, who is usually the winner in the lower court case (called the *respondent* or *appellee*). For example, in a trial court case affecting Smith (plaintiff) v. Jones (defendant), if Smith wins and Jones appeals that adverse judgment, the appellate court case would become Jones (petitioner) v. Smith (respondent).

Appellate courts, composed of judges but not juries, are usually limited to reviewing points of law rather than questions of fact or evidence. Appellate courts function to insure that the procedural and substantive legal rights of the parties were properly viewed at the trial court level. Therefore, the appellate court's decision is to affirm or reverse the lower court's decision. Sometimes the appellate court decision is to remand (i.e., to return) the case back to the lower court for retrial, with instructions concerning how the lower court should differently interpret a point of law or follow a legal procedure.

At both the intermediate appellate and Supreme Court levels, courts usually but not always accompany their decision with one or more written opinions. The opinion of the **court** states the reasoning accepted by the majority of the justices joining in the court's decision. Sometimes called a *majority opinion*, opinions of the court are announced by one member of the majority. In contrast, a *per curiam opinion* by the court signifies that all of the members of the Court of Appeals agree with the written opinion prepared by the court.

There also may be concurring and dissenting opinions. *Concurring opinions* express the reasoning of justices who agree with the court's decision but on differing grounds. *Dissenting opinions* present the arguments of justices who disagree with both the decision and the opinion of the court.

In all state court systems as well as in the Federal Court System, there is a "court of last resort" or *Supreme Court* to give a final review to appeals of adverse decisions handed down by lower courts. At either the state or federal level, such supreme courts accept for review relatively few appeals from lower court decisions. The losing party can, under certain conditions, petition a higher court to grant a writ of certiorari. A *writ* is a written court order requiring that some action be taken or be prohibited. A writ of *certiorari* is an order from a higher court to a lower court requiring that the record of a case be sent up for review. Most cases reach the U.S. Supreme Court on a writ of certiorari. The U.S. Supreme Court grants such a writ when four or more justices agree that the Court should review a case. When any higher court denies a petition for writ of certiorari, the decision of the lower court stands.

State or Federal Supreme Court decisions, in the relatively few cases where they are accepted for review, can have tremendous importance. They are binding on all lower courts and often involve constitutional or statutory interpretations of broad impact.

Legal Research

Laws are those rules governing relations between people. Given the complex distribution of law-making authority spread throughout the federal, state and local government entities, legal research can lead in many directions. Because of the constitutional division of power across levels of American government, the public procurement official may need to research laws at the federal, state, or local level. In this section, the focus will be limited to legal research at the federal level including international law involving the United States; however, the search skills and strategies appropriate to legal research at the federal level apply equally well to state and local laws.

Two Types of Legal Sources: Primary and Secondary Sources

As with other forms of library research, legal research requires locating and using primary and secondary sources. In legal research, *primary sources* are publications that present the law itself; i.e., the actual text of constitutions, statutes, regulations, court decisions, or treaties. *Secondary sources* are those publications that describe, summarize, and analyze the conflicts and consequences resulting from the application of those laws. It also includes finding aids for legal research in the form of indexes to court decisions and treaties.

Two Types of Primary Legal Sources: Chronological Series and Codes

Within all three areas of legal research, one will find that primary legal sources fall into two basic types of publications: (1) chronological series that compile the full text of statutes, regulations, and court decisions in the order in which they were adopted and (2) codes that collect or arrange the law according to topics or subjects.

Since statute, case, and administrative law are all continuously being adopted or modified, their respective legal chronological series are frequently updated. However, the most up-to-date published sources of federal and state law will usually be issued as a chronological series.

In contrast, legal *code* is a subject-organized, topical, or encyclopedic arrangement of the actual text of the laws in force. In effect, it is a very detailed subject index to the law. A code is usually published as a large, multi-volume compilation or set that is updated with *pocket parts* (paperbound supplements that update some legal codes and digests and are found in pockets attached inside the cover of hardbound volumes).

Examples of Legal Citations	
Chronological Series Citations	
(statute)	General state policy on public records, Chapter 119 of Florida Statues
(case)	Port Everglades Authority v. International Longshoremen's Association, Local No. 1922-1
Code Citations	
(statute)	Title X, Public Officers, Employees, And Records Chapter 119, Public Records
(case)	652 So. 2d 1169

Citation Format for Primary Legal Sources

The standard reference work on legal citations is *A Uniform System of Citation* (often called the "Blue Book"). At the time of this writing, the Blue Book was available to order online at www.legalbluebook.com/.

Since citations to all primary legal sources (chronological series or codes) follow a common pattern within each type, now is a good time to describe the two patterns. At a minimum, a citation to an entry in a legal chronological series should contain three elements in the following order of presentation:

1.	The short title or popular name of the statute, regulation, case	
2.	Three pieces of information about the publication in which the statute, regulation, case, or treaty is found:	
	a.	volume number
	b.	the abbreviation of the main title of the chronological series
	c.	the starting page number
3.	The year in which the statute was enacted, the regulation was issued, the case was decided, or the treaty was ratified (not necessarily the year of publication)	

At a minimum, citations to entries in legal codes contain just two elements: the facts of publication that inform the researcher where the entry is located in the code and the year of the edition or supplement. These facts of publication include: the title number, an abbreviation of the code's title, and the section number (§).

Chronological Case Law Sources

Court reporters are compilations of court decisions and opinions arranged by date of decision. The official court reporter for the U.S. Supreme Court is *United States Reports*. Until 1874, cases in *U.S. Reports* were cited by the last name of the editor (e.g., *Dred Scott v. Sandford* was cited as 19 Howard 393 [1857]). In 1875, the first 90 volumes of *U.S. Reports* (Dallas through Wallace) were renumbered consecutively, and both earlier and later cases began to be referred to by their *U.S. Reports* citations. However, citations prior to 1875 cases still frequently use the earlier form. All following volumes have continued the U.S. Reports numbering sequence initiated in 1875 (e.g., *Plessy v. Ferguson*, 163 US 537 [1896]).

Court orders are notices or directives issued by a court.

As the Court decides each case, first the U.S. Government Printing Office issues the decision and its accompanying opinion(s) as a separate *slip opinion*. To provide even quicker access to current Supreme Court decisions, your library may subscribe to either *The United States Law Week* or *Commerce Clearinghouse Supreme Court Bulletin*. Both mail to subscribers copies of all slip opinions within a week of release by the court. Slip opinions are subsequently compiled into paperbound volumes (also called *advance sheets or preliminary prints*). These, in turn, are replaced with hardbound volumes after the end of each *October Term* (which ends the following June or July).

The slip opinions are usually published within two to three weeks of their decision date. After each term of the court, a multi-volume, paperbound preliminary print of *U.S. Reports* is published. The paperbound preliminary print offers, in addition to the case reports, a subject index, a table of cases reported that is alphabetized by the names of both parties (except the United States), and court orders.

Court orders are notices or directives issued by a court. The most significant types of orders are those granting or denying petitions for writs of certiorari and motions to file *amicus curiae* (friend of the court) briefs. If allowed to submit amicus curiae brief, a person or organization — that is not a direct party to a case — is allowed to present to the court written arguments concerning resolution of the issues in dispute.

Unlike the slip opinions, the preliminary prints give the volume and pagination information used in case citations. After a time lag of about two years from the end of a term, the final version of *U.S. Reports* is published in hardbound volumes. These have the same additional sections as the preliminary prints. The bound volumes also contain both a "Table of Cases Cited" in the cases reported and a section listing orders announced by the court.

Besides *U.S. Reports*, your library may have one or both of the two commercially published, annotated court reporters. *United States Supreme Court Reports*, published by Lawyers

Cooperative Publishing, is cited with the abbreviation LEd or LEd 2d. The first LEd series contains all of the opinions in 1-349 US Volume I of LEd 2d. The second series starts with opinions in 350 US. *The Supreme Court Reporter*, published by the West Publishing Company, is cited as SCt. The first volume of this series begins with opinions reported in 106 US (1882).

In addition to reprinting the court's opinions that appear in *U.S. Reports*, the *U.S. Supreme Court Reports (LEd)* and *Supreme Court Reporter (SCt)* also present annotations and headnotes that precede each opinion. *Annotations* are brief essays that summarize and interpret the court's opinions. *Headnotes* are numbered, short paragraphs that each analyzes a separate point of law covered in an opinion. Annotations and headnotes offer the reader an overview of the legal issues decided in the case. Cases reported in both LEd and SCt provide cross-references to the corresponding volume and page for that case in *U.S. Reports*. Like the official reporter, the two commercial reporters provide advance sheets prior to publication of hardbound volumes at the end of each October term.

Secondary Sources for U.S. Supreme Court Decisions: Preview, Court Digests, Legal Encyclopedias, and Indexes

There are at least two characteristics of secondary sources that are useful when researching case law. First, they provide interpretative material to assist the reader in understanding the cause, nature, and consequence of case law on a specific topic. Second, they also offer finding aids to assist the reader in a more thorough search of the primary sources for relevant cases.

Some secondary sources for legal research might also be considered a primary source for other research purposes. An example is *Landmark Briefs and Arguments of the Supreme Court of the United States*. This multi-volume series reprints petitions, motions, written briefs, and oral arguments from selected, historically important cases decided by the U.S. Supreme Court. To a legal researcher, such material is not considered primary because, unlike the Court's decisions and opinions, it does not carry the force of law. However, to a political scientist researching the judicial process, this same material might well be considered a primary source because it is original information coming directly from the source unaltered by second party analysis or interpretation.

An excellent secondary source for keeping current on cases pending before the U.S. Supreme Court is the periodical entitled *Preview of United States Supreme Court Cases*. While the *Preview* briefs cases pending before the U.S. Supreme Court, two other basic types of legal secondary sources — case digests and legal encyclopedias — analyze decisions after the Court announces them. A fundamental difference between Supreme Court digests and legal encyclopedias is that the former only analyze cases decided by the U.S. Supreme Court, whereas the latter refer to decisions of lower level courts as well.

In addition, for research on case law that would be *controlling* in a specific geographic area, the reader would refer to the National Reporter System. This is a system of court case reports for the entire country. It divides the country into seven geographic regions and reports cases from each region after the decision is final. This sample citation—652 So. 2d 1169—would be read as volume 652 of the Southern Reporter (So.), second edition (2d), page 1169. The seven regions of the National Reporter System are as follows:

- Atlantic
- Southern
- South Western
- Pacific

- South Eastern
- North Eastern
- North Western

A **case digest** can be described as an index that classifies, by subject, reported case decisions and presents a brief abstract for each decision. Each case is analyzed to identify all specific findings and general principles, which may serve as precedent in future cases. These various points are then arranged by subject and indexed in a multi-volume set updated by pocket parts. As with court reporters, there are digests for all levels of federal courts as well as major state courts. The major case digests for the U.S. Supreme Court are *United States Supreme Court Digest*, published by West Publishing Company, and the *United States Supreme Court Reports Digest*, published by Lawyers Cooperative Publishing.

A legal encyclopedia presents introductory-level summary articles on hundreds of legal topics. They are a good place to go for information about both case and statute law when the researcher knows relatively little about a legal topic. Like the case digests, the topical articles in these encyclopedias can identify relevant cases for reviewing decisions and opinions.

The two major legal encyclopedias are *American Jurisprudence 2d (Am Jur 2d)* and *Corpus Juris Secundum (CJS)*. The "2d" in Am Jur and "secundum" in CJS refer to second edition, not second series as found in court reporters. Like more generalized encyclopedias, both *American Jurisprudence 2d* and *Corpus Juris Secundum* are multi-volume works that present hundreds of articles written in narrative form that are arranged alphabetically by topic title. Both use extensive footnotes to cite federal and state court decisions relevant to the article's topic. Pocket parts and replacement volumes to reflect the current law in force update both.

Conclusion

From this brief overview, it is clear that the law governing purchase contracts is complicated, comprehensive, and copious. The task for the public procurement officer is to successfully navigate through the legal maze of public procurement contracts by understanding and applying statutory, common, and administrative laws to each legal situation. As public procurement professionals gain an understanding and appreciation of the legal structure, they add substantial value to the procurement function as a source of authority.

References

American Bar Association (2000). *The 2000 model procurement code for state and local governments.* Chicago: American Bar Association.

Calmari, J. D., & Perrillo, J. M. (1998). *The law of contracts* (Hornbook Series, 4th ed.). St. Paul, MN: West Publishing.

Council of State Governments (CSG) (1988). *The book of states, 1988-89.* Lexington, KY: CSG.

Dolan, J. F. (1991). *Uniform commercial code: Terms and transactions in commercial law.* Boston: Little Brown Publishing.

Gavil, A. (1996). *An antitrust anthology.* Ottawa, Ontario: Anderson Publishing.

Gellhorn, E., & Kovacic, W. E. (1994). *Antitrust law and economics in a nutshell* (4th ed.). St. Paul: West Publishing.

Ginsberg, J. D., Litman, J., Goldberg, D., & Greenbaum, A. J. (1996). Trademark and unfair competition law. Available from www.lexisnexis.com.

Hynes, J. D. (2001). *Agency, partnership and the LLC in a nutshell.* St. Paul, MN: West Publishing.

Kempin, F. G. (1990). *Historical introduction to Anglo-American law in a nutshell* (3rd ed.). St. Paul, MN: West Publishing.

Keyes, W. N. (2000). *Government contracts in a nutshell* (3rd ed.). St. Paul, MN: West Publishing.

Marsh, G. A. (1999). *Consumer protection law in a nutshell* (3rd ed.). St. Paul, MN: West Publishing.

McManis, C. R. (1992). *Unfair trade practices in a nutshell.* St. Paul, MN: West Publishing.

Miller, A. R., & Davis, M H. (2000). *Intellectual property: Patents, trademarks and copyright in a nutshell.* St. Paul, MN: West Publishing.

National Association of State Procurement Officials (NASPO) (1997). *State and local government purchasing principles and practices.* Lexington, KY: NASPO.

Page, H. R. (1989). *Public purchasing and materials management.* Reston, VA: National Institute of Governmental Purchasing, Inc.

Pierce, D. E., Jr., & Gellhorn, E. (1999). *Regulated industries in a nutshell* (4th ed.). St. Paul: West Publishing.

Rohwer, C. D., & Skrocki, A. M. (2000). *Contracts in a nutshell* (5th ed.). St. Paul, MN: West Publishing.

Seavey, W. A. (1964). *Law of agency* (Hornbook Series). St. Paul, MN: West Publishing.

Weinstein, M., & Kimbrough, R. (1988). *Summary of American law* (rev. ed.). New York: John Wiley & Sons.

Weston, G. E., Maggs, P. B., & Schechter, R. E. (1992). *Unfair trade practices and consumer protection.* St. Paul, MN: West Publishing.

White, J. J., & Summers, R. S. (2000). *Handbook on the uniform commercial code* (5th ed.). St. Paul, MN: West Publishing.

Chapter 2

The Fundamentals of Procurement Law and Procurement Authority

Despite popular belief, government is not all-powerful! The power of a government to act is strictly limited to the authority granted to a government by the federal, state, or local constitution or charter; federal, state or local statute or ordinance; and administrative rule. Therefore, absent a specific grant of power from one of these sources, a government will not have the authority to enter into a purchase contract. In most instances, the power of a government comes from a legislative enactment authorizing specific state and federal officials and agencies to enter into purchase contracts.

The key to government or public procurement is the scope of the purchasing authority granted to a government official or agency. For example, if a county ordinance does not permit human resource personnel to enter into any kind of contract on behalf of the county, then those particular county employees must stay within that restriction. In contrast, many federal, state, and county laws grant the general power to enter into contracts to a particular official or agency. This would include the ability to establish general parameters and to set up a system for the administration and management of this power to contract. Over time, these legislative authorizations to contract have become more centralized with particular government officials and agencies. In short, the authority of a government official or agency to enter into a contract is only that authority granted to that official or agency by law.

Within the context of a legal framework, this chapter reviews the general principles for applying and interpreting public contract law and describes the relationship to civil and public law, criminal law, and tort law. Of particular importance to the public procurement official, this chapter also discusses the government's authority to contract, the provisions of the law of agency, and the relationship between the principal and its agents. The chapter also explores the differences between express, implied and apparent authority; and because statutory law defines the operational parameters of public procurement, it also discusses the framework and key concepts of the American Bar Association's (ABA) *Model Procurement*

Code for State and Local Governments in detail as well as other statutes, such as budgetary or federal funding laws that impact the public procurement function.

The Sources and Types of Contract Law

As a reiteration of Chapter 1, the source of a government official and agency's legal authority to enter into contracts is found in statutory law, administrative law and regulations, and common law.

Statutory Law

A key source of law in this country is the United States Constitution. Among other things, it establishes the relationship between the Federal Government and the states. The Constitution authorizes the U.S. Congress to enact laws within the powers granted by the Constitution. The authority not specifically granted to the U.S. Congress or other parts of the Federal Government are then reserved for the states.

The primary source of law and authority for public procurement officials is the legislatively enacted statutes. These legislative statutes not only grant contracting authority to a government official or agency but also may set out the specific policies and procedures for purchasing goods and services. For example, most state statutes contain a specific section concerning public works projects, which would include the requirements for the construction of public buildings and facilities.

Once the legislation is signed into law by the President of the United States at the federal level or the governor of a state at the state level, it is called a "public law." Public laws are organized by subject matter in the United States Code and the corresponding state statutory codes.

Administrative Law

Administrative rules and regulations established through proper procedures have the same legal effect as legislation passed by Congress. The primary set of procurement regulations at the federal level is called the *Federal Acquisition Regulation* (FAR). Like federal government agencies, state agencies may, through certain procedures, adopt regulations or rules to implement those statutes, which have the same legal force as legislation. Counties, cities and towns, to the extent that state statutes and their charters permit, enact ordinances and may also establish administrative rules and regulations.

Common Law

Just like statutory law and administrative rules and regulations, common law can be a primary source of authority for the public procurement official. The time-honored principles of common law have the same legal effect as statutory law in those cases where statutory law does not modify common law. The courts typically adhere to common law principles just as they do to those announced in statute.

When lawyers, judges and others refer to the common law, they are citing the collection of court decisions regarding a particular legal subject. It is from this collection that a legal rule of general application can be extracted. Once extracted, this "common law" rule would then apply as precedent in similar situations. In essence, the common law is law developed from the experience of lawyers and judges handling the same or similar legal disputes over several years. For example, the concept that a person who acts in bad faith (lies) when entering into a contract will not be entitled to receive the benefit of that contract is a legal principle based on the common law. With the exception of the State of Louisiana, which follows the French "civil code" model rather than the English "common law" model, judicial decisions that make up the common law establish legal parameters for public procurement officials.

Public Contracting

Within the context of public contracting, the most important source of the power to contract is statutory law and administrative rules and regulations. The genesis for public contract law is a statute or ordinance setting forth specific procedures that the government must follow in purchasing the goods, services, and construction that it needs. In many instances, statutes and administrative regulations will even incorporate by reference the common law of contracts; however, absent a specific statute or administrative rule, the common law of contracts will apply to public contracts.

Sources of Public Contract Law

Like the general law of contracts, the law of public contracts has its own body of common law. Decisions of courts on legal challenges to contract awards and on claims filed under contracts form much of that common law, but there are other important sources for it, as well. Certain governmental administrative entities, particularly within the Federal Government, have a responsibility to decide bid protests and contract claims; and the abundance of those administrative decisions is an important source of government contract law principles.

For instance, the U.S. General Accounting Office, an arm of Congress, has decided bid protests for the Federal Government since 1921. The legal principles of public procurement announced in its written decisions over the years have been the basis for many of the essential concepts that drive the practice of public contracting at the federal, state, and local government levels. Many of those concepts have now found their way into the language of statutes and ordinances.

Likewise, the decisions of the Federal Government's boards of contract appeals, responsible for deciding claims filed under contracts, are key sources of direction on contract interpretation and administration. While these administrative sources of public contract law do not have the same legal effect as do decisions of courts and, thus, do not meet a narrow definition of "common law," they are, nonetheless, important and often provide guidance to state courts on issues relating to public contracts.

...the principles of general contract law apply to the government procurement process...

Applying Contract Law to Public Procurement

As a general rule, the principles of general contract law apply to the government procurement process, except where the law of public contracts specifically displaces them. If statutes and rules that establish procedures for the award of public contracts are detailed, such as those that regulate the United States purchases, there is a broad displacement of general contract law and the requirements of public contract law apply. On the other hand, the public contract laws of most state and local governments are not as specific as those of the Federal Government; and, thus, general contract law will play a greater role in the procurement processes of those entities.

Other Laws Applicable to Public Procurement

This chapter illustrates part of the complex network of laws that define the responsibilities and authority of the procurement official. The procurement statute or ordinance explicitly authorizes a government official to contract for the government, but it is the law of agency that prescribes the extent of that authority and whether and how that official may delegate it.

There are other types of law that come into play in public procurement. Clearly, the law of contracts plays a key role, which will be discussed later in this chapter. Additionally, the final section of this chapter briefly describes some more specific categories of laws that often are part of the public contracting process. Following is a short summary of some types of law that apply.

Criminal Law

A crime is an act for which the law imposes punishment, such as imprisonment or fines. For the most part, criminal laws that affect public procurement may apply to any public procurement official or purchasing contract. Criminal law prohibits certain kinds of activities, such as kickbacks, bribery, false claims, false statements, mail or wire fraud, misuse of government property, and anti-competitive practices. Statutes set out what is a crime and then judicial opinions establish case law precedent interpreting the specific requirements of a crime.

Tort Law

Tort law is the counterpart to criminal law in that it permits parties to sue each other for damage to a person or property. Tort law is becoming increasingly more a product of statutory law but still mostly a product of common law. Under tort law, one person becomes obligated to another, not based on a contractual relationship, but due to various duties that the law creates. If a person runs a red light and crashes into another car, that person is financially liable to the owner of the damaged car and to any injured individuals because that person's actions fell below the standard of care that the law creates for someone driving a car.

For public procurement officials, the law of torts most likely comes into play during the administration of a contract or after a product has been purchased. For instance, a contractor constructing a public building discovers an error in the plans and specifications that will cost it more money to perform the contract. If the procurement official and the contractor do not resolve the dispute amicably, the contractor may file a claim for those additional costs. One of the legal theories that the contractor may include in its claim, in addition to the government's violation of the contract itself, is that the government negligently misrepresented the work to be performed.

Likewise, the government may wish to file a claim against a contractor and the engineer or architect hired to design a building where the roof of a new building leaks every time it rains. One of the legal bases that the government may assert, beyond simply breach of contract, is that the contractor negligently constructed, or the design professional negligently designed, the building.

By law, the time limits within which someone must bring a lawsuit against someone else for a negligent act generally are shorter than those set for bringing a lawsuit for a breach of contract. If the time has run out for pursuing a claim for breach of contract against a government contractor, there may not be time to pursue that contractor on the basis of negligence.

The government may purchase a piece of equipment that is defective and injures someone. There are bases in both contract law and the law of torts for recovering damages for those injuries. The tort basis is known as the law of product liability.

The Government's Authority to Contract

A government's power to contract is generally inherent in the powers that its constitution or charter grants it to govern. While a government has that inherent power, government officials do not. For purposes of public procurement, the legislative branch of government a legislature, board, or council must specifically authorize officials in the executive branch of government to enter into contracts. Without that authority, those officials may not do so. Thus, the existence of that authority is the foundation of any public procurement system.

State legislatures, by passing legislation that becomes statutes, and county, district or municipal boards or councils, by passing ordinances, define the scope of that authority and identify who may exercise it. The most effective procurement statutes and ordinances are those that establish the general parameters of an official's contracting or procurement authority and authorize that official to promulgate rules, regulations, or policies to implement it.

The Law of Agency

A ny entity, such as a corporation, a partnership or any level of government, must employ individuals to act on its behalf as it conducts business. These individuals are called "agents," and their roles and responsibilities are a set of legal principles referred to as the law of agency. The law of agency, which is essentially a product of common law, focuses not only on the creation of agent relationships but also the liability for losses suffered by others who deal with agents. Comprehensive coverage of the law of agency is beyond the reach of this book; however, every public procurement official needs to be familiar with some of the basic principles of the law of agency.

An agent is someone who acts on behalf of a principal. For example, the CEO of a corporation may act as an agent of that corporation. Further, a procurement officer may act as the procurement agent for the public entity that employs that procurement official. Within the context of public procurement, a local, state, or federal law will usually grant the power to contract to a government official or agency. In turn, the government official or agency will delegate, either by law, administrative rule or some other writing, the authority to enter into contracts to a public procurement officer. While such delegation of authority to an agent could be oral, it is highly recommended that the authority be provided in writing in order to clarify what the agent has been specifically authorized to do.

There are essentially two ways to create an agency relationship—*by agreement* between the principal and agent or *by law*. An agency relationship created by agreement requires the principal to perform an overt act, as evidence of the principal's intent for the agent to act on behalf of the principal. In addition, the agent must also accept the principal's offer to be an agent. In most instances, the principal and the proposed agent execute a written document in which the principal offers and the agent accepts appointment as the principal's agent.

An agency relationship created by operation of law can occur in two circumstances. First, a local, state, or federal statute may designate a government official as an agent, usually with the additional power to delegate that agency authority to another person. Second, a court of law may rule that an agency relationship exists as a matter of law, even though there is no agreement between a principal and an agent and there is no local, state, or federal law that creates an agency relationship.

This creation of an agency relationship by law usually occurs in the context of some dispute. In this case, the court rules that despite the lack of a formal agreement or other legal basis for the relationship, a person is acting on behalf of another person in relation to a third party. By way of illustration, if a government agency knows that one of its employees, who is not an agent by agreement or law, is entering into purchase contracts with vendors and fails to take steps to stop that employee from so acting, it may find that a court of law will rule that this employee was an agent. In this instance, the court ruling is based on the premise that the principal is obligated to know who its agents are, what those agents are doing, and must accept the consequences, both good and bad, of its agents' acts. This is sometimes called "agency by estoppel."

Types of Authority

Once an agency relationship is established, the agent's authority to act may be expressed, implied, or apparent.

Express authority means that the principal expressly confers, in writing, the authority of an agent to act on behalf of the principal. This express authority can be very specific. For example, the procurement agent may only have limited authority to enter into purchase contracts for less than $5,000. Express authority also can be generalized where the procurement agent has the authority to enter into all purchase contracts according to the needs of the principal.

Implied authority is a companion to any express authority conferred upon an agent. It permits an agent to do whatever incidental or customary actions are necessary to perform the expressly authorized acts. For example, an agent who has express authority to enter into a purchase contract will also have the implied authority to enter into a shipping and storage contract, if that is necessary.

Apparent authority is a trickier concept because it only applies when an individual has not been granted express authority to act on behalf of a principal. Rather, the principal, through some overt act, cloaks a person with the apparent authority in the eyes of a third party to act on behalf of the principal. For example, many businesses issue identification badges for all of their procurement office employees; however, some of these employees do not possess the express authority to enter into contracts on behalf of the business. If a procurement office employee wearing the procurement office badge enters into a contract with a vendor to bind the principal, the vendor may argue that this employee had the apparent authority to act as an agent for the principal. The key requirement for applying the concept of apparent agency is that the principal does some act to create a reasonable impression that a specific person is the principal's agent even though that person is not. Additionally, apparent agency can be created when the principal knowingly permits a person without express authority to act as an agent on the principal's behalf.

Generally, the principles of apparent authority do not apply to governments because they exist for the public good. The idea is that government operations are too large and varied to risk holding them responsible for the acts of unauthorized persons. However, courts are whittling away at that exclusion for governments and finding instances that, in fairness, hold the government responsible for the acts of its "apparent" agents.

In certain instances, a person with actual authority may bind the government to an otherwise unauthorized purchase by ratifying it. For ratification to occur, the authorized person must know, either actually or constructively, about the unauthorized purchase and approve it directly or by implication, such as by actions.

Public entities are strongly encouraged to avoid the legal consequences of apparent authority by maintaining vigilant supervision of its employees and providing clear and conspicuous disclosure of who has the express authority to act on behalf of a principal.

Liability of a Principal

In general, a principal will be bound by the acts of an agent performed within the course and scope of the agent's work. For example, a person may be a procurement agent for a public entity; however, when the person enters into a contract outside of business hours for personal goods or services and without any badge of apparent authority to act on the principal's behalf, the person is acting outside of the course and scope of the agent's work. Consequently, such a contract will not bind the principal to pay for the goods or services.

On the other hand, unauthorized acts performed by an agent within the course and scope of an agent's work will bind the principal. For example, many government agencies circulate lists of approved and unapproved vendors. If a procurement agent, during the course and scope of the agent's work, enters into a purchase contract with an unapproved vendor, the principal (i.e., the government agency) will be bound to that contract. The fact that the agent's act in entering into this purchase contract may be against policy or be "unauthorized" does not diminish the binding effect on the principal because the agent did act within the course and scope of the agent's work.

It is important to remember that a principal-agent relationship is different from an employer-independent contractor relationship. An independent contractor is not an employee of the principal but may still be an agent of the principal. An independent contractor is a person contracted by an employer to provide goods, services, or work for that employer. In this capacity, the employer does not have control over the details of how the independent contractor will perform the task but, rather, just pays for the goods, services, or work.

An independent contractor is a person contracted by an employer to provide goods, services, or work for that employer.

On the other hand, an employer has control over all of the details and the work to be performed by an employee. In this context, an employer could easily invest agent authority in an employee. This relationship between employer and employee is called **respondeat superior**. This classic agency relationship would directly apply to a public procurement official employed by a government entity.

In contrast, an employer is not ordinarily held accountable for the acts of an independent contractor. Further, it is unlikely that an employer, either through a grant of express authority or the creation of apparent authority, will confer any type of agent authority on an independent contractor. For example, it is unlikely that a plumber hired by an agency to do plumbing work would also be given the power to act as an agent for the employer.

The Impact of Statutory Laws

The constitutions and state laws of the 50 U.S. states describe the relationship between state government and the various county and municipal governments as well as special taxing districts, including public school districts. Additionally, these state statutes empower or restrict the authority of local governments. This relationship varies dramatically from state to state. In some situations, municipalities, special districts, or public school districts are an instrumentality of the state government and bound totally or partially by state statutes and laws. In other situations, the state statutes give wide latitude on the promulgation of local ordinances and regulations by providing an overarching framework of laws. Due to the complexity of these legal relationships, it is important that public procurement officials be fully aware of the relationship between their public entity and state statutes.

Key Components of the ABA Model Procurement Code

While each state and local government establishes its own statutes and regulations governing the public procurement function, it is important to note that there have been efforts to create a standardized template of rules and policies that can serve as a model for the development of state and local legislation.

In 1975, the Council of State Governments commissioned a study of procurement practices at the state and local levels. That study, entitled *State and Local Government Purchasing: Principles and Practices*, is updated and republished periodically by the National Association of State Procurement Officials (NASPO) (1997). The study became the foundation of a groundbreaking project undertaken by the American Bar Association, funded in major part by the U.S. Department of Justice, to draft model procurement legislation for state and local governments. The result of the project was the creation of *The Model Procurement Code for State and Local Governments*, approved by the American Bar Association's House of Delegates in 1979. The Code has helped to create transparent, competitive, and reliable processes by which billions of dollars in public funds are expended through contracts with private sector businesses (ABA, 2000, page iii).

In 1997, the ABA Sections of Public Contract Law and State and Local Government Law initiated its sponsorship of the Model Procurement Code Revision Project in collaboration with leading organizations, including the National Institute of Governmental Purchasing, Inc. (NIGP), the National Association of State Procurement Officials (NASPO), Public Technology, Inc. (PTI), the Construction Industry Roundtable (CIRT), the American Consulting Engineers Council, and the Council on Federal Procurement of Architectural and Engineering Services. There were a number of reasons cited for updating the Code including:

- A rapid increase in the volume of public procurement spending;

- Technological advances in the way in which public procurement transactions are processed via personal computers, email, and the Internet; and

- The need to purchase proprietary technology for public entities.

The goals of the revision project were to:

- reduce transaction costs for all governmental entities at the state and local levels;

- reduce transaction costs to private sector suppliers of goods and services;

- substantially increase available levels and ranges of competition through modern methods of electronic communications; and

- encourage the competitive use of new technologies, new methods of performing, and new forms of project delivery in public procurement, particularly in the construction area.

With assistance from the Massachusetts Institute of Technology (MIT), proposed revisions were circulated to interested parties through the Internet. In July 2000, the revised Code was released as *The 2000 Model Procurement Code for State and Local Governments*. The 2000 Code remains a short statute that provides the fundamentals of sound procurement that should be implemented by regulations consistent with the statutory framework (ABA, 2000, page xi).

The key modifications to the 2000 Code are as follows:

- *Electronic Commerce.* The 2000 Code modified definitions and added new definitions to Articles 1 and 3 that allow procurement processes to adapt to the electronic age.

- *Cooperative Purchasing.* The 2000 Code modified definitions and language in Article 10 to extend the benefits of cooperative procurement of suppliers and services among state and local governments.

- *Flexibility in Purchasing Methods.* The 2000 Code provided badly needed flexibility to senior procurement officials to adapt procurement procedures to unusual circumstances. Appropriate safeguards and reporting responsibilities are outlined in Article 3.

- *Processes for Delivery of Infrastructure Facilities and Services.* The 2000 Code provided more explicit guidance on the use of construction delivery methods. The revisions, as outlined in Article 5, provide best practice recommendations in the use of these alternative delivery methods as effective tools in managing an entire collection of a city's, state's, or county's infrastructure facilities.

It should be noted that the ABA developed the Model Procurement Code as a "model" rather than a "uniform" code so that state and local governments adopting the code could adapt it to their own organizational and political constraints. While implementation of Code-based legislation has fallen short of the vision of the initial supporters; consideration for enactment of Code-based legislation is present in ever-increasing numbers of jurisdictions. Two related ABA publications, *State and Local Government Procurement: Developments in Legislation and Litigation* (1986) and *Annotations to the Model Procurement Code* (1992), have served to keep information on the Code current.

The Model Procurement Code contains twelve articles that cover broad categories of the contracting process. Articles 1 through 10 cover basic policies for the procurement of supplies, services, and construction; management and disposal of supplies; and legal remedies. Article 11 provides socio-economic policies, which a state or local government may wish to amplify. Article 12 establishes ethical standards for public officials and contractors in connection with procurement. The following is a synopsis of the scope of each Article.

Article 1: General Provisions. Article 1 describes the general purposes of the Code, specifies its applicability, provides guidance for interpretations, and contains definitions of terms used in more than one Article.

Article 2: Procurement Organization. Article 2 sets forth the basic organizational concepts for establishing procurement policy and conducting procurement operations. It also contains several alternative proposals for establishing the policy-making office. In addition, Article 2 provides for certain exemptions from central procurement and authorizes the creation of a Procurement Advisory Council to suggest reforms and improvements and a Procurement Institute to train procurement personnel.

Article 3: Source Selection and Contract Formation. Article 3 describes the selection and contract formation methods authorized by the Code and authorized procurement officials to select and apply these methods. These source selection methods include: competitive sealed bidding, competitive sealed proposals, small purchase procedures, sole-source procurement, emergency procurements, and a competitive selection procedure for designated types of services. Although there is no longer statutory preference for competitive sealed bidding, Section 3-202 of the Code makes competitive sealed bidding a default source selection method.

With the 2000 edition, Article 3 provides flexibility in the extent to which competitive sealed proposals (CSPs) may be used as a source selection method. The Article requires the use of CSPs in the award of contracts for design-build, design-build-operate-maintain, and design-build-finance-operate-maintain services. Additionally, the modified edition requires that Request for Proposals (RFP) specify the relative importance of price and other factors and sub-factors that will be separately evaluated and scored by the procuring agency. The Procurement Officer is also authorized to conduct debriefings after source selection decisions and contract award. Finally, the revised Code substantially rewrote the requirements to reduce the burdens of submitting certified cost or pricing data.

The Model Procurement Code contains twelve articles that cover broad categories of the contracting process.

Article 4: Specifications. Article 4 contains requirements for development, monitoring, and using specifications. It requires that specifications be written in a manner to maximize competition to the extent possible.

Article 5: Procurement of Construction, Architect-Engineer and Land Surveying Services. Article 5 was substantially rewritten in 2000 and now establishes five project delivery methods that may be applied by the procuring agency to procure infrastructure projects and services: design-bid-build; design-build; design-build-operate-maintain; design-build-finance-operate-maintain; and operations and maintenance.

Article 6: Modification and Termination of Contracts for Supplies and Services. Article 6 authorizes the use of clauses in contracts for supplies and services covering changes and variations in estimated quantities and sets forth the criteria for making price adjustments pursuant to such clauses. It also authorizes the inclusion of other clauses, including liquidated damages, excusable delay, and termination.

Article 7: Cost Principles. Article 7 provides for the promulgation of regulations establishing cost principles to be used to determine types of costs reimbursable under cost-type contracts.

Article 8: Supply Management. Article 8 establishes requirements for control over the life cycle of supplies procured and establishes criteria for management, transfer, and disposal of surplus property.

Article 9: Legal and Contractual Remedies. Article 9 provides mechanisms for the resolution of disputes relating to solicitations and awards, contract performance, and debarment or suspension determinations. In addition, this Article provides procedures for handling contracts awarded in violation of law.

Article 10: Intergovernmental Relations. Article 10 contains provisions designated to facilitate cooperative procurement among the various units of government. It permits standardization of specifications for use by several jurisdictions, joint use of real and personal property, and sharing of personnel among local governments and between a state and its political subdivisions. The Article also provides that a state, at the request of other jurisdictions, may provide procurement information and technical services to those jurisdictions.

Article 11: Assistance to Small and Disadvantaged Businesses; Federal Assistance or Contract Procurement Requirements. Article 11 provides administrative procedures for assisting small and disadvantaged business in learning how to do business with the enacting jurisdiction. This Article also can be used to incorporate additional state socio-economic policies that are to be implemented through the procurement process. Article 11 requires compliance with Federal law and regulations not presently reflected in the Code when procurement involves the expenditure of federal assistance or contract funds.

Article 12: Ethics in Public Contracting. Article 12 contains ethical standards with accompanying sanctions that are applicable to all participants in the public procurement process. The proposed ethical standards cover conflicts of interest, gratuities and kickbacks, contingent fees, and misuse of confidential information. Additionally, this Article authorizes establishment of an Ethics Commission with authority to render advisory opinions to participants in the procurement process.

There are some key concepts within ABA's Model Procurement Code that are worth mentioning, as they are pervasive throughout the Code.

Competitive Sealed Bidding

Competitive sealed bidding has been and continues to be the preferred method of source selection. The Code embodies the fundamental principles that should be applied to the conduct of competitive sealed bidding, including the following:

Conditions for Use

Contracts shall be awarded by competitive sealed bidding except as otherwise provided in Methods of Source Selection.

Invitation for Bids

An Invitation for Bids (IFB) shall be issued and shall include a purchase description and all contractual terms and conditions applicable to the procurement.

Public Notice

Adequate public notice of the IFB shall be given a reasonable time prior to the date set forth therein for the opening of bids, in accordance with regulations promulgated by the Policy Office. Such notice may include publication in a newspaper of general circulation a reasonable time prior to bid opening.

Bid Opening

Bids shall be opened publicly in the presence of one or more witnesses at the time and place designated in the IFB. The amount of each bid and such other relevant information as may be specified by regulation, together with the name of each bidder shall be recorded; the record and each bid shall be open to public inspection.

Bid Acceptance and Bid Evaluation

Bids shall be unconditionally accepted without alteration or correction, except as authorized in this Code. Bids shall be evaluated based on the requirements set forth in the IFB, which may include criteria to determine acceptability, such as inspection, testing, quality, workmanship, delivery, and suitability for a particular purpose. Those criteria that will affect the bid price and will be considered in evaluation for award shall be objectively measurable. Examples include discounts, transportation costs, and total or life-cycle costs. The IFB shall set forth the evaluation criteria to be used. No criteria may be used in bid evaluation that is not set forth in the IFB.

Correction or Withdrawal of Bids; Cancellation of Awards

Correction or withdrawal of inadvertently erroneous bids before or after award, or cancellation of awards, or contracts based on such bid mistakes shall be permitted in accordance with regulations. Except as otherwise provided by regulation, all decisions to permit the correction or withdrawal of bids, or to cancel awards or contracts based on bid mistakes, shall be supported by a written determination made by the Chief Procurement Officer or head of a procurement agency.

Award

The contract shall be awarded with reasonable promptness by written notice to the lowest responsible and responsive bidder whose bid meets the requirements and criteria set forth in the IFB. In the event that all bids for a construction project exceed available funds as certified by the appropriate fiscal officer, and the low responsive bid does not exceed such funds by more than 5%, the Chief Procurement Officer, or the head of a procurement agency, is authorized, in situations where time or economic consideration preclude re-solicitation, to negotiate an adjustment of the bid price, including changes in the bid requirements, with the low responsive and responsible bidder, in order to bring the bid within the amount of available funds.

In summary, ABA's *2000 Model Procurement Code for State and Local Governments* serves as an excellent benchmark for the development of procurement statutes for state and local governments. If the public entity elects to develop its own statutes, the principles and concepts outlined in the Code should be seriously considered.

Other Impacts on Statutory and Administrative Laws

There are too many ancillary statutory or administrative laws that impact the procurement function on the federal, state and local level to mention specifically in this text. Nevertheless, the public procurement official must remain vigilant regarding these ancillary laws and their impact on their operations. There are some pervading key laws that are worth noting here.

Budget/Finance Laws

These laws are critical in public procurement. Budget statutes prohibit a governmental agency from spending funds beyond those that the legislative body appropriates for it. They are the impetus for encumbrance accounting that requires a purchase requisition or other form to be used which certifies that the agency has the funds. Additionally, finance laws address issues, such as the manner of paying vendors, whether the government will pay interest on late payments, and whether the government will make payments to vendors in advance of contract performance.

Federal Laws and Their Relationship to Federal Funding

Most state and local public agencies receive some level of governmental funding for the operation of their governmental units and services. In most cases, these funds must be expended consistent with the public procurement principles identified by the granting entity—typically, the federal or state government. Generally, these principles include:

- assurance of competition;

- adequate review procedures;

- use of appropriate procurement methods; and

- compliance with Federal Regulations governing equal employment opportunities and prevailing wages.

Prior to March 1988, public procurement agents faced a myriad of different rules when undertaking an acquisition using federal grant money. Not only were there different rules among the agencies, sometimes there were different rules within a single agency, depending on the source of the funds. Two related documents that were published in 1988 have helped to establish some consistency and uniformity.

- *The Uniform Administrative Requirements for Grants and Cooperative Agreements to State and Local Governments*

- *OMB Circular A-102: Grants and Cooperative Agreements with State and Local Governments*

Since the administrative laws of the Federal Government for granting funds to state and local governments are fairly dynamic, they will not be specifically addressed in this text. However, it is important to note that public procurement officials are required to abide by the procurement rules of the donor or granting agency. Further, procurement officials must remember that federal laws and statutes take precedence when the purchase is being made with federal funds.

Reform of Public Procurement Laws, Administrative Law and Enabling Legislation

As mentioned in *Introduction to Public Procurement*, produced by NIGP, public procurement officials are strongly encouraged to influence changes in statutory and administrative laws in order to enable the official to implement best practices for the profession.

There are a number of key issues for public procurement officials to consider when advocating changes to legislative and administrative laws:

- Statutes and ordinances fall within the purview of statutory law and reflect the highest level of authority for the public procurement function. Accordingly, statutes and ordinances should provide the overarching rules of conduct for public procurement.

- Statutes and ordinances are adopted by the legislative governing body (the state legislature, the city council, the county commissioners, etc.). As such, they are extremely difficult to change. In contrast, administrative laws (regulations, policies, and procedures) are typically developed and implemented by the executive or administrative body (governors, city managers, county administrators, school district superintendents, etc.). The public procurement official needs to be cognizant of the roles, responsibilities, and balance of power between the legislative and executive bodies that promulgate statutory and administrative laws. The official also needs to be cognizant of the political environment affecting these two groups, as most legislative bodies are elected while most executive bodies are appointed. Public procurement officials can best influence statutory laws through a consolidated effort of professional associations or collegial groups. In contrast, the public procurement official can have a greater individual influence on administrative law.

  ...the public procurement official can have a greater individual influence on administrative law.

- The authority granted by the legislative governing body to implement administrative law or regulations is often referred to as an "administrative procedures act." This series of statutes determines the manner and extent to which the procurement official has authority over the approval of procurement rules or regulations. To the extent possible, an administrative procedures act should enable the public procurement official to promulgate operational policies and procedures that enhance the value of the procurement function.

- Policy issues and procedural details that need to be dynamic in order to be effective (e.g., bid limits and contract authorization thresholds) should not be included in statutory law to the extent possible.

Reform of Public Procurement

Within the legal framework, the public procurement official should continually seek enabling legislation that empowers the public procurement function to add economic, efficient, and effective value to the public entity. As of this writing, new procurement concepts are transitioning from fresh, innovative practices developed by a few public entities to best practices serving as the standard for many entities. Undoubtedly, new concepts and practices will be implemented as the profession grows in stature and credibility.

Over the next several years, public procurement professionals should strive to ensure that their statutory laws and administrative laws enable them to offer the highest strategic value to their entities. Consider the following.

- Laws and regulations should provide ethical guidelines for conduct by public buyers, managers, elected officials, and suppliers.

- Laws and regulations should strive for the greatest efficiency and economy of the public procurement process by providing alternative methods of source selection, such as cooperative ventures and strategic sourcing.

- Laws and regulations should strive for the greatest effectiveness of the public procurement process by establishing realistic bid thresholds based on benchmarks of similar governmental entities.

- Laws and regulations should allow for evaluative methods that consider total cost of ownership and best value approaches to public procurements.

- Laws and regulations should promote public-private partnerships that encourage contract incentives and performance-based contracting.

- Laws and regulations should allow for fair negotiations for specified types of procurements.

- Laws and regulations should provide for the use of technology and electronic processes to create efficiencies and effectiveness.

References

American Bar Association (1992). *Annotations to the model procurement code* (2nd ed.). Chicago: American Bar Association.

American Bar Association (2000). *The 2000 model procurement code for state and local governments.* Chicago: American Bar Association.

American Bar Association (1986). *State and local government procurement: Developments in legislation and litigation.* Chicago: American Bar Association.

National Institute of Governmental Purchasing, Inc. (NIGP) (2000). *General public purchasing.* Herndon, VA: NIGP.

National Association of State Procurement Officials (NASPO) (1997). *State and local government purchasing: Principles and practices.* Lexington, KY: NASPO.

Chapter 3

The Basic Components of a Common Law Contract

This chapter focuses on the basic components of a common law contract. While Article 2 of the U.C.C. governs contracts for the sale of goods, the common law of contracts governs all other types of contracts, most notably, service contracts. Under the common law there are six essential elements needed to form a legal contract: offer and acceptance, definiteness, consideration, mutuality of obligation, capacity of the parties, and legality of purpose. In several cases, these contractual elements will be paralleled to the Uniform Commercial Code (U.C.C.) and public procurement practices. The chapter also addresses conditions that could lead to a voidable contract, including mistakes, misrepresentations, trade constraints, assignment, novation, frustration, and disputes. Additionally, the chapter reviews the conditions for oral and written contracts and contrasts the differences between private and public contracting.

What is a Contract?

Before delving into the legal specifics of the common law of contracts, it may be useful to define the basics of a contract. There is no simple definition of the term "contract." Non-lawyers generally tend to use the term to mean the written document signifying an agreement between two parties; but, in the eyes of the law, the term means the process by which the agreement is formed. Within the context of this chapter, the term "contract" refers to promises or agreements for which the law establishes enforceable duties and remedies.

A contract is nothing more than an agreement between two or more people to do something. The key to a contract is that there must be an agreement. A promise, proposal, or proffer with no agreement is not a contract. In the public procurement context, a contract is an agreement by a seller or vendor to provide goods or services to the public agency in return for receiving payment from the public agency.

The common law of contracts is not designed to make the process of conducting business difficult; rather, the purpose of the law of contracts is to facilitate business by establishing fair and efficient rules of contract law. On the one hand, the law of contracts wants commerce to flow smoothly so that everyone involved can make a reasonable profit or secure goods and services. On the other hand, the law of contracts does not want one person or firm engaged in commerce to create an unfair advantage towards another person or firm engaged in commerce. This constant tension between making sure business is not unduly hampered, yet making sure business people are legally protected, is the dynamic of modern contract law.

Contracts are primarily governed by state statutory, common law, and the contract itself. Parties to a contract have what is referred to as "the freedom of contract," which principally allows the parties to establish their own law for the performance of a specific contract. This private contract law may override many of the rules otherwise established by state law.

Statutory law may require that some contracts be detailed in writing and executed with particular formalities, such as contracts for the purchase and sale of real estate, guarantees, and contracts of employment in excess of one year. Otherwise, the parties may enter into a binding agreement without signing a formal written document. Contracts related to particular activities or business sectors may be highly regulated by state and/or federal law.

When Does a Contract Exist?

Before taking measures to enforce a contract, it must be established whether or not a contract actually exists. To determine existence, the opinion of the involved parties is ignored and the "reasonable person rule" serves as the basis for determination. By viewing the dynamic as a whole, the court decides if a "reasonable person" would have reason to believe that the parties intend to be bound to a contract. A binding contract requires an offer, acceptance and consideration. In addition, the parties must have an agreement as to the material elements necessary for the performance of the contract. This understanding and agreement is known as a "meeting of the minds."

In determining whether there is a valid contract, in addition to other factors, the court may consider testimony, written evidence such as notes, emails, letters, as well as any actions taken by or on behalf of either party in the performance of the disputed contract.

The court will attempt to determine the intentions of the parties; however, where the parties have not agreed to a key element of the contract, it is unlikely that a court will find an enforceable contract under the common law. A court will not decide terms of a contract for parties; it will rule on whether there was an agreement to terms and what constitutes that agreement.

A Letter of Intent is not a binding contract. However, if a Letter of Intent is written in such a way that it contains the consideration and requires performance, a court may find it to be a valid contract, especially if both parties sign off on the letter of Intent or one or both parties have fully or partially performed.

Privity of a Contract

Normally, only parties to a contract have the right to enforce its terms. This is known as the "privity of contract" rule. In some circumstances, third parties who are known beneficiaries to a contract may have rights to enforce and sue for breach of a contract. This would include agents or employees who obviously accept or offer a contract not in their own personal names but on another person's or a corporation's behalf. In these situations, it is said that an "agent" signed the contract. The person employing the agent is called the "principal," and the principal could sue or be sued under contracts entered into by his or her agent even though the principal did not sign the contract directly.

Forming a Contract

Contracts are formed through a variety of ways. There are express contracts, which may be written or oral, created when the formal elements for establishing a contract exist. Another kind of contract is an "implied-in-fact" contract, where some of the formal elements occur through conduct rather than express words. This type of contract occurs when someone takes a car to be washed at the local car wash. Although the formalities of an express contract are missing, it is implied that the person taking the car keys will wash the car and that the other person, who has handed those keys over, will pay for that service.

Sometimes, the law affords a person a legal remedy to pursue another person based on that second person's promise, even though critical elements of contract formation do not exist. An example of this type of contract is where a general contractor uses a subcontractor's quote in preparing a bid for a public construction project. Some courts have decided that, since the general contractor relied on the subcontractor's quote in preparing its bid, the subcontractor may not withdraw that quote until the general contractor knows whether it has been awarded a contract and has a reasonable opportunity to accept the quote.

In other instances, the law imposes an obligation on a person to achieve justice, even though there clearly is no contract. Those situations are called "implied-in-law" contracts. An example is a circumstance in which a doctor renders necessary medical treatment to someone who is unconscious and, thus, cannot enter into a contract for those services; the law implies a reasonable promise to pay the doctor for those services.

The principle of an "implied-in-law" contract does not generally apply to governments. There are exceptions. In one instance, a court required a city to pay a hospital for services rendered to an arrested person that city police had shot, on the theory that the city had a constitutional duty to provide medical services to that prisoner.

Elements of a Contract

There are six essential elements that must exist for an enforceable contract to be formed:

- Offer and Acceptance
- Consideration
- Capacity of the Parties
- Definiteness
- Mutuality of Obligation
- Legality of Purpose

Two of them — consideration and mutuality of obligation — are related.

Because of the formal nature of the public contracting process, there seldom is a dispute about whether the government and its vendor have complied with some of these elements. Nonetheless, issues arise from time to time. This text defines each element in the context of the common law of contracts.

Offer and Acceptance

Formation of a contract requires an agreement — two parties consenting to the same terms. The process by which persons reach an agreement is the offer and acceptance process. An offer generally involves a promise or commitment to do or not to do a specified thing in the future. That promise demonstrates a person's intent to assure that the thing promised will or will not be done.

Formation of a contract requires an agreement — two parties consenting to the same terms.

The words "I will sell you my black horse for $1,000" is an offer, because the speaker has made a commitment. A mail order catalogue that lists items for sale and their prices is not an offer, because the vendor has not used any language promising to supply a specific quantity at a specific price.

Acceptance occurs when the person to whom the offer is made exchanges his or her own promise or performance for the promise made in the offer. In the common law, the acceptance may not vary at all from the terms of the offer. If it does, then that kind of acceptance will not be valid as an acceptance but constitute a counteroffer and a rejection of the offer.

It should be noted that a contract accepted under threat of physical, mental, or the party so threatened as under "duress" will be void. Acceptance must be freely given. The same is true for contracts entered into between persons in a relationship of power imbalance. The law calls this "undue influence" and it will be presumed in some cases, such as parent-child, trustee-beneficiary, or doctor-patient contracts.

Offer and Acceptance within the Context of Public Procurement

In public procurement, a solicitation, such as an Invitation for Bids (IFB), is not an offer but, instead, is a request to vendors to submit offers. The bids or proposals submitted in response are offers. Acceptance occurs when the public official authorized to award contracts signifies that the jurisdiction has selected the vendor as the winner. That official may be the public procurement officer or may be a city council or board of supervisors.

Nothing needs to be signed for acceptance to occur; it takes place by merely communicating, by words or conduct, assent to the offer. Courts have held that an authorized procurement officer's letter notifying a vendor that it has been selected for award is the point at which a contract is created. Likewise, the vote of a city council may constitute acceptance. That is the case even where the government intends to enter into a signed, formal agreement at some later date.

On the other hand, a written notice of award does not form a contract where the public procurement official sends it so that the vendor receives it after the vendor's offer has expired. Similarly, a government official's statement to a vendor that the vendor has been awarded a contract does not constitute a valid acceptance if that official is not authorized to award contracts.

For small purchases, it is standard practice for the public procurement official to obtain written or verbal quotes and to issue a purchase order based on the best quote. The procurement official's issuance of a purchase order in response is generally an acceptance of an offer — the vendor's quote.

In other cases, the procurement official may simply send a vendor a purchase order for an item from the vendor's catalogue without obtaining quotes. Here, the purchase order constitutes an offer. The terms of the government's purchase order will likely vary with those on the vendor's order confirmation or in the documents shipped with the goods. Some vendors' documents state that acceptance is expressly conditional on assent to those varying terms. If the purchase order is for services rather than goods, the common law provides that the vendor has not accepted the government's offer because the vendor proposed terms that differ from those in the offer.

Definiteness

Under common law, an offer must include the important, or material, terms of the proposed agreement so that, when a person accepts the offer, the resulting agreement is enforceable. Important terms include subject matter, price, payment terms, quantity, quality, duration, and the work to be done. If the parties purport to agree on a material term but do so in a vague manner, as contrasted with omitting the term altogether, there is no agreement because it is too indefinite.

DEFINITENESS WITHIN THE CONTEXT OF PUBLIC PROCUREMENT

Because of the formal competitive process that most governments follow in purchasing items above a certain dollar limit, indefiniteness of the offer is not a problem. Remember that the bid that a vendor submits is the offer. Under the law of public contracts, that bid must be responsive; it must show the vendor's commitment to comply with the solicitation's requirements, which includes supplying a set price. If a vendor submits a bid that says the price will be that in effect at the time it supplies janitorial services, the bid is non-responsive; it is also indefinite.

Many public purchasers today are drafting "floating price" provisions in solicitations for goods subject to volatile price changes, such as with personal computers. Those pricing provisions state, for example, that price will be determined monthly, based on the manufacturer's commercial price plus the set fee or percentage increase that the vendor-bidder identifies in its bid. That type of pricing provision is not indefinite.

Consideration

The concept of consideration is a tough one for lawyers, and defining it in a meaningful way for non-lawyers is even more troublesome. It concerns the promises made during the offer and acceptance, which common law generally requires to be supported by "consideration." The term generally means that the person making the offer intends that the person to whom it is made does or promises to do something they are not legally obligated to do and that the person accepting the offer actually does or promises to do something not legally required. Simply stated, consideration is the "bargained for" exchange of promises. Under the common law, the key to consideration is that the person to be bound by the contract must make a promise or commitment to perform some act or actually perform some act.

CONSIDERATION WITHIN THE CONTEXT OF PUBLIC PROCUREMENT

A good example of a consideration issue in the government contracts setting arises under what are called term or indefinite quantity contracts. Public purchasers establish these contracts for items commonly used throughout the government. Under this type of contract, a vendor agrees to supply particular goods or services at a set price for a specific period of time, but the quantity of the goods or services that the government will need is unknown, only estimated. If a dispute arises because a vendor claims that the government has ordered too great a quantity of the items under the contract, the estimated quantities in the contract as well as the size of past orders will define whether the disputed order is reasonable.

If the contract does not require the government to buy all of those specific goods or services that it needs from that vendor, but reserves the discretion to buy them elsewhere, the government has not given any consideration; it has not obligated itself legally to the terms of the contract. That consideration problem is solved by mandating that the government purchase all of the specific goods or services it needs under the contract.

Mutuality of Obligation

This element is really a sub-element of consideration. It applies in situations where the offer requires the person accepting it to make a promise in return rather than by immediately performing. A simple statement of this element is "both parties must be bound or neither one is bound." It really means that both parties must supply consideration to the other. For example, if a contracting party reserves a means by which it may completely avoid performing, the contract may not be enforceable because both parties are not legally obligated to perform.

Competent Parties

There are certain classes of persons whom the law deems incapable of entering into a contract. A person who lacks the authority to contract for someone else under the law of agency is but one example. Others incapable of entering into binding contracts include infants and mentally infirm individuals. At common law, a person remains an infant until the age of 21. Today, statutes and court decisions set the age at 18.

Some scholars use the concept of "competency" interchangeably with the concept of "consent." Since a contract involves a "meeting of the minds," all parties must be capable of consent. Accordingly, minors and mentally challenged persons may void a contract at the minor's or mentally challenged person's option. If a minor ratifies a contract upon reaching the age of majority, he or she is then bound to it. A contract with an incompetent person is only voidable at the option of the incompetent person if the other party knew about the mental incompetence or ought to have known under the circumstances. An exception is made for contracts for the delivery of necessaries of life for which even a mentally incompetent person would be liable.

In like fashion, a drunk or intoxicated person also lacks the capacity to consent to a contract and has the option of voiding a contract signed while intoxicated, providing it is done at the earliest opportunity upon sobriety.

In the public procurement setting, the capacity issue generally arises because a government employee or a vendor's representative is not authorized to contract. In one instance, a government attempted to argue that a vendor was aware of the acceptable equipment components that the government's procurement official verbally described at a pre-bid conference but did not include in the solicitation. The vendor's sales manager, whom the vendor did not authorize to enter into contracts, attended the conference. The tribunal hearing the dispute determined that, since the sales manager had no contracting authority and did not prepare the vendor's bid, the vendor was not deemed to know about and, thus, was not bound by, the verbal description.

Legal Purpose

Courts generally will not enforce an agreement, or part of an agreement, that violates statutory law or public policy. The extent to which a court will assist one person to enforce an "illegal" contract against another will depend on the type of violation of law involved and the requirements of applicable statutes or ordinances.

For instance, a vendor may not have the appropriate license to enter into a contract to provide certain services to a government, but does so anyway. Another example is where a vendor submits a proposal to perform a study for a government and receives a contract to do the work. It includes in its proposal a requirement for the government to make payments to it in advance of the work, but the law of that jurisdiction prohibits advance payments. In the first case, the government, on discovering that the vendor does not have the proper license, must terminate the contract. If only part of a contract violates the law, as is the case in the second instance, the government may ignore that portion of the contract because the law will not enforce it.

Consideration of Conditions that May Lead to a Voidable Contract

Mistakes

The process for handling mistakes is discussed in Chapter 5; however, it should be noted here that a contract requires a meeting of the minds. If one or both parties have been mistaken about an element of the contract, then there is no such meeting of the minds. However, that does not necessarily mean that the contract is void. Such a rule could breed abuse. Therefore, the common law has attempted to develop a fairly sophisticated set of rules for dealing with mistakes. Unfortunately, as is the case with most contract law, the final determination of what those rules are is constantly changing.

A common mistake is where both parties make the same mistake. Each knows the intention of the other and accepts it, but each is mistaken about some underlying and fundamental fact. This is termed a "mutual mistake." When only one party to a contract is mistaken, this is termed a "unilateral mistake." The common law handles each of these types of mistakes in contracting differently.

When both parties are mistaken on a basic and fundamental element of the contract, the contract is void from the start...

When both parties are mistaken on a basic and fundamental element of the contract, the contract is void from the start if the mistake is of such significance that, in the words of the old English common law cases, it is a "false and fundamental assumption" of the contract. For example, if the identity of a contracting party is a fundamental element of the contract, such as an athlete or artist, a mistake in this regard will void the contract. Another example is a contract involving something that, unbeknownst to the parties, has been destroyed. In contrast, when only one party is mistaken, unless the other party to the contract knows or should have known of the mistake, the contract is still enforceable.

Misrepresentations

Misrepresentation is when one of the parties to a contract lies about or fails to disclose some material element of the contract and, in reliance on this statement, the other party entered into the contract. The common law of contracts treats this kind of fraudulent misrepresentation as grounds for rendering a contract unenforceable. The elements of fraudulent misrepresentation include:

> (1) that the representations were made by the wrongdoer to the victim before the contract; (2) that these representations were false in fact; (3) that the wrongdoer, when he made them, either knew that they were false or made them recklessly without knowing whether they were false or true; and (4) that the victim is damaged thereby.

Misrepresentation must be distinguished from sales language or "puffing." A salesperson's sales pitch that hypes a product may constitute a fraudulent misrepresentation. However, merely touting a good or service in generally favorable terms will most likely not constitute a fraudulent misrepresentation. It is also important to note that silence and the failure to disclose material facts can be construed as misrepresentations in certain circumstances, such as when the omission reasonably results in a misunderstanding or the omission is a fact that a reasonable person would want to know before entering into the contract.

Restraint of Trade Contracts

In contemporary commercial environments, restraint of trade contracts in the form of non-compete and non-circumvent agreements is common. On the face of it, such contracts, while not illegal, fly in the face of public policy as it is considered to be "good for the state" that people be free to ply their profession without restriction. Accordingly, state statutory law and the common law set forth the standards of fairness for such contracts. These standards include that such contracts must be reasonable in relation to the circumstances, time period, and geographical location or, now, Internet marketplace.

Confidentiality agreements, on the other hand, are typically enforced in favor of the restrainer if the information involves trade secrets.

Assignment and Novation

A person can transfer their rights, benefits and liabilities under a contract to another person, unless such assignment rights are limited or eliminated in the contract itself. Where the original contract stays intact and the party transfers rights, benefits, and liabilities under a contract (the assignor) to a new party (the assignee), this is called an "assignment." An assignment must be absolute with no contractual strings to remain attached between the assignor and the other original contracting party. However, the law favors assignment and imposes a duty that parties act reasonably when requested to approve an assignment. In addition, assignments can occur by operation of law, such as when a person dies or a firm declares bankruptcy or is purchased by another.

Novation is the replacement of one contract between two parties with another contract, either between the same parties or others. A novation extinguishes the original contract.

Frustration

No person can be held to a contract if, since acceptance, there has been a radical change which makes performance impossible or illegal. Under certain conditions, a person can be relieved of their contractual obligations under the common law doctrine of "frustration." This common law doctrine sometimes referred to as "impossibility of performance, will excuse one or both parties from performance of the contract. Impossibility of performance is judged by an objective standard. An act of God or a change in statutory law may render performance of the contract impossible or illegal. For example, Hurricane Katrina did render performance of many contracts for the delivery of goods to New Orleans impossible to perform. Further, when the law of Florida changed to disallow certain kinds of consumer and other financial loans, such contracts may have become illegal or impossible to perform.

However, frustration cannot be invoked just because the contract has suddenly become more difficult or expensive for one of the parties to perform. Likewise, frustration cannot be invoked just because it would be more advantageous for one party to not perform under a contract. For example, if one party to an agreement now believes that the contract price is too cheap and that the value of the goods or services contracted for demands a higher contract price, this kind of reason would not be sufficient to invoke a frustration or impossibility of performance defense to performance of the contract. Further, if a party to a contract was partly responsible for the intervening event, which destroyed the object of the contract, or if the event was foreseeable, the frustration or impossibility of performance defense would not apply. Finally, parties can, but would be well advised in most instances not to, contract away this defense by specifically baring such a defense in the contract terms.

Rules For Interpreting Contracts

The courts are frequently asked to resolve disputes about the meaning of certain words, sentences and provisions in contracts. A wide range of general interpretation rules guide the courts in the task of interpreting a contract. However, courts are reluctant to impose their view of what the terms of a contract mean between two parties unless the contract terms, as written, are ambiguous.

If both parties agree on a certain interpretation to be given to a term in a contract, a court has no reason or justification for pursuing the matter further and should accept this interpretation.

A court will always try to discover the intentions of the contracting parties using the plain, ordinary and popular meanings of the words used. Reference to a common usage dictionary is perfectly in order for a court making this kind of decision. A court will not try to re-write a contract using interpretation rules but, rather, to use these rules to pinpoint the intentions of the parties at the moment of contract. For example:

- Courts presume that no provision of the contract is void of any meaning or superfluous but rather must have some purpose. Only in those circumstances where no clear alternate interpretation is available to remove absurdity or ambiguity from a contract provision, will the court void any part of a contract.

- A court can refer to words that have been crossed out, or words in headings, margins, recitals, or a preamble for guidance in interpreting ambiguous contract terms.

- A court may refer to the factual circumstances under which the contract was signed or agreed upon to assist in interpretation of ambiguous contract terms. Such circumstances may include a review of letters exchanged between the parties and prior agreements between the parties. However, the courts will usually refrain from reviewing prior drafts of the existing contract.

- Business customs may also be considered.

- Where contract terms are ambiguous and open to more than one interpretation, the courts usually interpret the contract term against the author, especially if there is a power imbalance between the parties.

- A writing is given greater weight than oral testimony by the courts in interpreting ambiguous terms of a contract. In some cases, evidence of oral amendments or modifications will not be considered where a contract provides that it can only be amended or modified in writing.

- Obvious mistakes in spelling, punctuation and grammar will be corrected as long as such corrections do not change the meaning of a contract. For example, if a contract provision uses the word "may," the courts will not change that word to "shall" but will make sure that the word is spelled correctly and preceded or followed by the appropriate punctuation.

- Courts will interpret contract terms to carry out the general and specific purposes for which the contract was formed.

- Courts will always interpret ambiguous contract terms with a view towards carrying out the intentions of both parties to the contract.

Parol Evidence Rule

The Parol Evidence Rule prohibits a court from considering evidence outside of the language contained in the contract.

The ability of a court to interpret a contract may be limited by the Parol Evidence Rule. The Parol Evidence Rule prohibits a court from considering evidence outside of the language contained in the contract. This Rule is triggered by a finding of the court that the contract is the final and complete agreement of the parties and the final and complete expression of the terms of the contract. If the court finds that a contract is the final and complete agreement between the parties, then no extrinsic or outside evidence can be presented to a court to vary or contradict the terms of a contract. On the other hand, if the court finds that the contract is not the final and complete agreement of the parties, then the court will consider extrinsic or other outside evidence that proves the exact terms and conditions in a contract agreed to by the parties. Therefore, the bar of the Parol Evidence Rule does not prevent either party to a contract to present evidence to a court that the contract was not the final and complete agreement of the parties.

The customary application of the Parol Evidence Rule, as explained in the previous paragraph, can be altered by the parties to a contract. For example, many contracts will contain specific language that states the contract is the final and complete agreement of the parties. Further, many contracts will contain language that prohibit either party from presenting evidence to a court that the contract is not the final and complete agreement of the parties or evidence of different or additional terms applicable to the contract. Since the courts basic approach to interpreting a contract is to follow the intent of the parties, such contract provisions may limit both parties' ability to try to circumvent the application of the Parol Evidence Rule.

Parameters for Written Contracts

As a general rule, contracts may be written or oral. Under both the common law of contracts and other statutory law, certain types of contracts must be in writing. This requirement does not mean that two persons cannot enter into an oral agreement. It simply means that, for certain types of contracts that must be in writing, neither party may enforce an unperformed contractual obligation unless there is a written contract.

Statute of Frauds

At early common law, the king's courts in England generally did not enforce oral promises. This changed over time; but, in 1677, Parliament passed a law called the "Act for the Prevention of Fraud and Perjuries," requiring certain promises and agreements to be evidenced in writing. That law, generally known as the Statute of Frauds, became the common law of this country though court decisions and state legislatures have enacted their own versions of it.

Agreements that Must Be Supported by Written Documentation

The Statute of Frauds generally mandates that the following types of promises or agreements be evidenced in writing: agreements for the sale of land or of interests in land; agreements in consideration of marriage; a promise by the executor or administrator of a deceased person's estate to pay from his or her own pocket a debt of the deceased; certain promises made by a person to answer for the debt of another; and contracts that are not to be performed within one year from the time they are made, including leases and under the U.C.C., contracts for the sale of goods valued at more than $500. The key elements among that list for the procurement official are the sale of land or an interest in land, contracts not to be performed within a year and the sale of goods valued at more than $500.

Satisfying the Writing Requirement

The type of writing that will satisfy the Statute of Frauds varies. A memorandum, exchange of correspondence or receipt, for instance, may suffice if that writing identifies with reasonable certainty the contracting parties, the subject matter of the contract, and the contract's essential terms, especially a description of quantity when dealing with the sale of goods. The writing needs to be signed in some fashion by the party against whom the contract is being enforced. Any mark or sign that is written, printed, stamped, or otherwise placed on the writing may serve as a signature. Electronic signatures probably satisfy the requirement under appropriate circumstances.

Differentiating Between Private and Public Contracts

The extent to which the public procurement official's daily tasks require drafting a wide range of contract terms and conditions depends somewhat on the procurement law and policies in place within the particular jurisdiction. For instance, if the law does not require certain purchases to be acquired competitively, the procurement official may engage in extensive negotiations with vendors for those purchases, including drafting and redrafting the contract's terms. A procurement office may have established a set of terms and conditions that are standard for all contracts, and the procurement official need only attach a copy of them to solicitations issued for competitive procurements.

Whatever responsibilities the public procurement official has in writing contract terms and conditions, they will differ from the responsibilities, and the flexibility, that parties have in the private setting. Briefly, here are the general differences between how contracts are formed in the public and private settings.

Formation of Private Contracts

In the commercial world, parties create contracts in one of three ways. One party may present the other with a prepared document for signature, and the second party has little bargaining power to change the terms of the agreement. Many consumer sales agreements fall within this category.

The second way that a contract is formed is when each party sends the other its prepared document, setting forth differing terms. For example, one party may issue a purchase order for certain goods, and the other sends a confirmation that contains terms that vary from the purchase order. The goods are often shipped despite the differences in the documents, and those differences do not become important unless a problem arises.

The third way that a contract may be created is through the process of negotiation, in which the parties bargain for the contract's terms. Both parties sign the agreement that results from that negotiation. The contract may be a complex document with pages of tightly drafted clauses, or it may consist of a letter that one party drafts for the other to sign.

Formation of a Public Contract

Public contracts are, for the most part, created through a different process. However, just like in private commerce, a public procurement official may issue a purchase order to a vendor for some small-dollar purchases based on items and prices in that vendor's general catalogue. The vendor may ship the goods requested with a confirmation or invoice that contains terms that vary from the purchase order. This scenario generally creates a contract, despite the fact that the parties did not reach an agreement on its precise language. This type of transaction occurs both in private and public contracting.

For larger-dollar purchases, a contract arises as a result of a formal, arms-length process. The public entity issues a solicitation that "invites" vendors to make an offer that complies with the specific terms of that solicitation. Where the public entity seeks a contractor through the competitive sealed bids process, there is no real bargaining. Under the competitive sealed proposals method, the opportunity for discussions and negotiations exists but is limited.

Even in a qualifications-based selection process, where the procurement official negotiates price after selecting the most qualified professional service vendor, the subject matter of the negotiation is generally restricted to price or fee. Thus, in much of public contracting, the bargaining that is a normal part of private commerce is absent, due in large part to the mandate placed on public procurement officials to ensure that the contractor-selection process is fair to all.

Once the public procurement official selects the winning bid or proposal and notifies the vendor submitting that bid or proposal of its selection, a contract comes into existence in most cases. Where the awarding of a contract requires the vote of a town council or board of supervisors, that vote is the event that creates a contract. The solicitation and the bid or proposal becomes the contract voted upon.

In some public entities, procurement officials prepare a separate contract document for signature once they have selected and notified the winning vendor. A separate contract document is unnecessary because a contract arises under the principles of contract law once the entity indicates acceptance of the vendor's bid or proposal.

For complex projects, the public procurement official, their client-agency user, and the vendor may wish to have one document, instead of the solicitation and the proposal that spells out the obligations of the parties. The public procurement official should understand that the document is not the contract but may be a more concise version of it. Problems may arise with this practice. The creation of a separate document opens the door for mistakes to occur in the transfer of information from one document to another. An example is the inadvertent change of "125 calendar days" for performance to "125 working days." To the extent that the new document changes the terms of the solicitation or the bid or proposal, it may amend the contract.

Sometimes, public procurement officials issue a solicitation without many terms in it, particularly when buying goods, and award a contract through a simple blanket purchase order. Unless the solicitation addresses issues, such as termination of a contract because of an act of God, contract remedies including termination, and payment, such terms may not be adequately covered, or covered at all, depending on the language of the blanket purchase order. This practice of issuing an incomplete solicitation may also provide leverage for the vendor in any argument to include the vendor's terms and conditions in the contract. In addition, some vendors or contractors innocently, or maybe not so innocently, seek the public procurement official to sign a separate agreement for "housekeeping" or other similar reasons. The best approach is for the procurement official to include in the solicitation all the terms that will become part of the contract. The procurement office should have a set of approved, standard contract terms addressing issues common to all of its contracts, and may wish to draft additional standard terms applicable, for instance, to contracts for the purchase of goods. The public procurement official must either include those standard terms in every solicitation or simply include language in the solicitation that incorporates them by reference, making copies available to vendors online, via fax-on-demand, or at the procurement office.

Common Law Breaches and Remedies

A breach of contract comes in many forms. There is a "complete breach" or "material breach" of contract where one party fails to perform the essential and fundamental part of their undertaking or so underperforms the contractual obligation that the purpose of the contract is not satisfied. In other situations, a party to a contract performs most of the obligations under the contract but omits or refuses to completely perform under the contract. This "minor breach" of contract, because the party to the contract "substantially performed" the contractual obligation, has the effect of binding the other party to the contract to also perform under the contract, at least in an equivalent manner.

The common law measure of damages for a breach of contract can be set out in the contract itself or can be based on other various applicable legal principles. For example, the parties to a contract can set out the measure of money damages in a contract through a valid liquidated damages provision. A valid liquidated damages provision under the common law must be a reasonable measure of the actual damages suffered by either party if the contract is breached. The courts will not validate a liquidated damages provision in a contract if the amount of damages recoverable under such provision does not correspond to the actual damages suffered by a party due to the breach of contract. Predicting at the time of the formation of a contract what the actual damages will be upon the breach of a contract can be difficult. The court, in hindsight, will evaluate a liquidated damages provision to insure that the application of the provision which may limit or enhance the amount of damages a party may receive, is not a penalty.

In addition, the parties to a contract can agree that specific performance of the contract is required because the value of performance of the contract is unique and that money damages would be an inadequate remedy. For example, the remedy of specific performance applies most often in a sale of land contract or in a contract for unique goods or services. In all cases, each party has a responsibility to mitigate their losses. That means that even if the contractual partner is not keeping their end of the bargain, the affected party should use reasonable effort to keep its losses at a minimum.

An injunction is another coercive legal remedy, which can be used in some breach of contract cases where a direct order is required to stop a party from continuing an ongoing breach. An injunction will only be granted where monetary damages would not protect the injured party.

The most common form of contract damages are compensatory money damages, the out-of-pocket expenses caused by the breach. Money damages are an attempt by the court to compensate the innocent party to the contract; that is, the party that suffers the breach. The purpose is compensation — not punishment.

Generally, there are two main methods of calculating money damages:

- The diminution of value test: the difference between what was contracted for and what was received.

- The cost of performance method: whatever it costs to put the plaintiff in the position he would have been in had the defendant fully performed his contractual obligations. The defendant is ordered to pay the cost of fixing the defect necessary to complete the contract.

References

National Institute of Governmental Purchasing, Inc. (NIGP) (1999). *General public procurement*. Herndon, VA: NIGP.

National Institute of Governmental Purchasing, Inc. (NIGP) (2000). *Intermediate public procurement*. Herndon, VA: NIGP.

Chapter 4

The Uniform Commercial Code

Commercial business activity in the United States, whether private or public, began at the local level. Local businesses sold goods and services to neighbors, and local government purchased from local businesses. With the industrial revolution and the ability to travel and communicate on a national level, the mechanics of conducting a simple business transaction either involved a maze of local customs or remained completely unregulated. It became apparent that a uniform business transactions law would make the business of buying and selling more predictable, more efficient, and less risky.

In response to this need, the American Law Institute and the National Conference of Commissioners on Uniform State Laws published a uniform code of commercial law in 1951. This uniform code, called the Uniform Commercial Code, referred to simply as the "U.C.C.," essentially incorporated the common law of commercial transactions into a uniform law. The U.C.C. was presented to, and adopted by, all 50 states.

The most important part of the U.C.C. for the public procurement official is Article 2, entitled "Sale of Goods." Absent a specific state or federal statute or administrative regulation, Article 2 will govern the public procurement official's contract for the sale of goods. It is important to note that Article 2 only covers contracts for the sale of goods and not contracts for the sale of services. Therefore, a contract to purchase 200 boxes of pencils will be covered by Article 2, but a contract for the purchase of a financial auditor to review data will not be covered by Article 2.

The U.C.C. plays an essential part in the daily tasks of the procurement official. It particularly does so whether there is or is not a formal, written contract between the public entity and the vendor for the purchase of goods. Small dollar purchases in which the purchaser solicits verbal price quotes and issues a purchase order; and formally competed, higher dollar purchases where the purchaser issues a simple blanket purchase order to the winning vendor without any underlying, comprehensive contract terms in place are examples of public procurement contracts that may not be memorialized in a written contract document. The public purchaser must be familiar with some basic U.C.C. requirements.

This chapter provides a general overview of key contractual concepts affecting public procurement in the areas of contract performance, warranties, breaches, and remedies. However, the text does not intend to provide a comprehensive review of these concepts, so the public procurement official is strongly encouraged to become very familiar with pertinent sections of Article 2 of the U.C.C.

Scope of Article 2 of the U.C.C.

Section 2-102 of the Code defines the scope of Article 2 to include "transactions in goods." "Goods" that are the subject of sales under Article 2 consist of all things, whether specially manufactured or not, that are movable at the time the contract is executed (U.C.C. Section 2-105[1]).

The use of the term "transaction" rather than "sale" in U.C.C. Section 2-102 is significant in that it makes clear that the reach of Article 2 goes beyond those transactions where there is a transfer of title. Thus, Article 2 sections have been applied in decisions involving transactions that are not bona fide sales, but which are used as substitutes for a sale or which have attributes analogous to a sale, such as leases, bailments, or construction contracts.

It is clear that Article 2 of the Code is intended to have broad application; however, it also follows from the Code's continued focus on "goods" that a contract which calls merely for the rendition of services is not subject to the sales provisions of the Code. Therefore, the fact that the party supplying a service does so in conjunction with the delivery of goods does not necessarily mean that the transaction falls within the scope of the Code. Even though the definition of goods includes goods that have been specially manufactured, "(not) all contracts for special manufacture qualify as contracts for the sale of goods under the Uniform Commercial Code" (*Curtis Publishing Company v. Sheridan*, 53 F.R.D. 642, 644 [S.D.N.Y. 1971]). Even in the context of a contract for special manufacture, initial inquiry should focus not on the fact of special manufacture, but on whether the contract is for the sale of goods or for the rendition of services. Most state court's use the "predominant purpose" test to determine if the contract falls within the coverage of Article 2 of the Uniform Commercial Code. For example, a pool service contract may also include the purchase of a pool pump or other pool equipment. In this case, the predominant purpose of the contract is to purchase a pool service while the purchase of the pool equipment is an incidental purchase.

It should be noted that, while Section 2-318 attempts to define the scope in which buyers are entitled to the protections afforded by Article 2 warranty provisions, this is largely a question of state law. Each state is free to extend or restrict the application of the Article 2 warranty provisions as it sees fit.

The U.C.C. and Contract Warranties

Article 2 U.C.C. warranties are important because they create the seller's legal obligations regarding the transfer of title to and the quality and characteristics of the goods sold. A warranty is a seller's promise or representation that the goods will be of a stated quality or character. Warranties may also involve an obligation to repair or replace unsatisfactory goods. The U.C.C. permits sellers to disclaim warranties if done in compliance with the U.C.C. requirements.

The key Article 2 U.C.C. warranties are:

- Warranty of Title (Section 2-312)
- Express Warranties (Section 2-313)
- Implied Warranties of Merchantability (Section 2-314)
- Implied Warranties of Fitness for a Particular Purpose (Section 2-315)

Warranty of Title

The warranty of title, which is implicitly incorporated in Article 2 U.C.C. contracts, is really three different warranties in one. The warranty of title not only warrants good title to the goods sold but also warrants that there are no security interests or other liens on the goods other than those known to the buyer. The warranty of title also warrants against any patent infringement or similar type claim. The U.C.C. also expressly provides the mechanism for disclaiming or excluding this warranty of title by a seller.

U.C.C. Section 2-312 states:

(1)Subject to subsection (2) there is in a contract for sale a warranty by the seller that:

(a) The title conveyed shall be good, and its transfer rightful; and
(b) The goods shall be delivered free from any security interest or other lien or encumbrance of which the buyer at the time of contracting has no knowledge.
(2) A warranty under subsection (1) will be excluded or modified only by specific language or by circumstances which give the buyer reason to know that the person selling does not claim title in himself or that he is purporting to sell only such right or title as he or a third person may have.

For example, if a county purchases from a vendor a tracking system used to track inventory of paper products and other goods and the vendor fails to obtain the various patent clearances before selling the system, the manufacturer/owner of the patented system would have the right to recover the tracking system from the county. The county's legal cause of action would be against the vendor for breach of the U.C.C. Warranty of Title.

Express Warranties

A seller's oral or written statements or promises made to a buyer which relate to the characteristics, qualities or performance of the goods, creates an express warranty. It occurs when a seller either promises or asserts as fact that the goods will provide a certain level of performance or quality, and that promise or assertion becomes a reason that the buyer enters into a contract.

The key to whether a seller's statement or promises create an express warranty is that the seller's statements or promises must be of such substance that the promise or statement is capable of measurement or proof. Descriptive literature or a product sample that a bidder submits with its bid describing or showing a certain quality or performance level of the bidder's product may constitute an express warranty.

Section 2-313 defines an express warranty, in pertinent part, as follows:

> Express warranties by the seller are created as follows: (a) Any affirmation of fact or promise made by the seller to the buyer which relates to the goods and becomes part of the basis of the bargain creates an express warranty that the goods shall conform to the affirmation or promise.

The key... is that the seller's statements... must be of such substance that the... statement is capable of measurement or proof.

For example, suppose a school district purchases erasable wallpaper to cover the walls in various pre-school classrooms. The vendor of the wallpaper not only shows and demonstrates a sample of the wallpaper to the public procurement official but also demonstrates how easily the wallpaper is applied. The vendor writes and draws on the wallpaper with special marking pens. The vendor then represents and shows that the wallpaper can be wiped clean and re-used. The school district purchases the wallpaper and hangs the wallpaper in various classrooms. However, after the first use, the wallpaper does not wipe clean and cannot be reused. The school district, based on the representation, sample and demonstration by the vendor, would have a legal claim against the vendor for breach of a U.C.C. Express Warranty.

Implied Warranties

An implied warranty arises by operation of law without the need for any action by the buyer or the seller. The U.C.C. creates, other than the warranty of title, two very important implied warranties: The Implied Warranty of Merchantability and the Implied Warranty of Fitness for a Particular Purpose.

IMPLIED WARRANTY OF MERCHANTABILITY AND USAGE OF TRADE

If the person selling the goods is considered a merchant of those goods under the U.C.C., there is an implied warranty that the goods will meet certain industry standards. The warranty is that they will "pass in the trade under the contract description" and be "fit for the ordinary purposes" for which those types of goods are used. This concept is commonly referred to as "usage of trade."

The implied warranty of merchantability, as codified under Section 2-314 of the U.C.C., states, in pertinent part:

> Unless excluded or modified,... a warranty that the goods shall be merchantable is implied in a contract for their sale if the seller is a merchant with respect to goods of that kind. Under this Section the serving for value of food or drink to be consumed either on the premises or elsewhere is a sale.

Section 2-314(1) states that, for goods to be merchantable, they "must be at least such as... are fit for the ordinary purposes for which such goods are used." In accordance with Section 2-314(2), to prove a breach of implied warranty of merchantability,

> a plaintiff must prove, first, that the goods bought and sold were subject to an implied warranty of merchantability; second, that the goods did not comply with the warranty in that the goods were defective at the time of the sale; third, that his injury was due to the defective nature of the goods; and fourth, that damages were suffered as a result. The burden is upon the purchaser to establish a breach by the seller of the warranty of merchantability by showing that a defect existed at the time of the sale.

There is an interesting note about the application of this warranty in the public procurement arena. Some courts have decided that, if the government regularly sells certain goods as surplus property, it may be a "merchant" under the U.C.C. In those cases, the implied warranty arises, unless the government disclaims it as part of the sale.

For example, suppose a county purchases yellow and white paint from a vendor to be used to paint the yellow and white lines at the local airport. However, after the paint had been applied and dried, the paint gave off not only a noxious odor but also the fumes of the paint were toxic and caused many airport workers to suffer respiratory illness. In the county's lawsuit against the paint seller, although most paint will give off a smell, if the county can prove that fumes from this paint were toxic, then the paint purchased by the county would breach the U.C.C. Implied Warranty of Merchantability.

THE IMPLIED WARRANTY OF FITNESS FOR A PARTICULAR PURPOSE

While the implied warranty of merchantability applies to goods used for their ordinary purpose, the implied warranty of fitness for a particular purpose applies to an instance where the seller, at the time of contracting, has reason to know that the buyer wants the goods for a particular purpose and is relying on the seller's skill or judgment to select or furnish suitable goods.

An example is a case involving a sawmill operator who described in detail the mill's hydraulic system and asked a major oil company's representative to recommend a proper oil. After some time, the operator discovered that the oil was not the proper product and was the cause of the hydraulic system's frequent breakdowns. The oil company's representative had to pay damages to the mill operator due to a breach of the implied warranty of fitness for a particular purpose.

> Section 2-315 of the U.C.C. provides:

> Where the seller at the time of contracting has reason to know any particular purpose for which the goods are required and that the buyer is relying on the seller's skill or judgment to select or furnish suitable goods, there is unless excluded or modified under the next section an implied warranty that the goods shall be fit for such purpose.

Disclaimer of Article 2 Warranties

> Section 2-316(3) of the U.C.C. provides:

> (a) Unless the circumstances indicate otherwise, all implied warranties are excluded by expressions like "as is," "with all faults," or other language which in common understanding calls the buyer's attention to the exclusion of warranties and makes plain that there is no implied warranty.

The key to disclaiming either the Implied Warranty of Merchantability or the Implied Warranty of Fitness for a Particular Purpose is that such disclaimer must be conspicuously written in any document. It should be noted that the clause "unless the circumstances indicate otherwise" provides the buyer an opportunity to prove that the seller did not properly disclaim any implied warranty.

Performance of an Article 2 U.C.C. Contract

Overview

The performance of a U.C.C. Article 2 contract for the sale of goods is pretty simple — the seller will deliver the goods contracted for to the buyer, and the buyer will pay the seller for the goods (U.C.C. Sections 2-301, 2-507, and 2-511). When the Code provisions are read together literally, it appears that neither the buyer nor the seller of goods is obligated to do anything unless the other acts. This is because Article 2 anticipates that the seller's delivery of the goods to the buyer and the buyer's payment for the goods will happen simultaneously. Although many commercial transactions may occur in this manner, some commercial transactions do not happen this way.

Under the common law, a party may require that the other party "tender" his or her performance in a certain way; and, if that second party does not do so, the first party may reject the performance. For instance, if the contract requires payment in dollars and a party makes payment in pesos instead, the other party may reject the payment without violating the contract. That rule often is called the "perfect tender" rule.

The U.C.C. adopts that rule, but substantially limits it. If none of the U.C.C. exceptions apply, the buyer may say "take these goods away; there is a defect." The rule also applies to installment contracts and permits a buyer to reject goods in a single installment under a contract calling for the goods to be delivered in lots. However, only if the installment substantially impairs the value of the entire contract may a buyer, in effect reject the entire contract and cancel any obligation to accept any other installment. Unlike under the common law, the buyer must permit the seller to fix, or "cure," the non-conforming tender of delivery of the goods.

If the buyer accepts the goods, he or she no longer has the right to reject them. Acceptance occurs in several ways. On receiving the goods, the buyer must inspect them, identify the defects, and notify the seller in a timely manner. Timeliness depends on the circumstances, such as the difficulty in discovering defects, but the buyer must be diligent about inspection. If the buyer is not diligent or fails to send a timely notice of the defects, he or she has accepted the goods. The buyer also may accept the goods if he or she uses them after knowing about the defects.

The U.C.C. permits the parties to a contract to agree to terms different from those that the U.C.C. specifies. It may be, for instance, that a government wishes to require "perfect tender" in an installment contract; that is, to declare the contract breached if any one delivery is defective. To do so, there must be contract language in the solicitation or purchase order reserving that right to the government.

Article 2 creates room for the parties to fashion not only the terms but also the performance of a contract for the sale of goods to fit their needs. Article 2 attempts to codify existing general commercial practice so that, absent a contrary agreement between the parties, all buyers and sellers know how a contract will be performed. Therefore, the study of the performance obligations of a U.C.C. Article 2 contract for the sale of goods establishes a framework for commercial activity to flourish.

As previously mentioned, it is strongly recommended that the public procurement official become knowledgeable of all concepts contained in Article 2 of the U.C.C. Within the context of performance issues, the official should focus on the 500 and 600 sections of Article 2. Some key parameters regarding contract performance are highlighted below.

Tender of Delivery

The "tender of delivery" describes the seller's obligation regarding the provision of goods as specified in a sales contract. Section 2-503(1) provides: "Tender of delivery requires that the seller put and hold conforming goods at the buyer's disposition and give the buyer any notification reasonably necessary to enable him to take delivery."

Buyer's Right to Inspection of the Goods

In accordance with Section 2-513, the buyer of goods has a right to inspect the goods at a reasonable place and time and in a reasonable manner before acceptance or rejection of the goods and before making payment for the goods. This "reasonable" time for inspection will vary with the type of goods delivered. For example, the time permitted for a buyer to inspect perishable goods, like food, will be shorter than the time to inspect durable goods, like nails and bolts and screws.

Buyer's Rightful Rejection of Goods

Sections 2-601 and 2-602 of Article 2 define the buyer's right to reject goods delivered by the seller if the goods fail to conform to a contract for any reason and also require the buyer to timely notify the seller of rejection of the non-conforming goods. For example, if a school district purchases athletic equipment and the logo on each piece of athletic equipment identifying the school district is not exactly as contracted for, the school district has the right under the U.C.C. to reject the non-conforming delivery of athletic equipment.

Buyer's Obligations as to Rightful Rejected Goods

Sections 2-602, 2-603, and 2-605 of Article 2 impose an obligation on the merchant buyer and a non-merchant buyer to use reasonable care in holding the rejected goods. The merchant buyer's duties also include following the seller's instructions regarding the goods, including reshipment to the seller at the seller's expense. Both the merchant buyer and the non-merchant buyer may, in the absence of seller instructions, sell perishable goods at the seller's expense. For example, if a county operated jail facility purchases frozen food from a vendor and rightfully rejects the frozen food as non-conforming to the contract terms, the county must use reasonable care in holding onto the frozen food and reasonable care would include making sure that the frozen food does not spoil. In addition, the county would be able to charge back the cost of storing the frozen food so that it does not spoil.

Buyer's Acceptance of Goods

Section 2-606 specifies what constitutes the acceptance of goods.

> (a) Acceptance of goods occurs when the buyer:
> (1) after a reasonable opportunity to inspect the goods signifies to the seller that the goods are conforming or that he will take or retain them in spite of their nonconformity; or
> (2) fails to make an effective rejection (Subsection (a) of Section 2.602), but such acceptance does not occur until the buyer has had a reasonable opportunity to inspect them; or
> (3) does any act inconsistent with the seller's ownership; but if such act is wrongful as against the seller it is an acceptance only if ratified by him.
> (b) Acceptance of a part of any commercial unit is acceptance of that entire unit.

In essence, Section 2-606 stipulates that the buyer may accept the seller's delivery of goods; regardless of whether the seller's goods conform or do not conform to the contract. For example, if the county police department purchases and receives from a vendor radar guns to detect speeding cars and uses these radar guns despite the fact that the guns are bigger and bulkier than the contract specifies, by using the radar guns the county has accepted the delivery of the radar guns under the terms of the U.C.C. However, it is also important to note that by accepting the radar guns, the county has not waived its legal right to sue for breach of contract.

Buyer's Revocation of Acceptance of Goods

Even after a buyer has accepted the seller's delivery of goods, the buyer can revoke acceptance of the goods when the buyer discovers that the seller's non-conforming goods substantially impair the value of the goods. Revocation of acceptance by the buyer requires that notice be given to the seller within a reasonable time after the buyer discovers the goods are non-conforming or that the seller will not correct the non-conforming delivery of goods. The key to revocation of acceptance is that the non-conformity of the goods must substantially impair the value of the goods. The following is a comparison of the U.C.C. sections regarding rejection of goods and revocation of acceptance of goods

Section 2-602 provides the manner and effect of rightful rejection as follows:

(a) Rejection of goods must be within a reasonable time after their delivery or tender. It is ineffective unless the buyer reasonably notifies the seller.

(b) Subject to the provisions of the two following sections on rejected goods (Sections 2-603 and 2-604).

(1) after rejection, any exercise of ownership by the buyer with respect to any commercial unit is wrongful as against the seller; and
(2) before rejection, if the buyer has taken physical possession of goods in which he does not have a security interest, he is under a duty after rejection to hold them with reasonable care at the seller's disposition for a time sufficient to permit the seller to remove them; but
(3) the buyer has no further obligations with regard to goods rightfully rejected.

Sections 2-601 outline the buyer's rights on improper delivery to (1) reject the whole; or (2) accept the whole; or (3) accept any commercial unit or units and reject the rest.

Section 2-608 Revocation of Acceptance in Whole or in Part

(a) The buyer may revoke his acceptance of a lot or commercial unit whose non-conformity substantially impairs its value to him if he has accepted.

(1) on the reasonable assumption that its non-conformity would be cured and it has not been seasonably cured; or
(2) without discovery of such non-conformity if his acceptance was reasonably induced either by the difficulty of discovery before acceptance or by the seller's assurances.
(b) Revocation of acceptance must occur within a reasonable time after the buyer discovers or should have discovered the ground for it and before any substantial change in condition of the goods, which is not caused by their own defects. It is not effective until the buyer notifies the seller of it.

(c) A buyer who so revokes has the same rights and duties with regard to the goods involved as if he had rejected them.

For example, suppose the county accepts the tender of delivery of ink cartridges from a vendor only to discover upon opening the cartridge packages as needed that the cartridges are not full of ink. If this failure to provide full ink cartridges could only be reasonably discovered upon opening the cartridge packages and affects 75% of all of the ink cartridges delivered, the county would have the right under the U.C.C. to revoke its acceptance of the ink cartridges.

Seller's Right to Cure a Non-conforming Delivery of Goods

The seller's right to cure is perhaps the best example of how far U.C.C. Article 2 will go to give the buyer and seller a chance to complete a deal. The seller has two different Article 2 rights to cure (i.e., "correct") a seller's delivery of non-conforming goods.

If the time for performance by the seller under the contract has not expired and the seller has received notice of a rightful rejection or revocation of acceptance of the goods by the buyer, then the seller, upon notice to the buyer, can make a delivery of conforming goods before the seller's time for performance expires. Furthermore, the buyer must accept this delivery of conforming goods.

Where the buyer rejects or revokes acceptance of non-conforming goods delivered by the seller, and the seller reasonably believed that the buyer would accept the non-conforming goods, with or without some money adjustment, the seller upon timely notice to the buyer, may have a reasonable time to deliver conforming goods to the buyer.

In either case, a seller's notice to a buyer that the seller intends to cure the non-conforming delivery of goods and the seller does in fact cure this non-conforming delivery, the buyer must accept the "cured" delivery.

Section 2-508 of the U.C.C. regarding the cure by the seller provides:

> (1) Where any tender or delivery by the seller is rejected because non-conforming and the time for performance has not yet expired, the seller may seasonably notify the buyer of his intention to cure and may then within the contract time make a conforming delivery.

> (2) Where the buyer rejects a non-conforming tender which the seller had reasonable grounds to believe would be acceptable with or without money allowance, the seller may, if he seasonably notifies the buyer, have a further reasonable time to substitute a conforming tender.

The seller's right to cure under the U.C.C. is a major departure from the common law of contracts.

Risk of Loss

The risk of loss provisions of Article 2 addresses the issue of who bears the expense of the loss if the goods are damaged or destroyed in delivery of the goods by the seller to the buyer.

Article 2 attempts to allocate the risk of loss to the goods in transit fairly between the buyer and the seller. The key factor in placing the risk of loss with the seller or the buyer is to first determine if the seller's tender of delivery of the goods was of conforming or non-conforming goods. The allocation of the risk of loss to the buyer will depend in large part on whether the buyer would have had the right to reject or revoke acceptance of the goods delivered by the seller.

Section 2-509 of the U.C.C. regarding the risk of loss in absence of a breach provides:

(1) Where the contract requires or authorizes the seller to ship the goods by carrier

(a) if it does not require him to deliver them at a particular destination, the risk of loss passes to the buyer when the goods are duly delivered to the carrier even though the shipment is under reservation (Section 2-505); but (b) if it does require him to deliver them at a particular destination and the goods are there duly tendered while in the possession of the carrier, the risk of loss passes to the buyer when the goods are duly tendered so as to enable the buyer to take delivery.

(2) Where the goods are held by a bailee to be delivered without being moved, the risk of loss passes to the buyer

(a) on his receipt of a negotiable document of title covering the goods; or (b) on acknowledgment by the bailee of the buyer's right to possession of the goods; or (c) after his receipt of a non-negotiable document of title or other written direction to deliver, as provided in subsection (4)(b) of Section 2-503.

(3) In any case not within subsection (1) or (2), the risk of loss passes to the buyer on his receipt of the goods if the seller is a merchant; otherwise the risk passes to the buyer on tender of delivery.

(4) The provisions of this section are subject to contrary agreement of the parties and to the provisions of this Article on sale on approval (Section 2-327) and on effect of breach on risk of loss (Section 2-510).

Section 2-510 of the U.C.C. addressing the effect of a breach on the risk of loss provides:

(1) Where a tender or delivery of goods so fails to conform to the contract as to give a right of rejection the risk of their loss remains on the seller until cure or acceptance.

(2) Where the buyer rightfully revokes acceptance he may to the extent of any deficiency in his effective insurance coverage treat the risk of loss as having rested on the seller from the beginning.

(3) Where the buyer, as to conforming goods already identified to the contract for sale, repudiates or is otherwise in breach before risk of their loss has passed to him, the seller may to the extent of any deficiency in his effective insurance

coverage treat the risk of loss as resting on the buyer for a commercially reasonable time.

Impossibility of Performance of a Contract for Sale of Goods

Article 2 uses the concept of "commercial impracticability" as the standard by which to judge whether a contract has become "impossible to perform."

"Commercial Impracticability" does include the common law contract notion of "act of God" or "force majeure." Note that Article 2 provides for other situations when performance of a contract may be excused; including Sections 2-613, 2-614, 2-615, and 2-616. A prime example of commercial impracticability can be seen in the aftermath of weather disasters like Hurricane Katrina. There is little doubt this provision of the U.C.C. applies to the inability to deliver goods to New Orleans after Hurricane Katrina. For example, contracts let for the delivery of new school busses by a New Orleans bus company to a New Orleans school district would be "commercial impracticable" not only because the roads were impassable but also because many of the school buildings had been destroyed.

> *"Commercial Impracticability" does include the common law contract notion of "act of God" or "force majeure."*

Remedies for Breach of an Article 2 Contract

Overview

Before identifying remedies for a breach of contract, there should be a general acknowledgement and understanding of what constitutes a breach of contract. As stated in Section 2-301, the basic obligation of the seller is to deliver conforming goods, and the basic obligation of the buyer is to accept and pay for conforming goods delivered by the seller. Therefore, by definition, a seller's breach of contract would be the failure to properly deliver conforming goods to a buyer, and a buyer's breach of contract would be the failure to accept and pay for conforming goods delivered by the seller. Regardless, both a seller and a buyer must provide notice to the other that a breach of contract has occurred.

Generally, if a breach occurs by either the seller or the buyer, the party hurt by the breach may pursue all legal remedies that the U.C.C. has devised, including canceling the contract.

In general, the purpose of the remedy provisions of the U.C.C. is to hold the party that breached the contract liable for the damages that he or she has caused the other party, namely, the losses caused and the gains prevented. However, the party who has been wronged by a breach of contract may not unreasonably sit by and let damages accumulate. He or she has a duty to take actions that reduce the damages caused.

Under common law, the general remedy for breach of contract is money damages representing the monetary value of gains lost and losses sustained. This is also a remedy available under the U.C.C.

The determination of whether a breach of contract by either party has occurred can be tricky. Section 2-610 stipulates that a buyer or seller may definitely refuse, prior to when the performance of a contract obligation is due, to perform a contract obligation. This refusal to perform a contract obligation not yet due amounts to an anticipatory repudiation of a contract. In this instance, either a buyer or seller may choose to leverage Section 2-609 and seek, in writing, adequate assurance from a party that the party will honor its contractual obligation.

The failure on the part of either a buyer or seller to provide this adequate assurance of performance within a reasonable time not to exceed 30 days will amount to repudiation of a contract. Under Section 2-611, a buyer or seller may retract a repudiation of a contract by providing a clear indication to the other party that the repudiating party intends to perform its contract obligations. Such retraction of a repudiation of a contract will be effective, unless the non-repudiating party has already canceled the contract or otherwise changed its position in reliance on the repudiation. An anticipatory repudiation of a contract will also trigger the remedies for breach of contract under the U.C.C.

The provisions of Article 2 cover the basic remedies available for sellers and buyers. The basic remedies are addressed below and are detailed within this section of the chapter.

- For the seller's non-delivery or defective delivery of goods, the buyer may recover the difference between the market price of the goods and their contract price, or between the price of substitute goods and the unpaid contract price.

- For the seller's breach of warranty, the buyer may recover the difference between the value that the goods would have had if they had been as warranted and their actual value.

- For the buyer's breach in not accepting the goods, the seller may recover the difference between the contract price and the market price, or the difference in price obtained in reselling the goods and the contract price for the goods.

- The buyer is obligated to pay the price of the goods to the seller if the buyer has accepted the goods or if goods are destroyed after the risk of loss has passed to the buyer.

Essentially, the remedies provided by the U.C.C. are to be liberally administered to make sure that the injured party is put in the same position as if the other party had fully performed the contract.

Seller's Remedies for Buyer's Breach of Contract in General

Section 2-703 establishes the menu of remedies available to a seller for a buyer who breaches a contract. This Section states that the seller's remedies can be triggered when a buyer:

- Has wrongfully rejected the goods; or
- Has wrongfully revoked acceptance of the goods; or
- Fails to pay for conforming goods properly delivered; or
- Repudiates the contract for the sale of goods.

Where appropriate, the seller's first option is to withhold delivery of any undelivered amount of the goods. Where appropriate, the seller can also identify conforming goods to the contract and may even, in some circumstances, complete production of unfinished goods intended for the particular contract that has been breached by the buyer (Section 2-704).

SELLER'S REMEDY - MARKET PRICE AND CONTRACT PRICE DIFFERENTIAL

Section 2-708 provides the traditional measure of damages when the breach of contract by the buyer amounts to non-acceptance of conforming goods delivered by the seller or the buyer's repudiation of the contract.

SELLER'S REMEDY – RESALE PRICE AND CONTRACT PRICE DIFFERENTIAL

Section 2-706 provides the uniquely U.C.C. measure of damages for a buyer's breach of contract. The U.C.C. permits the seller to resell the goods in a private or public sale and then claim the difference between the resale price of the goods and the contract price of the goods as the amount of damages.

It is important to note that applying either the market price-contract price differential or resale price-contract price differential as the measure of a seller's damages for a breach of a U.C.C. contract may not sustain a legal claim for damages. For example, if the market price or the resale prices is <u>more</u> than the contract price, the seller would actually make money due to the buyer's breach of contract. This scenario has occurred when the goods to be sold jump in price. An example of this would be oil.

SELLER'S REMEDY - SPECIFIC PERFORMANCE: THE PRICE OF THE GOODS

Section 2-709 addresses two concepts. First, the seller, upon a buyer's failure to pay, is entitled to recover the actual purchase price of the goods if the goods are accepted, lost, or damaged within a commercially reasonable time after the risk of loss has passed to the buyer. Second, a seller is entitled to the purchase price of goods identified to a contract that the seller, despite a reasonable effort, could not resell because of the unique character of the goods. This remedy provision literally forces the buyer to perform the buyer's contract obligation — pay the purchase price.

Buyer's Remedies for Seller's Breach of Contract in General

Section 2-711 establishes the roster of remedies available for a buyer upon a seller's breach of contract. The section specifically states that the seller's failure to make delivery of goods or the seller's repudiation of the buyer's contract or the buyer's rightful rejection or revocation of the goods permits the buyer to cancel the contract with the seller. In addition to cancellation of the seller's contract, the buyer, where appropriate, will be entitled to the other remedies provided in Sections 2-712, 2-713, 2-714, and 2-716.

BUYER'S REMEDY - COVER

This clause is the counterpart to the U.C.C. Article 2 that creates a resale remedy for sellers in Section 2-706 and is unique to the U.C.C. In this instance, the buyer under Section 2-711 is permitted to seek the purchase of substitute goods based on the seller's breach of contract. It should be noted that the failure of a buyer to choose "cover" under Section 2-712 as a remedy does not preclude the buyer from other remedies listed in Section 2-711.

BUYER'S REMEDY - MARKET PRICE AND CONTRACT PRICE DIFFERENCE

This provision is similar to the seller's remedy contained in Section 2-708. It should be noted that the market price is determined at the time when the buyer learned of the breach. Section 2-713 also provides the buyer's remedy for a seller's repudiation of contract obligations.

It should also be noted here that either applying the market price-contract price differential or the cover price-contract price differential as the measure of damages may not sustain a legal claim for damages under the U.C.C. For example, when the cover price or market price is <u>less</u> than the contract price, the buyer would actually save money because of the seller's breach of contract. This scenario occurs when the price of the contracted goods drop, like the drop in the sales price for automobiles.

Buyer's Remedy - Breach of Warranty

This provision provides the measure of damages for a seller's breach of contract in which the buyer has accepted the goods but the goods are either non-conforming or fail to live up to the Article 2 warranties. Note that in all cases of a breach of contract under Article 2, the injured party to the contract must provide notice of breach to the breaching party. The proper measure of a buyer's damages under this section simply amounts to the difference between the value of the goods at the time and place of acceptance and the value of the goods if the goods had been as warranted.

Buyer's Remedy - Specific Performance: Seller Must Deliver the Contracted for Goods

Section 2-716 is the counterpart to the seller's remedy of specific performance, which requires that the buyer pay for the goods. Under this provision, the buyer's remedy of specific performance requires the seller to deliver conforming goods to the buyer.

Special Remedies for Buyer and Seller Breach of Contract

Liquidated Damages

The parties to an Article 2 contract may agree to set the amount of damages for a seller or buyer breach of contract. As a general rule, a liquidated damages clause is upheld unless it is determined to be a penalty.

Liquidated damages constitute a sum which the parties to a contract contemplate should be paid to satisfy any loss or injury following a breach of the contract. Under Subdivision 1 of Section 2-718 of the U.C.C., a liquidated damages clause is valid if the amount is reasonable in light of (1) anticipated or actual harm caused by the breach; (2) difficulties of proof of loss, and (3) inconvenience or non-feasibility of otherwise obtaining an adequate remedy.

With respect to the first requirement,

> a liquidated damages provision will be valid if reasonable with respect to either (1) the harm which the parties anticipate will result from the breach at the time of contracting or (2) the actual damages suffered by the non-defaulting party at the time of the breach.

It should be noted that it is incumbent upon the buyer to demonstrate, through quantifiable means, that damages did exist. According to the U.C.C., "it is not material whether the parties themselves have chosen to call the provision one for 'liquidated damages.'" In short, liquidated damages must meet the U.C.C. test of actual damage or harm in order to be enforceable.

Seller's Incidental and Consequential Damage

Since one of the purposes of the Article 2 remedy provisions is to make a seller "whole" after a buyer's breach of contract, Section 2-708 regarding lost profits and 2-710 concerning incidental damages are important remedy provisions.

Section 2-708 of the U.C.C. regarding the seller's damage for non-acceptance or repudiation provides:

> (1) Subject to subsection (2) and to the provisions of this Article with respect to proof of market price (Section 2-723), the measure of damages for non-acceptance or repudiation by the buyer is the difference between the market price at the time and place for tender and the unpaid contract price together with any incidental damages provided in this Article (Section 2-710), but less expenses saved in consequence of the buyer's breach.

> (2) If the measure of damages provided in subsection (1) is inadequate to put the seller in as good a position as performance would have done then the measure of damages is the profit (including reasonable overhead) which the seller would have made from full performance by the buyer, together with any incidental damages provided in this Article (Section 2-710), due allowance for costs reasonably incurred and due credit for payments or proceeds of resale.

Section 2-710 of the U.C.C. regarding the seller's incidental damages provides:

> Incidental damages to an aggrieved seller include any commercially reasonable charges, expenses or commissions incurred in stopping delivery, in the transportation, care and custody of goods after the buyer's breach, in connection with return or resale of the goods or otherwise resulting from the breach.

Buyer's Incidental and Consequential Damages

These two sections contrast with the seller's damages by providing the buyer the right to be made whole. U.C.C. Section 2-715 provides:

> (2) Consequential damages resulting from the seller's breach include any loss resulting from general or particular requirements and needs of which the seller at the time of contracting had reason to know and which could not reasonably be prevented by cover or otherwise.

In order for consequential damages to be recoverable under the Code, they must not only be causally related to the breach, but also result from the buyer's requirements, which the seller had reason to know at the time of contracting — in other words, foreseeable damages.

Seller's Stoppage of Delivery

Sections 2-702 and 2-705 permit a seller to withhold or stop delivery of goods to a buyer who is insolvent. Section 2-705 also permits the seller to stop the delivery of goods to a buyer who has repudiated the buyer's contract obligations. Insolvency is defined in Section 1-201(23) as either a person who has ceased paying debts incurred in the ordinary course of business or cannot pay debts as the debts become due. Section 2-702 also permits a seller to reclaim goods delivered to a buyer upon notice and within 10 days of receipt of the goods by the buyer. The 10-day time limit does not apply to the seller's reclamation rights if the buyer fraudulently misrepresented the buyer's solvency to the seller within three months before delivery of the goods.

Other Key Concepts Contained in Article 2

In addition to the provisions for performance, warranties, breaches, and remedies, the public procurement official should be knowledgeable of the following additional concepts.

The Parol Evidence Rule (Reference Section 2-202)

The basic thrust of the Parol Evidence Rule is to ascertain, in an orderly fashion, the specific terms of an agreement between two parties. This is not always easy, as parties to a written contract often converse over a long period of time about the terms of an agreement. Unfortunately, after a careful review of a written contract, either or both parties to the contract may think the written contract means different things or contains the wrong terms or is missing terms. The ability of either party to produce evidence of orally agreed upon additional terms to a written contract is governed by the Parol Evidence Rule.

Section 2-202 contains the Code's version of the Parol Evidence Rule:

> Terms with respect to which the confirmatory memoranda of the parties agree or which are otherwise set forth in writing intended by the parties as a final expression of their agreement with respect to such terms as are included therein may not be contradicted by evidence of any prior agreement or of a contemporaneous oral agreement but may be explained or supplemented:

(a) By course of dealing or usage of trade (Section 1-303) or by course of performance (Section 2-208); and

(b) By evidence of consistent additional terms unless the court finds the writing to have been intended also as a complete and exclusive statement of the terms of the agreement.

The U.C.C. plainly distinguishes between "final" expressions of agreement and "complete and exclusive" statements of agreement between the parties. The completeness of a written contract is entirely a function of the parties' intent.

If a court determines that the parties agreed that the contract was final and complete, the Parol Evidence Rule applies. Under the rule, a court will not admit evidence, either written or oral, of prior understandings or negotiations that vary or contradict the contract's terms.

The Parol Evidence Rule is the reason that public procurement officials will often see a clause in their jurisdiction's boilerplate contract language that the contract is a "complete and final" expression of the parties' intentions. That type of clause is called a merger clause. Should there be a contract dispute, that boilerplate language is an important factor that a court will consider in determining whether the parties intended for the contract to be complete and final.

The "Battle of the Forms" (Reference Section 2-207)

The goal of Section 2-207 of the U.C.C. is to recognize that a contract may be embodied in more than one written document and that a contract may be formed even if the parties to the contract do not use matching forms. In short, just because the "standard" contract form used by one party is different from the "standard" form used by another party does not necessarily mean that the parties do not have an agreement or contract. Section 2-207 clarifies when a contract will and will not exist when the forms do not match.

For example, suppose the school district contracts with Waterworld, Inc. on a one-time basis to supply bottled water for a school picnic. The acceptance form sent by Waterworld states that any dispute arising from the performance of this contract shall be referred to binding arbitration. The school district contract contains no provision regarding the handling of disputes. When Waterworld delivered contaminated bottled water to the school district for the picnic, the school district brought suit against Waterworld. Waterworld argues that, based on its acceptance form, the school district's lawsuit must be dismissed and any claim by the school district must be referred to binding arbitration. Under 2-207 of the U.C.C., if the school district and Waterworld are considered merchants, that is, entities that regularly deal with these kinds of goods and both could be considered merchants, then if the arbitration provision in the Waterworld acceptance form "materially alters" the rights and obligations of the parties, then this provision would not be binding on the parties but represent a counter-offer by Waterworld. However, if this arbitration provision would not "materially alter" the rights and obligations of the parties to the contract, then the arbitration provision would become part of the contract between the school district and Waterworld. Courts have consistently viewed a binding arbitration clause as a "material alteration" of the rights and liabilities of contracting parties.

Missing Terms – The Gap-Filling Provisions of the U.C.C.

Article 2 contains provisions to fill out the terms of a contract for the sale of goods when some contract terms may be missing. These Article 2 provisions are called "gap filler" provisions, as exemplified below:

- Section 2-305 makes provisions for supplying a missing price term by reading into a contract a commercially reasonable price in line with the particular circumstances of the contract.

- Section 2-307 states that unless otherwise agreed to by the parties, goods called for by the contract shall be delivered in a single lot with payment due upon delivery.

- Section 2-308 states that unless otherwise agreed to by the parties, the place of delivery of goods is the seller's place of business; or, if the seller does not have a place of business, the seller's residence will serve as the place of delivery.

- Section 2-309 provides that time of delivery or shipment or any other reference to time, absent an agreement of the parties, shall be a reasonable time.

- Section 2-310 requires payment for goods at the time and upon delivery of the goods, absent a contrary agreement between the parties.

- Section 2-311 permits option contracts, which permit a designated party to specify in a timely manner the specific terms and performance requirements for a contract.

- Section 2-306 stipulates that output and requirement contracts are sufficiently specific to satisfy the quantity requirement.

Unconscionability (Reference Section 2-302)

This Article 2 provision is a consumer protection provision designed to deal with "adhesion contracts." Adhesion contracts are those kinds of contracts (typically, form contracts) where the consumer who is buying the goods is in no position to bargain effectively with the seller. In this context, the seller presents a "take or leave it" contract for the purchase of goods with the intent to take advantage of the consumer's lack of knowledge and sophistication in order to get the consumer to sign a patently unfair contract. For example, when a seller of a $25 watch convinces the consumer that the watch is worth $1,000 and gets the consumer to sign a contract to purchase the watch for $1,000, the unconscionability provision of Article 2 of the U.C.C. may apply. If a contract or a term of a contract, such as price, is found to be unconscionable as determined by a court, the contract or contract term is voided.

In the context of public procurement, the concept of unconscionability, a strictly U.C.C. invented term, may not as readily apply to a public agency or municipal corporation. In many instances, the public agency as a buyer may have superior bargaining power over a vendor. This many times stems from the attractiveness to sellers of contracting with public agencies. However, in other instances a public agency, acting as buyer, may also be subjected to the superior bargaining power of, for example, a single source, and multi-national supplier. Therefore, the U.C.C. doctrine of unconscionability may apply equally to an ordinary consumer buyer and a public agency buyer.

Chapter 5

The Legal Context for Formal Solicitations

This chapter contains sections from the text entitled "Fundamentals of Federal Contract Law" authored by Eugene W. Massengale (199) and has been reproduced with permission of Greenwood Publishing Group, Inc. Westport, CT.

Overview

The inter-dependent links between the legalities of contracting and the functional outcomes of contracting for a public entity are obvious. The public procurement official who develops bid and proposal solicitations must do so with two legal end results in mind:

- Does the solicitation document address all of the legal requirements for my agency?

- Does the solicitation document contain all of the legal protections and clarifications required by my agency in order to produce a contractual document that achieves the desired outcomes of the customer?

The National Institute of Governmental Purchasing, Inc. (NIGP), addresses these two questions in various ways within its 2004 foundation texts. Specifically, *Sourcing in the Public Sector* discusses in great detail the framework on developing specifications, standards, and assembling a final sourcing document, and *Contract Administration* emphasizes the critical nature of developing a solid sourcing document as an essential component for minimizing risks during the contract administration phase. The intended outcome of this specific chapter, therefore, is not to replicate the work of these companion texts. Rather, it is to emphasize that sourcing documents typically are converted into contracts with the selected supplier and, as such, need to be developed within the context of a legal framework.

An Overview of the Formal Solicitation Process

Formal, sealed bidding is a method of acquisition that involves:

- the preparation of the Invitation for Bids (IFB);
- the publicizing and issuing of the IFB;
- the submission of sealed bids by qualified prospective contractors;
- a formal bid opening; and
- the contract award to responsive and responsible contractors based on price and price-related factors.

Acquisition by the sealed bid method results in the award of contracts based on a variety of methods. The two most common methods are firm-fixed-price contracts and fixed-price contracts with some form of economic price adjustment features that are normally tied to the Consumer Price Index (CPI) or Producer Price Index (PPI).

To be effective, the IFB must describe the requirements clearly, accurately, and completely. Unnecessarily restrictive specifications or contract terms and conditions should be avoided because they unduly restrict and limit competition. The IFB must also include all documents, whether attached or incorporated by reference, necessary to enable prospective bidders to prepare and submit bids. In preparing IFBs, acquiring agencies may be statutorily required to include a statement of all significant factors, including price-related factors, which the procurement agent reasonably expects to consider in the evaluation of bids, as well as the relative importance assigned to such factors. The following price-related factors may be applicable to the evaluation of sealed bids and may be included in the IFB, when appropriate:

- foreseeable costs or delays to the agency resulting from such factors as differences in inspection, location of supplies, and transportation. If bids are on an F.O.B. origin basis, transportation to the designated destination should be considered to determine the lowest cost to the agency.
- changes made, or requested by the bidder, in any of the provisions of the IFB, if such change does not constitute a ground for rejecting the bid.
- advantages or disadvantages to the agency that might result from making more than one award. Individual awards are to be made for the items or combination of items that result in the lowest aggregate cost to the agency.

Invitations are publicized through the distribution of IFBs to prospective bidders, postings in public places, and such other means as may be appropriate. This could include publication in the local newspapers with general circulation, agency Web sites, electronic distribution lists, and electronic distribution by third parties. Since many agencies are deleting the requirement for publication in a local newspaper due to the cost and the low return, the public procurement official may want to consider modifying related statutes or regulations if this is still a requirement. The IFB must be publicized sufficiently in advance of the public opening to enable prospective bidders adequate time to prepare and submit their bids.

To be considered for award, a bid must comply in all material respects with the requirements of the IFB. This policy enables all bidders to stand on an equal footing and maintains the integrity of the sealed-bidding method of acquisition.

Once bids are received by the acquiring agency, they are publicly opened at the specified time and place by the procurement agent or other official and read aloud. Public opening and reading of bid submittals maintains the transparency that is expected in government bidding. All bids received and opened should be recorded in some form of public tabulation, which includes the IFB number, the bid opening time and date, a general description of the acquisition, the names of bidders submitting timely bids, the prices bid, and any other pertinent information required for bid evaluation. Once completed, the sharing of the bid opening information should be handled in accordance with local regulations and state statutes.

After bids are opened and recorded, they are evaluated without discussion with bidders, except where necessary to determine if a mistake in bidding has occurred. An award will be made with reasonable promptness to the responsible bidder(s) whose bid, conforming to the requirements of the IFB, is most advantageous to the agency, considering only the price and the price-related factors set forth in the IFB.

Drafting the Contract

What follows is a series of legal issues that should be considered by public procurement officials as they begin to develop contracts. In those circumstances where the solicitation document becomes a component of the contract, these considerations should be given at the time of solicitation development. As mentioned previously, *Sourcing in the Public Sector* (NIGP, 2004) offers detailed parameters for drafting sourcing documents that are converted into contracts once a supplier is selected. The intent of this section, therefore, is to emphasize the value of including legal terms in the solicitation document because this document frequently becomes the contract. Accordingly, the terms "solicitation document" and "contract" will be used interchangeably to mean that legal concepts must be contained in both sets of documents.

More often than not, there are two types of public officials who develop the language of a public contract on behalf of a public entity. The public procurement official, or the client agency with the procurement official's review, prepares the specifications for goods, describing the item to be purchased as well as language addressing related issues, such as delivery, packaging, repair, and maintenance. For service contracts, the procurement official prepares the "scope of work," including service elements and delivery, desired contract outcomes, and the level of expertise required from the supplier and its staff. The public entity's attorney drafts those portions of the contract generally directed at the law that affects the formation and operation of the contract, such as indemnification; certifications about independent, non-collusive pricing and gratuities; contract termination; and preservation of remedies. Sometimes, procurement officials draft those types of terms and the attorney reviews and approves them.

For service contracts, the procurement official prepares the "scope of work,"

While the actual responsibility for scripting contract language will vary, depending on the size and resources of the government and the level of training of the procurement official, it is important for the procurement official to remember two key concepts. First, the specifications or scope of work that describes the item or service being purchased serves to tell potential suppliers what the public sector wants. Second, the specifications or scope of work become a part of the contract that results from the competition and establishes whether the supplier/contractor is complying with the contract's requirements.

Additionally, the public procurement official should continuously monitor whether other specific contract language is addressing the overall mission of the procurement operation. While it may be more appropriate for an attorney to draft, or at least review, certain contract terms such as an indemnification clause, the procurement official needs to determine whether those terms are reasonable. If suppliers are taking exception to a clause or deciding not to compete because they consider the clause too onerous, the procurement official should alert the attorney and discuss whether there is other suitable language that will both protect the public entity and be more palatable to suppliers.

Developing a Drafting Strategy

Before drafting any contract language, the procurement official should understand the objective of the purchase and the contract and develop a strategy based on that objective. It is critical that the procurement official have a good understanding of both the marketplace and the requirements of the internal customer before preparing language that will govern how the purchase and delivery of an essential service or product will operate. Copying language or templates used in the past or from forms is not helpful if the language does not achieve the objective.

Drafting Language to Fit the Type of Contract Used

Another decision that will affect some of the language that the procurement official must draft is the selection of the type of contract to use. For instance, different contract types necessitate various types of cost or pricing provisions as well as contractor documentation requirements. A contract for a simple commodity that establishes a firm fixed price may not need to state anything further than that the price is fixed for the period of the contract and, perhaps, describe situations in which there may be a price increase or decrease.

On the other hand, a firm-fixed-price contract for a consulting study may state that the contractor is not entitled to anything but the fixed price for its services, unless the government directs changed or additional work that increases the cost. Additionally, the contract may provide that the contractor must, nonetheless, submit monthly time sheets evidencing work performed, particularly if the contract allows progress payments or requires the contractor to meet specific milestones to obtain progress payments.

The procurement official should ensure that the terms included in the solicitation advise competing vendors of the type of contract to be awarded and address all of the other issues that relate to that type of contract. Vendors need to know the public entity's performance and documentation requirements for payment because those requirements may be, depending on the type of contract used, key components of the costs that the vendors need to factor into their prices.

Use of Legal Counsel

Finally, before drafting contract language, the public procurement official should consider whether any of the issues intended to be addressed in the contract's terms require the assistance of an attorney. The language of a contract may change the outcome that the common law or other statutory law, including the U.C.C. may otherwise dictate on a matter. If the public procurement official decides, in keeping with the objectives of the purchase, that the contract should address a legal issue in a particular way, that official should consult with the jurisdiction's attorney to make sure that the language drafted achieves the legal objective sought.

Organization of a Basic Contract

Good organization of a contract's terms is as essential to its meaning as are the words used in the contract itself. Most basic contracts result from the parties to it bargaining equally and, through a "give and take" process, writing a document that reflects their bargain. Public contracts generally do not arise in this fashion; but there may be situations in which a procurement official must negotiate directly with a vendor to create a contract, such as purchases exempt from the procurement law, sole-source procurements, or intergovernmental agreements. In those instances, the procurement official should find this general description useful.

Description of the Document

Contracts have subject matters. If the title of a contract merely says "Agreement" at the top of the page, it does nothing to describe for the reader the type of agreement involved. The better practice is to identify the type of agreement in the title, such as "Contract for Professional Services," or "Agreement for the Lease of Software."

Caption

The caption in a contract identifies the parties to the contract and the legal action they are taking. This section of the contract need not be literally identified as the caption, but it should contain the appropriate language, for example:

AGREEMENT FOR THE PURCHASE OF GOODS AND SERVICES PARTIES

The City of Timbuktu (City) and Contractor X (Contractor) enter into this agreement on October 11, 2005, for the purchase of certain software upgrades and services (Agreement). The City and Contractor (Parties) agree as follows:

The procurement official may put the date of the agreement in the caption, or at the end of the contract. Note that the date of the contract may not be its effective date. A contract term may provide a different date for the agreement to become effective; that is, for performance to begin.

Recitals

Sometimes, drafters include a "recitals" section in a contract to state the background for it, often for the purpose of clarifying the parties' intentions. It is not necessary to do so. Traditionally, recitals begin with "whereas" clauses. The procurement official should not use the term "whereas" because it does not meet the "plain language" principle of contract drafting.

Recitals should be short and consist of a bare statement of key facts. They should not contain representations, indicate agreements, or contain substantive contract terms and conditions. Those should appear in the body of the agreement, for example:

Background

1. The (public entity) maintains its automated financial system on an XYZ mainframe computer that operates exclusively on BBB operating software. That software requires upgrading and maintenance from time to time.

2. Contractor manufactures BBB software.

3. The (public entity) and Contractor want to enter into an agreement for the purchase of BBB software upgrades and maintenance.

The parties agree as follows:

Definitions

The procurement official may want to follow the caption section, or the recitals section, if used, with definitions of key terms in the contract. The official should ensure that throughout the contract the words or terms as defined are consistently used.

Operative Language

This section of the contract should consist of the terms that answer the "what, where, when, and how" questions about the purchase. The procurement official may wish to divide this section into subsections with separate headings. Those subsections might separately address matters, such as specifications or scope of work; performance of the contract delivery, warranty, maintenance, and payment for commodities contracts; or, for a consulting contract, for instance, documentation of work hours, milestones for any progress payments, and format for a final report; and standard and special terms and conditions, such as those addressing indemnification, conflicts of interest, termination of the contract, and liquidated damages.

Offer and Acceptance

In public procurement, a solicitation, such as an IFB, is not an offer but, instead, requests vendors to submit offers. The bids or proposals submitted in response are offers. Acceptance occurs when the public official authorized to award contracts signifies that the jurisdiction has selected the vendor as the winner. That official may be the procurement officer or an agency council or board of supervisors.

Accordingly, the contract language should be drafted in a way that ensures that contract terms define the point at which acceptance occurs. Letters identifying a vendor as, or inferring that the vendor is, the apparent awardee do not constitute acceptance. If the procurement official needs to send a letter to an apparent awardee, such as to request certain financial information for determining that vendor's responsibility, the letter should explicitly state that it is not an acceptance of the bid or proposal.

Solicitations should include wording, generally in the instructions section, stating that in submitting the bid or proposal, the vendor agrees to hold its bid or proposal open for a stated period of time. That language clarifies that the vendor's "offer" is irrevocable; that is, the vendor may not withdraw it and must hold it open for a specified period of time. If the solicitation does not contain that language, a jurisdiction may have no recourse against a low bidder who wishes to withdraw its bid after hearing the other bidders' prices. Some procurement laws or rules limit the instances in which a vendor may withdraw its bid or proposal after submitting it, which may provide the jurisdiction with a remedy. The better practice is to include language in the solicitation making the bid or proposal irrevocable for a period of time.

To help ensure the proper contract terms for small purchases, there should be a standard term in every purchase order stating that the offer (which in certain cases is the order itself) expressly limits the vendor's acceptance to the offer's terms.

Competency

There are certain classes of persons whom the law deems incapable of entering into a contract. A person who lacks the authority to contract for someone else under the law of agency is an example. In the public procurement setting, the capacity issue generally arises because a government employee or a vendor's representative is not authorized to contract.

The wording in the solicitation addressing vendor signatures on a bid or proposal should state that the person signing for the vendor should be an authorized representative. Additionally, the solicitation should state that only an authorized procurement official may make a contract award. Contract terms should also state that only an authorized procurement official can make a modification of the contract.

Legal Provisions

Statutes and ordinances often require public contracts to contain certain terms. Examples of the subjects that those types of terms may address are rights to audit and inspect contractor records, retention of records, and availability of funds, indemnification, and conflict of interest. The procurement officials should ensure that their solicitations, contracts, and purchase orders contain those required terms. More often than not, the statutes that require these clauses are not the procurement laws of the jurisdiction. Instead, the requirements will be in laws that address, for instance, ethics or budgetary matters.

Obligations

Statements of obligation concern things that the vendor has promised to do in the future signified by use of the word "shall." They will appear in the contract's specifications or scope of work and in the description of the type or course of performance required.

Representations and Warranties

Representations and warranties should reside in the contract in the same place that the obligations do. The procurement official should include in the contract language any representations about the vendor and the vendor's product that the public entity has relied on in entering the contract. Unlike obligations, the official must demonstrate in that language that the representations are in the present and are a basis for the public entity contracting with the vendor.

For instance, if the contract is for consulting work, the contract language should include something like "the contractor represents that it has ten years' experience in conducting, and the specific expertise to conduct, a study on the nesting habits of the endangered blue and pink owl." By placing all essential representations in the contract, the procurement official avoids having parol evidence problems if a dispute arises.

The same is true of warranties. Warranties may either be representations of current facts or may relate to a promise of something in the future. The language in the "owl consultant" example above could also be a warranty as well as a representation. If the procurement official wishes to ensure that it is, the words "and warranties" should be inserted after the word "represents."

Warranties may either be representations of current facts or may relate to a promise of something in the future.

In public procurement, many warranties involve performance over time or future performance of commodities or items, such as computers, ergonomic chairs, copiers, fax machines, and carpet. The manufacturer and dealer may offer their own warranties but the procurement official may wish to include one in the contract as well. Those types of warranties are promises of something in the future, for example:

> In addition to all other warranties, Contractor warrants that its ergonomic chairs will be free of any defects in mechanics or materials for one year after each purchase.

Remember to ask whether the contract term ought to include a remedy for the situations in which the promise is not kept or the fact is not as represented. If so, the term should spell out the consequences.

Declarations

Declarations address the legal principles that govern the parties' agreement. In most cases, those declarations will be the standard terms and conditions and any special ones developed for the particular contract, such as liquidated damages. To ensure that the contract contains all of the necessary declarations, the procurement official should examine whether those terms and conditions answer the possible situations that could arise under the contract.

Closing

The closing of a contract should show that the parties consent to the agreement. It is the place where their signatures are placed, demonstrating that consent. The parties who sign the agreement should be the same ones whose names appear in the caption. Since neither a corporation nor a public entity can actually sign an agreement, the closing should designate their "signatures" as follows:

THE CITY OF TIMBUKTU   ABC CORPORATION
By_____   By_____

The closing should include the date that the parties signed it, represented by simply stating at the end "Signed November 11, 1998." If the parties are likely to sign the contract at different times, the procurement official should place a line for the date under each signature line, such as "Date _____."

Drafting Terms and Conditions

Terms and conditions are the "heart" of any contract. They define and describe the rights and responsibilities of the parties. This chapter teaches the procurement official how to write good terms and conditions.

The phrase "terms and conditions" is only one of the terms that lawyers use to identify the substantive parts of a contract. Other terms used are "clauses," "provisions," "paragraphs," and the word "terms" by itself. These words describe a whole range of things, such as specifications or scopes of work, delivery and repair response time lines, warranties, pricing for contract option or renewal periods, milestones for performance, termination of the contract, assignment of the contract to another vendor, indemnification, ownership of work products, and notification of debarment or suspension.

For most purchases, the public procurement official will not draft a complete contract but will assemble a solicitation that will result in the formation of a contract and be part of it. The drafting principles and tips that this chapter has already discussed apply equally to this important exercise. The solicitation is the starting point for a good contract.

The organization of the solicitation is just as important as it is for a basic contract. Each of the parts of the solicitation should be distinct to make the document clear and easy to use. Instructions to bidders, for instance, should not include language defining the circumstances under which the procurement official may terminate the contract. Instead, those instructions ought to be restricted to advising bidders and offerors about the how, when, where, and what of preparing and submitting their bids or proposals. Likewise, the procurement official should not mix specifications defining the commodity to be supplied with other performance requirements that the contract may establish, such as documentation to be submitted with payment requests.

One key to creating a good contract document is the identification, development, and use of some general solicitation provisions (instructions to bidders/offerors, terms and conditions, etc.) that the procurement official may use consistently for every solicitation. The procurement official should involve their attorney in the drafting process, and that attorney should approve the end product.

Standard Terms and Conditions

It is fairly easy for the seasoned procurement official to identify those terms and conditions that are basic for every contract. By asking the question "What if?" the public procurement official along with the jurisdiction's attorney should identify those legal issues that they want to be consistent in all contracts. Those legal issues should become terms and conditions that are standard in every contract that the jurisdiction awards.

Laws often require that certain terms appear in every contract of the public entity, and those clearly are candidates for the standard terms and conditions. Here are some other possible topics that the procurement official may wish to address:

- Definitions of terms;
- The law applicable to the contract (generally the law of the contracting state or, for other public entities, the law of the state where they are located);
- Authority of the procurement official;
- Contract interpretation (excluding parol evidence called a "merger" clause and providing that instances in which the public entity ignores a contractor's noncompliance with the contract does not waive that entity's right to enforce the contracts requirements called a "no waiver" clause);
- Public records laws (describing that the contract is a public record);
- Severability (stating that, if a court deems part of the contract as invalid, the

remainder of the contract is still valid);

- Relationship of the parties (providing that the contractor and its employees are independent contractors and not employees of the public entity);

- Assignment and delegation (prohibiting the contractor from assigning its contract rights or delegating its contract duties without the written approval of the authorized procurement official);

- General indemnification (stating that the contractor will hire an attorney to represent the public entity and pay any damages or other costs that the entity incurs due to the negligence of the contractor under the contract);

- Indemnification for patent and copyright infringement (requiring the contractor to indemnify the public entity for any violations of patent and copyright law that arise out of performance of the contract);

- Sub-contracts (requiring the authorized procurement official's approval of sub-contracts);

- Compliance with applicable laws (stating that the contractor must comply with all laws applicable to the performance of the contract);

- Force majeure (identifying those instances in which the public entity will excuse the contractor's noncompliance with the contract, such as acts of God and strikes);

- Amendment of the contract (providing that the sole manner for changing the requirements of the contract is through a written amendment to the contract that the authorized procurement official signs);

- Nondiscrimination (prohibiting the contractor from discriminating on racial, sex, religious, or disability grounds, and identifying specific laws and executive orders that are pertinent);

- Advertising and promotion of the contract (requiring approval of the authorized procurement official before using the contract for promotional purposes);

- Ethics, including conflicts of interest, gratuities, and kickbacks;

- Availability of funds in the next fiscal year;

- Right of the public entity to audit and inspect the contractor's books and records;

- Retention of records (requiring the contractor to maintain records relating to the contract for a set period of time);

- Termination for default (authorizing the public entity to terminate the contract for nonperformance or defective performance);

- Termination for the convenience of the government (authorizing the government to terminate the contract with proper notice and providing recovery of certain contractor costs and profit); and

- Nonexclusive remedies (reserving to the public entity all remedies for violation of the contract that the law allows).

There are some additional terms and conditions that a procurement official may wish to include as standard in every solicitation for the purchase of commodities. Those terms address issues that arise under the U.C.C., such as:

- Risk of loss (defining which party must bear the cost of the commodities if they are lost or destroyed during delivery or before the public entity accepts them);

- Inspection and testing (allowing the public entity to test the commodities and thoroughly inspect them without being deemed to have accepted them); and

- Nonconforming tender (permitting the public entity greater leeway than the U.C.C. allows to reject an untimely delivery or delivery of defective commodities under an installment contract calling for multiple deliveries).

Additionally, the reader should refer to NIGP's (2004) *Sourcing in the Public Sector*, which addresses statutory and legal terms that should be incorporated into the sourcing document, such as:

- Workers' Compensation;
- Occupational Safety and Health—Infractions and Compliance;
- Workplace Hazards;
- Ownership and Intellectual Property;
- Disclosure, Confidentiality, and Public Information;
- Indemnity;
- Personal Harassment; and
- Infringement.

Incorporation by Reference

It is clear from the list above that the standard terms and conditions may be lengthy. One good way to reduce the size of the solicitation is to incorporate those terms and conditions by reference. The way to do that is to place a term in the solicitation stating:

> This solicitation incorporates by reference the Standard Terms and Conditions, Form _____, and those terms and conditions are a part of the solicitation as if it specifically set them forth. Copies of them are available.

The procurement office may make copies available at its office, online, or via fax-on-demand.

Special Terms and Conditions

It is often useful to include in a solicitation a category of terms and conditions designated "special" because they, like the specifications or scopes of work, are unique to that particular purchase or type of purchases, or require adjusting for particular purchases. The public procurement official should be careful not to react to a one-time problem previously encountered with a bidder, offeror, or contractor by drafting a special term to include in every solicitation for printing The term drafted in those situations is often too narrow and may simply confuse the meaning of the contract without achieving any commensurate benefit.

An example of a special term is one addressing liquidated damages. While the parameters for applying liquidated damages is specifically addressed in Chapter 3 and 4, it should be mentioned here that the public procurement official should insert a liquidated damages term in a contract only where it will be difficult for the public entity to determine what its actual damages are if the contractor breaches the contract. Liquidated damages are a substitute for actual damages and must be a reasonable approximation of the amount that actual damages might be. If the dollar amount of the liquidated damages is too high, a court will view it as a penalty and refuse to enforce it.

Interpretation of Terms and Conditions

A court uses the common law rules of interpretation to determine and implement the intention of the parties to the contract as noted in Chapter 3 of this book. As a starting place for drafting, the procurement official should be familiar with those rules to understand how a court will interpret a contract's language if it is ambiguous or not drafted carefully.

Clearly, the best approach is to avoid using language that may require relying on these rules. If a dispute arises, a court will view the language for its objective meaning — the meaning that a reasonable person would give it — and not necessarily the meaning that the drafter intended.

A simple way that Burnham (1993), in *Drafting Contracts*, suggests for a drafter to objectively review what he or she has written is to engage in a "dialogue" with the contract language by constantly asking three questions:

- What am I trying to say?
- Could the language be interpreted in more than one way?
- How could I say it better?

It is also a good idea for the procurement official to let someone else read and critique the draft contract language.

Time Provided To Submit a Bid

In order for the sealed-bidding method of procurement to function effectively, prospective bidders must be given a reasonable period of time in which to prepare and submit bids. Normally, enabling legislation provides that the time between the issuance of the solicitation and the opening of the bids should be at least 30 calendar days, unless the public procurement official determines that a shorter period is reasonable or is both reasonable and necessary to satisfy an urgent requirement. The situation must be urgent to justify compressing bidding time because competition may be restricted. Further, bidders responding to the IFB may be forced to include contingencies in their bids that, with additional time, could have been eliminated.

Amendments to IFB

An IFB may be amended prior to the time set for bid opening if it becomes necessary to make changes in quantities, specifications, delivery dates, and contract terms or to correct an ambiguous or defective invitation. Prior to issuing the amendment, the public procurement official is required to consider whether a reasonable extension of time is necessary, and consideration should be given to extend the bid preparation time if only a short time remains between the issuance of an amendment and the time set for bid opening. What is reasonable must be determined on a case-by-case basis. In one case, a Federal Contracting Officer was found to have acted reasonably when bidders were given one day to consider an amendment that was simple in nature and when no bidder objected to the time allowed (Pacific Contractors, 78 CPD 297). However, in another, the award was set aside where the amendment was issued two days before the bid opening date and no additional time for bidding was granted, even though six bidders did receive and were able to acknowledge receipt of the amendment (Comptroller General Opinion B-158766 [1966]).

Bidders should be required to acknowledge receipt of amendments. Failure to do so could result in the rejection of their bids as being non-responsive to the requirements of the IFB. For example, a low bidder's failure to acknowledge receipt of an amendment to an IFB for containerized seedlings could not be waived as a minor informality because the amendment significantly reduced the specified quantity of trees and had more than a trivial effect on price. Minor informalities can be treated as such only if the agency can waive the provision.

A bidder's failure to expressly acknowledge receipt can be waived under the constructive acknowledgment theory if the bid clearly indicates that the bidder received the amendment. Such would be the case where the amendment added another item to the solicitation and the bidder submitted a bid on that item. The agency may also waive formal acknowledgment where the amendment involves only a matter of form or has no or negligible impact on price, quantity, quality, or delivery of the item(s) to be bid.

Timeliness of Bid Submission

A bid is timely only if it is received in the office designated in the IFB no later than the precise time set for the opening of bids. A bid received after the time set for bid opening is a late bid and cannot be considered for award unless the public entity expressly permits such consideration in their statutes or regulations. In these cases, a late bid may be considered if received before contract award. For example, in Virginia, the courts have specifically legislated that late bids/responses cannot be received or considered. However, in Florida, the courts have stated that agencies do, in fact, have the discretion to waive the receipt of the late bid, after all factors are considered, and if the acceptance of the late bid is in the best interest of the agency. (Refer to *Hewitt Contracting v. Melbourne Airport Authority*, 1988.)

The "firm bid rule" is one of the most rigid features of the sealed-bidding method of acquisition. Its purpose is to prohibit modification or withdrawal of bids for a reasonable period of time after bid opening. Public policy traditionally prohibits the revocation of a bid after the public opening and during the acceptance period. Public Procurement Agents should be allowed a reasonable time after the opening to ascertain whether collusion or fraud has been perpetrated against the entity by the bidders. Withdrawals after the results of the bidding could open the way to fraud against the agency. (See *Scott v. United States*, 44 Ct. Cl. 524 [1909].) For example, a bidder could be permitted to attend a public bid opening, determine the prices offered by his competitors, and then either submit a modified bid undercutting the other bidders' prices or withdraw his bid. For this reason, the modification or withdrawal of bids should be prohibited in order to preserve the integrity of the sealed-bidding system.

Responsiveness of Bids

The key element in any public bidding system is the requirement that all bidders must bid on the same effort. This requirement is embodied in both federal statutes, in the statement that award may only be made to a bidder "whose bid conforms to the invitation," and also in most agency rules. The major purpose of this provision is the promotion of objectivity and fairness in the procurement system assuring that a bidder cannot win the competition by offering to perform the work in a less expensive way than other bidders could also have posed had they known that the agency was willing to accept such work.

Allowing such bidding on alternate levels of work would inevitably involve the contracting officer in further discussions with bidders to ascertain the precise nature of their offers and in the ultimate discretionary decision which offer was low, taking into consideration both price and level of performance that was offered. It would also provide low bidders with an opportunity to withdraw their bids after seeing the bids of their competitors by interpreting their offer in a way that would not meet the agency requirement. Such a system is tantamount to negotiated procurement with neither the safeguards from unequal treatment of bidders and favoritism that are considered to be essential in formal advertising nor the protection from open disclosure of competitive price that is thought to be a necessary part of negotiated procurement. The responsiveness requirement has grown to embody much more than the concept that the successful bidder must bid on the precise level of work called for by the invitation. It has come to stand for the proposition that the contracting officer must reject any bid that fails to comply with the invitation in any material manner. Such deviations may occur in many ways.

Required information may be omitted. The bid may contain mistakes or may not be prepared in accordance with bidding instructions. Conditions or provisions not authorized by the IFB may be included. It is immaterial whether these irregularities occur by design or chance or whether the bidder is willing to correct or modify the bid to conform to the terms of the invitation. The bid must be rejected unless the bidder has unequivocally and unambiguously agreed to perform the work and his bid was submitted in accordance with the bidding instructions.

...a bid must respond and conform to the requirements of the IFB.

These critical requirements have made responsiveness a focal point for award controversies. If a low bidder can be disqualified, the next bidder in line stands to receive the award at a higher price. The chances for this occurring are much greater in the area of responsiveness where procurement officials have much less discretion than in other areas, such as specifications or responsibility. There, objections are likely to be rejected on the grounds that the matter falls within the discretion of the procuring officials. Much of the controversy, therefore, focuses on whether a particular issue is one of responsiveness. To be eligible for award, a bid must respond and conform to the requirements of the IFB. Compliance with every aspect of the IFB is essential to assure that all bidders are treated equally and fairly during the evaluation phase. Accordingly, bids submitted under the following circumstances should be considered non-responsive:

- A bid that fails to meet the essential requirements of the IFB;

- A bid that does not conform to the specifications, unless the IFB authorizes an alternate bid and the alternate meets the requirements specified;

- A bid that fails to conform to the delivery schedule or the permissible alternatives set forth in the IFB;

- A bid received from any person or concern that is suspended, debarred, or ineligible for contract award if the period of suspension, debarment, or ineligibility has not expired as of the bid opening date;

- A bid requiring the submission of a bid bond if none was furnished in conformance with the IFB; and

- A bid seeking to qualify the terms and conditions of the IFB, or otherwise seeking to limit contractor liability, or to limit the agency's rights.

The question of responsiveness is extremely critical when dealing with the interrelationship between responsiveness and responsibility. Responsiveness, with no contracting officer discretion, deals with the question of whether the bidder has promised to do exactly what the agency has requested. Responsibility involves the question of whether the contractor can or will perform as promised, and the contracting officer has a great deal of discretion. Questions of responsiveness are determined only on the basis of information submitted with the bid and on the facts available at the time of bid opening. Conversely, responsibility determinations are made on the basis of all information that may be submitted or available up to the time of award.

The rejection of a non-responsive bid has very harsh consequences for the bidder and deprives the agency of the advantage of the rejected bid (usually the low bid). Thus, where other alternatives are present, there is a reluctance to classify a problem as one involving responsiveness, unless to do so is essential for maintaining the integrity of the bidding process. For these reasons, procuring agencies have also adopted a policy of not rejecting bids when the deviation is not material.

A minor informality or irregularity is one, which is merely a matter of form and not of substance or pertains to some immaterial or inconsequential defect or variation of a bid from the exact requirement of the IFB, the correction or waiver of which would not be prejudicial to other bidders. The defect or variation in the bid is immaterial and inconsequential when its significance as to price, quantity, quality, or delivery is trivial or negligible when contrasted with the total cost or scope of the supplies or services being procured. The contracting officer shall either give the bidder an opportunity to cure any deficiency resulting from a minor informality or irregularity in a bid or waive such deficiency, whichever is to the advantage of the government. Examples of minor informalities or irregularities include:

- Failure of bidder to return the number of copies of signed bids required by the invitation for bids;

- Failure to furnish required information concerning the number of bidders' employees;

- Failure of bidder to sign its bid, but only if (a) the unsigned bid is accompanied by other material indicating the bidder's intention to be bound by the unsigned bid document, such as the submission of a bid guarantee, or a letter signed by the bidder with the bid referring to and clearly identifying the bid itself; or (b) the firm submitting a bid has formally adopted or authorized, before the date set for opening of bids, the execution of documents by typewritten, printed, or stamped signature and submits evidence of such authorization and the bid carries such a signature;

- Failure of a bidder to acknowledge receipt of an amendment to an IFB, but only if (a) the bid received clearly indicates that the bidder received the amendment, such as where the amendment added another item to the invitation for bids and the bidder submitted a bid thereon; or (b) the amendment involves only a matter of form or is one which has either no effect or merely a trivial or negligible effect on price, quantity, quality, or delivery of the item bid upon; and

- Failure to execute a required certificate.

Mistakes in Bids

One of the most troublesome areas in sealed bidding is that of mistakes in bids. Whereas a bidder for a commercial contract may be able to withdraw or submit a corrected bid at any time prior to the acceptance of his offer, bidders for public agency contracts are generally not permitted to withdraw or modify their bids after the public bid opening. In sealed bidding, the type of mistake most often made is generally reflected in, or confined to, bid prices. This is attributable to the fact that IFBs are normally quite explicit as to what is required of the bidder, to include specific terms and conditions of the contemplated contract. Other types of mistakes (i.e., failure to sign the bid or failure to acknowledge receipt of amendments) relate to bid responsiveness.

The rules applicable to correction of mistakes in bid prices apply only to bids that are otherwise responsive to the requirements of the IFB. Accordingly, the procurement agent is required, after bid opening but prior to contract award, to examine each bid received to determine if it contains a mistake. If the procurement agent has actual knowledge, or should have known, that a mistake has been made, the procurement agent cannot in good faith bind the bidder to the erroneous bid price by awarding the contract.

Clerical mistakes, apparent on the face of the bid, may be corrected by the procurement agent upon verification of the bid actually intended by the bidder. Examples of apparent clerical mistakes include obvious errors in the placement of a decimal point, obvious figure transposition, obvious discount errors, and mathematical errors in the computation of unit and total prices. Other types of mistakes could involve failure to include a vendor or subcontractor quotation or failure to price out some critical aspect of the work to be performed.

Once a mistake is suspected, the purchasing agent is required to request verification of the bid. This is accomplished by notifying the bidder that a mistake is suspected, calling the bidder's attention to the mistake or to the reason a mistake is suspected, and requesting that the bidder verify the correctness and accuracy of the bid. As to suspected clerical errors, the purchasing agent may permit correction of the mistake by verification of the bid intended. Correction of all other mistakes may be made upon a determination by the Agent and/or Legal Counsel that clear and convincing evidence establishes the existence of a mistake and of the intention of the bidder, unless the correction would result in displacing one or more bids.

In most cases, a bidder's unequivocal confirmation of his bid price is sufficient to enable the agency to award a contract to him. There are instances, however, where a bidder's confirmation of the bid may be inadequate to dispel doubts as to its accuracy, requiring the agency to reach a determination as to its acceptability. Bids may be corrected where there is clear and convincing evidence of a mistake, and a reasonable person should be aware of the mistake. However, if correction would displace a lower acceptable bid, the correction may not be made unless the mistake and the bid actually intended are ascertainable.

Termination for the Convenience of the Agency

The ebb and flow of international commitments, constant changes in requirements for goods and services, funding limitations, and continuing advances in science and technology demand that the agency possess the flexibility to cancel contracts, in whole or in part, when it is in the public interest to do so. The concept of contract termination for the convenience of the agency has evolved over time and is intended to protect the agency from unneeded acceptance of equipment, material, or supplies that, through usage, no longer suit its needs or that have been made obsolete by advances in technology. Such a termination may be ordered when the public procurement official determines that, for reasons other than the default of the contractor, it is in the agency's best interest to discontinue all, or some part, of the remaining work under the contract.

Clerical mistakes...

may be corrected

by the procurement

agent upon

verification of the

bid actually intended

by the bidder.

The Termination for Convenience article permits the agency to discontinue performance of a contract with only limited liability. If, in a private contract, a party attempts to terminate an agreement without a contractual right to do so, that party would be liable for breach of contract damages. The Termination for Convenience article in the public agency contract converts what would otherwise be a breach into an administrative claim cognizable under the contract. The fault concept is of only minor, if any, significance in termination for convenience actions. Although a small number of contractors have appealed Terminations for Convenience, alleging bad faith or arbitrariness, they have been uniformly unsuccessful. Concepts of fault or improper actions usually are related indirectly to terminations for convenience, generally when a wrongful default termination is converted into one for the convenience of the agency.

Methods for Invoking Convenience Terminations

A termination for the convenience of the agency may be invoked by the public procurement official delivering a formal notice of termination to the contractor or by operation of law. If the termination is directed by written notice, the notice must indicate: (1) that the contract is being terminated for the convenience of the agency pursuant to the contract provisions authorizing the termination, (2) the effective date of the termination, (3) the extent of the termination, (4) any special instructions applicable to the termination, and (5) steps that the contractor should take to minimize the impact on personnel if the termination, together with all outstanding terminations, will result in a significant reduction in the contractor's work force.

A termination for the convenience of the agency may arise by operation of law in a number of ways. Whenever a termination for default is found to be improper, or whenever a constructive termination has occurred, the termination may be converted by regulation and the clause itself into one for convenience. If, after termination for default, it is found that the contractor was not in default or that the default was excusable, the rights and obligations of the parties are the same as if the termination had been for the convenience of the agency.

The courts, to obtain jurisdiction in those situations where the contract had either been erroneously canceled or not properly entered into, rely on the doctrine of constructive termination for the convenience of the agency. For example, the courts have accepted the agency's argument that cancellation of a contract was required, based on a finding that the contract has been improperly solicited, and treated the cancellation as a constructive termination for convenience even though the Purchasing Agent did not follow regulatory requirements. It cannot be contrary to the "best interests of the Agency" — the controlling standard of the termination clause — to end a contract that has been incorrectly advertised. (See *John Reiner & Co. v. United States*, 163 Ct. Cl. 381, 325 F. 2d 438 [1963].) The contractor is not entitled to recover anticipatory profits because the agency could have invoked the termination for convenience provision regardless of whether the contract involved was of the "requirements" type or the "indefinite quantity" type. In comparable circumstances, it has been held that the failure of the agency to invoke the convenience termination article makes no difference and that that clause, nevertheless, sets the limit for any possible recovery. (See *Nesbitt v. United States*, 179 Ct. Cl. 666, 345 F.2d 583 [1965].)

The doctrine of constructive termination for convenience has also been relied on in those factual situations where the agency is prevented by the application of equitable estoppel from repudiating a contractual arrangement. This is especially true if the agency fails to comply with regulatory procedures governing the award of contracts by sealed bidding, particularly where a lower successful bid has been accepted after bid opening. If the agency fails to timely notify the otherwise low bidder of a late, lower acceptable bid, and if that contractor relies on the agency's inaction to its detriment, an equitable adjustment will be authorized under the Termination for Convenience article. (See *Emeco Industries v. United States*, 202 Ct. Cl. 1006, 485 F.2d 652 [1973].)

Limitations on the agency's right to terminate a contract for its convenience are normally not prescribed in the standard termination clauses. The convenience termination clauses provide for termination "whenever the public procurement official or entity shall determine that such termination is in the best interest of the Agency." They are designed to provide a mechanism whereby the agency may end its obligations on a contract and yet limit its liability for the contractor's costs and profit on the preparations made and the work done. It may well be that the agency does not promote confidence when it terminates a contract and deprives the contractor of its profits, but the determination of the interest and convenience of the agency is by the contract clause left to the Purchasing Agent and the entity. Absent bad faith, or some other wrong to the contractor or illegal conduct, the agency alone is the judge of its best interests in terminating a contract for convenience, pursuant to the discretionary power reserved to the agency by the clause. (See *Colonial Metals Co. v. United States*, 204 Ct. Cl. 320, 494 F.2d 1355 [1974].)

The agency, accordingly, has virtually unrestricted rights to cancel a contract, providing that the cancellation is in its best interests and was made in "good faith." Bad faith or arbitrariness is significantly more difficult to establish in an agency contract environment than under commercial standards. Nevertheless, the courts have acknowledged that, under appropriate circumstances, the contractor may be able to overcome the limitations of the Termination for Convenience article by showing that the termination was, in fact, made in bad faith.

In the absence of clear evidence to the contrary, it is presumed that public officials involved in the termination of the contractor's agreement were acting conscientiously in the discharge of their duties when the contract was terminated for the purported convenience of the agency. (See *Librach & Cutler v. United States*, 147 Ct. Cl. 605 [1959].) The courts have always been loath to find to the contrary, and it requires "well-nigh irrefragable proof" to induce the courts to abandon the presumption of good faith dealing. In cases where the courts have considered allegations of bad faith, the necessary irrefragable proof has been equated with evidence of some specific intent to injure the plaintiff (contractor). Bad faith, in many respects, is comparable to actions that are motivated by malice alone (i.e., the court has found bad faith in a civilian pay suit only in view of a proven "conspiracy to get rid of the plaintiff" or conduct that was "designedly oppressive"). Applying this standard, bad faith does not exist in such cases where (1) the Purchasing Agent/entity awards a contract to another company after terminating a plaintiff's contract or (2) there is an incorrect reading of the contract by the agency, which is not tantamount to bad faith.

De Facto Debarment

A further restraint on the agency's right to terminate a contract for convenience is that the termination cannot act as a de facto debarment. It is well settled that while no individual or corporation has a right to be awarded a specific agency contract, one who has been dealing with the agency on an ongoing basis may not be blacklisted from further contracting, except for valid reasons and in conformity with the procedural safeguards established by law. It is clear that due process of law requires that before a contractor may be blacklisted (whether by debarment or by suspension), the contractor must be offered specific procedural safeguards, including a notice of the charges against him, an opportunity to rebut those charges, and, under most circumstances, a hearing. Absent a factual basis in the record, the courts will not allow the agency to hide behind the cloak of such conclusory phrase as "termination for the convenience of the agency" to justify its actions. (See *Art-Metal-USA v. Solomon*, 473 F. Supp. 1 (D.C. Cir. [1978].)

It is equally well established that, where the agency has breached the contract, anticipatory profits are recoverable. This rule applies in those cases where the agency's action to cancel a contract cannot be legally justified either by the terms of the contract or by the reasons given in support of cancellation. If the contractor was at all times ready, willing, and able to perform his obligation under the contract, but was prevented from doing so by the unauthorized act of cancellation on the part of the agency, there is no question that the cancellation is a breach of contract by the agency. An unqualified and positive refusal to complete performance of a contract may be treated as a complete breach and entitle the injured party to bring action at once and be compensated. Under these circumstances, the measure of the contractor's damages is the amount of profit that would have been earned had the contract not been cancelled. (See *David J. Joseph Co. v. United States*, 113 Ct. Cl. 3, 82 F. Supp. 345 [1949].)

When the agency enters into a contract, it has rights, and it ordinarily incurs responsibilities similar to those of a private person who is a party to a contract. If the agency terminates a contract without justification, such termination is a breach of the contract, and the agency becomes liable for all of the damages resulting from the wrongful act. The damages will include not only the injured party's expenditures and losses in partially performing the contract, but also the profits that such party would have realized if completion of the contract had been permitted. The objective is to put the injured party in as good a position pecuniarily as they would have been in if the contract had been completely performed.

If the agency has reserved the right to terminate a contract for convenience and then does so, there is no breach, and normally there can be no recovery for the profits that would have been made if the agency had not exercised its reserved right. The termination clause limits profit to work actually done and prohibits the recovery of anticipated, but unearned, profits. That limitation is a deeply ingrained strand of public procurement policy.

Moreover, anticipatory profits are not allowed in those cases where a default termination has been converted into one for the convenience of the agency even though the default articles provide for an "equitable adjustment" for wrongful default terminations. It has long been held that the cancellation of a contract under the power reserved to the agency does not include anticipatory profits as justified compensation. A major reason for the initiation and use of Termination for Convenience articles has been to allow the agency to avoid paying unearned profits. Thus, any recovery of profits on a terminated contract is limited to profits on work actually performed prior to the termination. (See *General Builders Supply Co. v.*

United States, 187 Ct. Cl. 477, 409 F.2d 246 [1969] and *Accord Dairy Sales Corp. v. United States*, 593 F.2d 1002 [1976].)

Bid Protests and Disputes

Bid protests, the disputes process, and the equitable remedy of extraordinary relief are statutorily-based remedies available to the contractor, or prospective contractor, doing business with the agency. Each remedy has its application during a specific phase of the acquisition process. Bid protests are associated with the award phase and are generally concerned with some irregularity in the selection of a bidder or offeror for contract award or with allegations of defective specifications or terms and conditions of the proposed contract. Contract disputes arise during the performance phase, where extraordinary relief is only available when all other means have been exhausted.

Bid Protests

The bid protest process is based on the implied contract theory. The issuance of a solicitation instrument and the submission of a bid or offer result in the creation of an implied contract. This implies that the agency will fairly and honestly consider each bid or offer received in accordance with the express criteria set forth in the solicitation and in accordance with the agency's rules and regulations and appropriate statutes. Failure on the part of the agency to abide by these criteria is generally viewed as a breach of an implied contract. The bid protest process is also an avenue through which interested bidders or offerors can bring irregularities in the specifications or the terms and conditions of the proposed contract to the attention of the procuring agency. Thus, protests may be filed in either the pre-award or post-award phase of the acquisition process.

The public entity's enabling legislation should encourage protesting contractors to seek resolution of their complaints with the purchasing agent prior to filing a protest with the City/County Commission or the Courts. When a protest is filed with an agency, an award normally should not be made until the matter is resolved, unless the purchasing agent or other designated official determines that: (1) the supplies or services to be contracted for are urgently required; (2) delivery or performance will be unduly delayed by failure to make an award promptly; or (3) a prompt award will otherwise be advantageous to the agency.

A "protest" is defined as a written objection by an interested party to a solicitation issued by an agency for bids or proposals for a proposed contract for the procurement of goods or services or a written objection by an interested party to a proposed award or the award of such a contract (31 U.S.C. Section 3551[1]). "Interested party" means an actual or prospective bidder or offeror whose direct economic interest would be affected by the award of the contract or by the failure to award (31 U.S.C. Section 3551[2]).

A protest by a "concerned citizen" who argued that only one bidder on a challenged procurement provided an appropriate response to the solicitation could not be considered by the agency because the protestor did not qualify as an interested party. The requirement that a party be "interested" is designed to assure diligent participation in the protest process so that the issues are sharply presented, the record is complete, and frivolous protests are avoided. In making the determination as to what "interests" entails, the courts may consider the nature of the issues raised and the direct or indirect benefits to the protestor.

The public entity's enabling legislation should authorize the purchasing agent to determine whether the solicitation, proposed award, or award complies with statutes and regulations governing the procurement process. If it is determined that the solicitation, proposed award, or award does not comply with appropriate statutes and regulations, it should be required that the agency:

A "protest" is... a written objection by an interested party to a solicitation issued... for bids or... written objection... to a proposed award...

- refrain from exercising any of its options under the contract;

- recompete the contract immediately;

- issue a new solicitation;

- terminate the contract;

- award a contract that is consistent with such statutes or regulations; or

- perform any combination of the foregoing.

Debarment and Suspension

It is the general policy of government agencies to award contracts to, and consent to subcontracts with, only responsible contractors. Debarment and suspension are discretionary actions that are appropriate means to effectuate this policy. The serious nature of these sanctions requires that they be imposed only in the public interest for the agency's protection, not for purposes of punishment.

From the agency's perspective, debarment and suspension are among the most effective administrative remedies available to a procuring agency to protect the agency's interest. From the contractor's perspective, they are the most serious form of sanction that can be imposed because they bar a contractor from doing business with the agency either for a specified period, in the case of debarment, or temporarily, in the case of suspension.

Debarment and suspension may be authorized by statute as well as by regulation, and the validity of both measures is well established. In the case of both statutory and administrative debarment, it has been held that such are not penalties; rather, if the procedures are reasonable, debarment represents proper regulatory measures for protecting the interests of the agency. Debarment and suspension, although harsh measures from the contractor's perspective, are the essential administrative mechanisms, whereby the procuring agencies and departments maintain the integrity of the acquisition system. Suspension may be imposed as a preliminary step to debarment or as the only action, and immediately precludes the contractor from participating in the acquisition activities (ABA, 2000).

The ABA Model Procurement Code recommends that legal advice be sought concerning any proposed suspension or debarment (ABA, 2000).

Suspension is normally for a shorter period of time, such as 12 months or, if legal proceedings have commenced during that period, until the completion of such proceedings.

The agency may suspend a firm or individual upon evidence of commission of fraud or a criminal offense in connection with obtaining, attempting to obtain, or performing a public contract or subcontract. Under this criterion, a contractor may be suspended upon indictment for fraud. For an agency to suspend a contractor there must be adequate evidence, which has been defined as information sufficient to support the reasonable belief that a particular act or omission has occurred. Evidence required to sustain a suspension is less than that which must be shown to convict the contractor of fraud, but is more than uncorroborated suspicion or accusation.

In *Horne Brothers v. Laird*, 463 F.2d 1268 (D.C. Cir. 1972), the court examined what it described as the serious and fundamental questions regarding the fairness of procedures utilized by the agency in suspending contractors. It stated as a general proposition that an action that suspends a contractor and contemplates that the contractor may remain suspended for a period of one year or more is a condition that requires the agency to ensure fundamental fairness to the contractor whose economic life may depend on the ability to bid on agency contracts. Fairness requires that the bidder be given specific notice as to at least some charges alleged against the bidder and be given, in the usual case, an opportunity to rebut those charges. It suggests that, generally, a temporary suspension for a short period, not to exceed 30 days, without notice and opportunity to rebut charges may be acceptable. It also suggests that the kind of evidence the agency may be required to produce to comply with due process and to ensure there is adequate evidence to support the suspension is a question of judgment.

Debarment

A contractor may be debarred following conviction of, or civil judgment for:

- commission of fraud or a criminal offense in connection with obtaining, attempting to obtain, or performing a public contract;
- violation of federal or state antitrust statutes relating to the submission of offers;

- commission of embezzlement, theft, bribery, falsification or destruction of records, false statements, or receipt of stolen property; or

- commission of any other offense indicating a lack of business integrity or business honesty that seriously and directly affects the contractor's present responsibility as an agency contractor or subcontractor.

A contractor may also be debarred for violating the terms of an agency contract or subcontract, but the violation must be of such a serious nature that debarment is fully justified. Such violations include: (1) willful failure to perform in accordance with the terms of one or more contracts or (2) a history of failure to perform, or of unsatisfactory performance of, one or more contracts.

An individual or firm whose business or livelihood is largely dependent upon government contracts is entitled to procedural due process. This includes the rights to notice of specific charges and an opportunity to present evidence before the contractor can be blacklisted or barred from securing such contracts for actions demonstrating lack of integrity. The agency cannot act arbitrarily, either substantively or procedurally, against a person. That person is entitled to challenge the processes and the evidence before being officially declared ineligible for agency contracts. Disqualification from bidding or contracting directs the power and prestige of an agency towards a particular person and may have a serious economic impact on that person. Such debarment cannot be left to administrative improvisation on a case-by-case basis. The agency power must be exercised in accordance with accepted basic legal norms. Considerations of basic fairness require that administrative regulations establish standards for debarment and procedures that include notice of specific charges and opportunities to present evidence and cross-examine adverse witnesses. These procedures should culminate into administrative findings and conclusions based on the records so made. Conceivably a temporary suspension for a reasonable period, pending investigation prior to a hearing, might be constitutionally permissible in some circumstances when procedural safeguards are accorded before a final decision is reached; but how long a temporary suspension could be sustained would depend on the need and other circumstances. (See *Gonzales v. Freeman*, 334 F.2d 570 [D.C. Cir. 1964].)

Due process includes the right to be notified of the specific charge concerning the contractor's lack of integrity so as to afford the contractor an opportunity to respond to and attempt to persuade the agency, in whatever time is available, that the allegations are without merit. Since a determination that a contractor lacks integrity may not be made without reference to specific charges or allegations, it will impose no burden on the agency to notify the contractor of those charges. In so doing, the contractor will at least have the opportunity to explain his or her actions before adverse action is taken. A simple misunderstanding or mistake may be clarified before both the agency and the contractor experience significant injury.

References

American Bar Association (2000). *The 2000 model procurement code for state and local governments.* Chicago: American Bar Association.

Burnham, S. J. (1993). *Drafting contracts: A guide to the practical application of the principles of contract law* (2nd ed.). New York: Matthew Bender and Company.

National Institute of Governmental Purchasing, Inc. (NIGP) (1999). *General public procurement.* Herndon, VA: NIGP.

National Institute of Governmental Purchasing, Inc. (NIGP) (2000). *Intermediate public procurement.* Herndon, VA: NIGP.

National Institute of Governmental Purchasing, Inc. (NIGP) (2004). *Contract administration.* Herndon, VA: NIGP.

National Institute of Governmental Purchasing, Inc. (NIGP) (2004). *Sourcing in the public sector.* Herndon, VA: NIGP.

Chapter 6

Ethics and Professionalism in Public Procurement

This chapter was written by Mr. Leroy Harvey, Ph.D. candidate at Florida Atlantic University and is reprinted with his permission.

Introduction

One of the most illusive concepts in human organization, from the societal level to the family unit, is that of ethics. Whether it is the task of defining ethics, or the challenge of deciding when it is being adhered to or violated, there seems to be several nebulous areas of indecision. There are questions relating to who decides what is ethical, how it should be decided, and why some standards are more appropriate than others. There are also questions that relate to the religious origins of the basis for ethical standards, whether these standards should be relevant to secular affairs and why other standards originating from other perspectives are not considered sound. In addition, there are questions of whether ethical constraints reduce or advance interactions in some organizations, and therefore how useful they are in the effective functioning of those organizations. Finally, there is the ultimate question of whether everything ethical is good, and everything good ethical.

While this chapter cannot answer all questions that abound regarding ethics, it aims to address some of the most frequently encountered ones. No attempt will be made to compile a list of ethical or unethical practices, but examples of what they are will be given. This chapter will look at the relationship of ethics and law, the relationship of ethics and professionalism, and the role of ethics in government procurement. Ethics will be shown to be an important component of professionalism and how it should extend beyond the working environment of the professional to be a part of the lifestyle of the individual. Throughout the chapter, it will be shown that there are important advantages to adhering to high ethical standards, even if the short-term benefits may not be manifestly attractive or appreciable. The benefits from such standards, realized over the long term, usually outweigh any short-term gains made through questionable practices. Despite the old adage, the fact of the matter is that good guys do not always finish last.

Origins of the Concept of Ethics

The question of what is good and bad behavior most likely originated in pre-societal and pre-religious human history. Long before humankind decided to form organizations to achieve collective security, economic goals, and religious systems, humans learned to appreciate or disagree with the activities and actions of other humans. They came to like those who acted in a certain manner, while disliking others who acted contrary to the preferred behaviors. The concept of trust developed through the reliability of an individual to engage in behavior consistent with desirable conduct, and the behavior of those who were not consistently reliable gave rise to mistrust and apprehension. As described by philosophers like Thomas Hobbes and John Locke, this mistrust led to fear being a constant factor in the "state of nature." The state of nature as described by these philosophers may be overdramatic, but it helps to place the issue of trust in perspective and how human beings have come to deal with right and wrong.

For Thomas Hobbes, constant fear led humankind to agree to form a commonwealth or society in which certain basic preferences (rights) would be protected. Everyone preferred to live without the constant fear of death; and, in order to secure this right, everyone had to give up any other preferences (rights) that could potentially jeopardize the agreed-upon right. For John Locke, the preference (right) of having private property led mankind to agree to a social contract in which people were expected to abide by certain guidelines. Early in their development into a civilized society, mankind consciously or unconsciously started to develop a code of ethics (Aljian, 1974). These guidelines were expected to benefit everyone, while not harming anyone. John Stuart Mill, in his *Utilitarianism* (1861), suggests that we should maximize good by doing that which will provide the greatest good for the greatest number of people.

Mistrust in the state of nature, therefore, led to the formation of rules or laws to guide the proper conduct of individuals and to a definition of what is right and wrong behavior. However, there are instances in which the pursuit of ethical obligations may require that certain laws be ignored. During the time of slavery in the United States, many people broke the law in assisting runaway slaves, in order to fulfill what they considered their moral obligations. This means that many people hold ethics, from a moral perspective, in higher esteem than they do laws. On the other hand, while laws have the coercive force of authority, they do not obviate the possibility of inappropriate behavior. Those who want to circumvent ethical standards can sometimes find ways to do so within the confines of the law, and without being punished under the law.

Defining Ethics

As a field of philosophical inquiry, ethics is the study of morality. Morality is different from law, obedience to authority, religion, and opinion or preferences. In a more in-depth inquiry into ethics, one would encounter philosophical branches such as meta-ethics, theoretical normative ethics, and applied ethics (Callahan, 1988). Conceptual approaches to teaching ethics can also be broken down into categories like social philosophy and political theory, ethical issues and social morality, professional and administrative ethics, and meta-ethics and ethical analysis (Bowman & Elliston, 1988). For the basic purpose of this chapter, it can be accepted that there are generally three separate approaches or schools of thought to ethics. Though these approaches have been given different names by people around the world, a simple classification used by Dobrin (2002) describes them as: (1) the virtue approach, (2) the consequentialist/empirical approach, and (3) the principled approach.

Virtue ethics focuses on individual integrity and character and is based on human beings being true to themselves and to others. It is concerned with what should be the nature of a person's character and what must be done to achieve this. Among philosophers of antiquity, Aristotle is the most well known proponent of this approach. The consequentialist approach looks at the results of the actions that the person takes. David Humes is perhaps the earliest leading champion of this approach. Two tributaries to this approach are the utilitarian perspective, which is the European approach, and pragmatism as theory, which is the United States form of that school of thought. The utilitarian focus is on providing the greatest good for the greatest number of people, while pragmatism values outcomes over process, meaning the end justifies the means. The principled approach relies on rationality and seeks universal and consistent principles on which to base ethics. Ethics generated through this approach should be a temporal and appropriate to all people in all places. German philosopher Immanuel Kant is the most famous advocate of this approach to understanding ethics.

Despite the different approaches to understanding ethics, professions have long established acceptable standards by which they are governed. Within organizations, ethics concerns itself with the concept of what is right versus what is wrong behavior. It is a reality that what is considered wrong behavior in one organization, country, or region may not be seen as wrong in another. Standards vary from culture to culture and from organization to organization. For instance, in some countries it may be acceptable for a public administrator to accept a gift as a token of appreciation for expediting a process for an acquaintance. As expressed by Rose-Ackerman (1999), "in many countries a telephone, a passport, or a driver's license cannot be obtained expeditiously without a payoff. Sometimes the service is available only to the corrupt, but not to the patient but honest citizen" (p.15). In other countries, this behavior is considered unethical, if not illegal. Compounding this is the fact that what is considered unethical in a government agency may not be seen as wrong behavior in a private sector firm, even in the same country.

For some cultures, if it is not illegal, then it is fair game; and anything short of bribes, kickback, blackmail, unauthorized payoff, and other outright lawlessness may be seen as one hand washing the other. To some people in Third World countries and the former communist block, it is tactical to have someone on the inside of government to look out for your interests; and, as they say, one good favor deserves another. In the United States and other countries, there has been a movement away from this To Insure Prompt Service (T.I.P.S.) approach to expediting transactions with governmental organizations. Laws have been enacted to ensure that flagrant disregard for appropriate conduct is not proliferated in government functions. While ordinances have become a guiding light in navigating the treacherous waters of professional behavior, they are not lighthouses. They cannot be solely depended upon, and both written and tacit ethical codes exist and must be heeded. What then is the difference between what is unethical and what is illegal?

Laws versus Codes of Ethics

W*ebster's New Collegiate Dictionary* defines *law* as a rule of conduct or action prescribed or formally recognized as binding or enforced by a controlling authority. It is the binding custom or practice of a community that is advisable or obligatory to observe. The concept of law connotes coercion and control, and needs an authoritative body to ensure its compliance. An action or activity is considered *lawful* if it is authorized, established, or in harmony with the relevant law. Issues pertaining to the law are considered *legal* issues; and, in practice, the term is extended to describe an action that is lawful. Any activity that is sanctioned by law is generally considered good for the society, but sometimes there is room within legal parameters for unethical practices to occur. For example, while freedom of speech provisions under the Constitution may allow workers to have discussion on topics with sensitive sexual content, it is unethical to conduct such discussion in the presence of others who do not indicate their desire to hear such content. Therefore, while laws are not broken in such a case, ethical standards are violated.

Webster's New Collegiate Dictionary defines *ethic* as a set of moral principles or values, a theory or system of moral values, and the principles of conduct governing an individual or a group. In non-professional vocations, ethics may not be codified, and are sometimes tacit mores that descended through historical practices. Even when there is no formal approach to educating the individual on the organization's ethics, the person entering the occupation will be acculturated over time. Within professional organizations, conduct is considered *ethical* if it conforms to accepted professional standards. Quite often, these standards are codified and promulgated and can be learned as part of the professional development of the individual or group. There are usually laws enacted to govern the activities within long established professions, and additional guidelines are often set by the profession to complement these laws.

To put it simply, differences between legal and ethical issues may be related to the severity of the offenses and the consequences for violating each. Illegal offenses usually have the potential of affecting society at-large in a negative way, or so the laws claim. Violation of laws can carry consequences that are enforceable by the governing authority and require that the offender repay a debt to society. This can also ruin an individual's legal and social status in society. Unethical offenses that are within the law may only affect a limited segment of the society and quite often a small number of people situated close to the incident. The offender in an ethical matter may be castigated within the profession and among interested parties, but may not be required to repay a debt to society at large. As with law, some ethical violations are more serious than others, and the most serious ethical guidelines are sometimes elevated to the status of law. For example, the problem of kickback was once an unethical issue; but, when it became a widespread and major problem (graft), laws were enacted against it.

> *...actions can be unethical without being illegal, though everything illegal should be considered unethical.*

Making a practice a legal issue does not mean that laws will be vigorously enforced, but it shows that it has been identified as a problem that deserves the coercive force of the governing political body. The irony of the situation is that there are legal but unethical issues that could potentially harm society more than other situations that are addressed through law. At the time of writing this chapter, human cloning is not illegal in most countries, yet laws in some of these same countries do not allow the sale of human organs. Cloning, which some consider unethical, could potentially have a greater negative effect on society than the sale of organs. Most people in the medical profession do not condone either activity, and this is because both the legal and illegal activities mentioned above violate the ethical standards of the profession.

The bottom line is that actions can be unethical without being illegal, though everything illegal should be considered unethical. Therefore, the professional should not rely solely on whether or not an action is legal, but should determine what is right or wrong behavior. This requires the constant adherence to professional standards. Callahan (1988) proposes that the law permits many immoralities that could not withstand even the most basic ethical scrutiny, yet we would not want these actions to be made illegal, since that would interfere with individual liberties. Notably, the difference between laws and ethics does not stop there; and there are even instances when the law requires, or at least encourages, immoralities. Law enforcement officers are allowed to abandon moral principles in carrying out investigations or sting operations. Police officers can use or sell drugs if that will aid them in law enforcement activities. In extreme cases, secret agents are allowed to commit murder in order to fulfill their duties.

In public service there is sometimes a tradeoff between efficiency and social obligations, and an increase in one oftentimes results in a decrease in the other. In government procurement, an effective balance must be established in the effort to reduce malfeasance while increasing efficiency. Allowing procurement personnel to operate in a competitive environment without their hands being tied by overly stringent codes or ordinances can pursue this. However, in a time when some commentators advocate for or against a high level of discretion to be granted to public administrators, as demonstrated in the well known Frederick-Finer public administration debates, it must be noted that "discretion increases corrupt incentives" (Rose-Ackerman, 1999, p. 59). Still, rigid ordinances or codes may not always be the answer, and "reforms [are] needed to encourage discretion and improve incentives for good performance" (p. 61).

Ethics and Professionalism

How then do ethics relate to professionalism and what are the elements of a profession? There has been extensive discussion on the concept of professionalism and what constitutes a profession. One simple definition of a profession is that it is any calling or occupation by which a person habitually earns their living. However, some have pointed out that in days of yore the term "profession" was reserved for the privileged occupations, such as doctors, lawyers, professors, and the clergy. To reconcile the difference in definitions, some researchers have long accepted the notion of a professional continuum with different categories like non-professions, marginal professions, would-be-professions, emerging professions, new professions, and old-established professions (Thai, 1983). In today's world of advanced information and technology, the concept of professionalism has once again emerged to mean more than just being a member in an occupational group labeled as a profession (Brody, 1989). What then do we look for when we seek professionalism in the public sector?

 Characteristics of a Profession

Echoing the views of many experts in the field, Rabin (1983) considers the following elements as integral components of any profession:

- A body of knowledge that supports the practice and study of the profession;

- An established code of ethics that promulgates acceptable standards;

- Autonomy over one's actions as a member of the profession;

- Altruistic service to society and the profession; and

- Regulation of entry into the occupation.

This is not an exhaustive list, and academicians like Thai (1983) believe that the following are also distinct and necessary attributes of a profession:

- Authority over clients;

- Community sanction; and

- An intrinsic culture.

While some scholars believe that the body of knowledge can be specialized and theoretical (Buck, 1976), many others like Glickauf (1971) believe that the professional should be well educated, with a broad educational background. Having a knowledge base that draws from allied fields complements the specialized training in the administrator's specific area and differentiates the professional from the trained technician. While the technician concentrates on the approach in which he or she is trained, the professional should be broad based and well informed about issues related to his or her actions and decisions. Included in this broad body of knowledge should be a clear understanding of laws and ethical standards relevant to the field of work. This is especially true of personnel involved in pivotal governmental activities like public procurement, since the level of interaction with other governmental departments and the private sector is such a high one.

The attribute of autonomy can be realized when practitioners in their field separate themselves from the laity with the necessary expertise and develop a certain level of immunity from manipulation by others. Some have argued that professionals in fields like procurement cannot function from a position of autonomy, since it is by cooperating with others from management that the greatest effectiveness is realized (National Institute of Governmental Purchasing [NIGP], 1991). However, while some fields like procurement are intertwined with other areas of government, they have to demarcate their territory and exercise control over their responsibilities, activities, and duties. For professionals, the principle of autonomy over their actions in procurement should not be impaired by the actions of other members, from management, or any political entity. Being consistently astute regarding ethical standards is a big plus in the area of professional autonomy. This does not mean that public officials, special interests, and the public at large will not seek to influence the most highly professional public procurement official, but doing so will not be easily accomplished if the public purchaser truly believes in their professionalism.

The altruistic component will be questioned in these highly individualistic and opportunistic times, but the practitioner's pride of doing what he or she does should culminate in the delivery of service for the sake of civility. Many trained public officials go beyond the call of duty to properly serve their community, without seeking any additional opportunity for self-aggrandizement. Hart and Wright (1994) liken this to the courageous behavior of military personnel defending the integrity of their nations. If society can expect soldiers to be courageous in situations that can result in their deaths, then society should also be able to expect benevolence from its public servants and administrators.

Gaining the public's trust, recognition, and acceptance should be the desire of any true professional, and the push for sanction by the community they serve should be an ongoing effort. For public administration in general, sanction by the community helps legitimize its role in the governance of society. For procurement in particular, it justifies not contracting out the procurement function as is done by some federal departments like the Department of Defense. Besides competency, ethical soundness (incorruptibility) may be the leading criterion in gaining the public's trust. In fact, without the public's acceptance of their integrity, competence, and authority, the public procurement officer will constantly be required to defend actions and decisions.

Another attribute of professionalism that is directly related to ethics is the "authority over clients" factor. Being closely linked with the "community sanction" attribute, authority over clients does not come only through the powers delegated to the bureaucracy by the three branches of government, but also by the professional's image in the organization and the legitimacy ascribed by the public at large. NIGP's Code of Ethics (Appendix A) states that all its members should be "governed by the highest ideals of honor and integrity in all public and personal relationships in order to merit the respect and inspire the confidence of the organization and the public being served." The Code also admonishes members "to believe in the dignity and worth of the service that their organizations provide, and to recognize and respect the responsibilities entrusted upon them as public servants."

...a major

component of the

procurement culture

involves the issue of

ethical standards.

Regulation of entry into the field of public procurement will become a necessity as the practice is advanced along the professionalism continuum. Most government agencies have established mechanisms to screen entrants into the field, based strongly on concerns for ethical behavior in the future. There has been great progress in developing academic programs that prepare public servants, administrators, and scholars for the practice in and study of public administration. For public procurement to be recognized as a new profession, it will have to prove that its practitioners have acquired a high level of competency through specialized training and education. The common body of knowledge and skills necessary for accomplishing this task is being accumulated and includes studies in professional ethics.

Each profession's intrinsic culture is perpetuated through professional associations, esoteric publications, accepted practices that are passed on through acculturation, and fraternal relationships. Through all of these experiences, the professional learns what actions facilitate effective and desirable results and is made aware of activities that can be deleterious to one's own career and the profession in general. The profession actively seeks to bolster its image and prestige and gives recognition to people who make this possible. Public procurement as a profession is no different, and its culture permeates its membership through conferences, seminars, publications, workplace interactions, and formal and informal organizations. Professional procurement associations campaign to keep all their members on the same plane as far as the professional culture is concerned. For new members, it takes only a short time to be able to determine what is tolerated and what is unacceptable behavior, and a major component of the procurement culture involves the issue of ethical standards.

Ethics in Public Procurement

The existence of a code of ethics for the professional public purchaser is important because of the level of responsibility that is attached to the duties of the purchaser. There are always opportunities for improper conduct within the occupation, and the professional must be seen as unimpeachable and of an irreproachable character (Glickauf, 1971). Many public administration schools offer courses in administrative ethics, and agencies have increased ethics awareness in the workplace, which has resulted in improvements over the past decades. The development of a body of knowledge for procurement professionals and the establishment of ethical standards are not left up to academia. Many government organizations, professional associations and societies, and many suppliers have accumulated a set of ethical standards as parts of their operating policies.

Professional bodies such as the NIGP and the Universal Public Procurement Certification Council (UPPCC) have exercised leadership in establishing and fostering professional codes of conduct for public procurement officials. Special interest groups are also actively seeking conformity to certain standards by those involved in public procurement. A few elected officials are proactive in assuring accountability for the activities of procurement officials and have made it their personal prerogative to guard against inappropriate procurement practices within their jurisdiction. One area in which special interest groups, politicians, and administrators find common ground is in the area of protecting certain disadvantaged businesses seeking to do business with government.

In government, the procurement function involves a great deal of power, which stems from the fact that procurement officials determine how government business is to be awarded among suppliers. The decisions made by these officials have an important impact on business structures ranging from sales commissions, sales managers' performance records, and a company's profit structures to suppliers' access, competitiveness, and survivability (Dowst, 1972). There are opportunities for power to be abused and for purchasers to use their positions for personal gains. Since the activities of these officials cannot always be controlled by procedural rules or auditing, there are always opportunities for kickbacks, personal purchases at special prices, entertainment paid by suppliers, gifts in return for favors, and other unethical behaviors. It is, therefore, important for all public procurement officials to be cognizant of their obligations to their employers, to suppliers, and to the profession.

Obligations to Your Employer

It should be noted that unethical actions in procurement do not always occur as a reciprocal gesture aimed at benefiting both parties. As a matter of fact, a person could even act unethically without gaining from the action. Sometimes it is even difficult to tell if the person intended to act in a manner deemed unethical. For example, a purchaser could inadvertently divulge information on competitive prices or misrepresent the agency's requirements.

Public purchasers should not underestimate the intent of individuals or groups to extract information on the procurement activities of their agency. This is why it is important for the public purchasers to be consistent in their practices, and not allow deviation from guidelines, even when such deviation seems harmless. Most importantly, the professional must always be wary of seemingly harmless offers or gifts from vendors. This means that receiving benefits, even when it does not place anyone at a disadvantage, should be avoided.

It is the purchaser's obligation to protect confidential information belonging to both the agency and real and potential contractors up until the time that such information becomes public information by law. Most information gathered in government contracts becomes public information once the bids are officially opened, but this does not mean that the purchaser cannot become aware of information before the opening. For example, suppose, in seeking clarifications regarding a Request for Proposal (RFP), a vendor inadvertently reveals information intended for a sealed bid. If such a situation should occur, the purchaser is expected to respect the privacy of such information until the bid is officially opened. The purchaser may want to avoid addressing such information in granting the clarification, and any clarification given should be shared with all competing vendors. This will prevent anyone from accusing the purchaser of coaching a competitor, or for taking part in collusion. The purchaser must remember that the information that is worked with belongs to the employer and should be treated as such.

The public agency as an employer is entitled to undivided loyalty from its employees, and it can be considered unethical to disagree with the agency's policy in public (Aljian, 1974), or when representing the agency in private presentations. Disagreements should be addressed within the organization and among peers and superiors. Public purchasers should conduct themselves in such a fashion that they never become more obligated to anyone other than to their employer. In addition, there is no excuse for treating the confidentiality of procurement information lightly or using it for personal reasons. This also involves securing sensitive procurement information from other members of the organization who are not involved in the procurement process. Information gathered on a vendor is information that has been entrusted to the agency, and that trust should not be broken by an employer who uses it for personal gain or for granting an advantage to another vendor.

Purchasers have an obligation to reveal any conflict of interest that can affect the fair conduct of procurement activities by their employers. For instance, a purchaser who has ownership of stock in a company seeking to do business with the agency should make this known to the employer. Such disclosure should also be extended to conflicts of interest involving relatives of the purchaser or the purchaser's past employment with a company that is seeking to do business with the public entity. If appropriate, the purchaser may be asked to excuse him or herself from participation in the transaction in question. This would ensure that the agency is not led into a contractual arrangement that is not fully competitive and that may not be in its best interest. Even in conflict of interest cases where the purchaser's adherence to strict professional standards can prevent any disadvantage to the agency or any other competing vendor, the perception problem may be too overwhelming to risk such an involvement.

Obligations to Vendors/Suppliers

Treating the supplier fairly should be the goal of all public purchasers. What is fair to all suppliers, the public, and the buyer is usually ethical. The public purchaser has many obligations to the vendors and suppliers, and a few are worth noting here. It is important that suppliers be furnished with reliable information at all times. Deliberately misleading a supplier is unethical, even if it is a way to avoid addressing other difficult questions. Under no circumstance should an actual or potential vendor be given erroneous information, since such an incident will result in the kind of negative reaction that could impair future competitive bidding. In addition, every reasonable consideration should be given to the suppliers and their products. To invite a supplier to the procurement process with a *priori* decision to exclude them from consideration is considered unethical (Aljian, 1974). Unless serious considerations are being given, a purchaser should avoid making requests for free samples or demonstrations from vendors.

Disenfranchising legitimate vendors, denying them access to the procurement process, and even causing undue waiting is also unethical. Open discrimination and preferential treatment was once a common occurrence, even in government procurement. So severe were these problems that many jurisdictions have enacted laws against those practices and have actively sought to guard against such activities. Equal opportunity rules and affirmative action have helped tremendously in this aspect. Individual jurisdictions have established their own outreach programs for disadvantaged business enterprises, women-owned business enterprises, and minority-owned business enterprises. It is considered unethical for public purchasers to blatantly circumvent these ordinances and outreach programs aimed at promoting inclusiveness.

Disenfranchisement of legitimate vendors does not always take on a blatant appearance, and many suppliers have been kept out of the competitive process in subtle ways. For instance, there are times when needed merchandise may be proprietary, causing the buyer to develop a relationship with the sole supplier. This relationship may be a good one and could last for a long time with the buying agency being appreciative of the goods or service. Eventually, a time will come when that commodity in question is no longer a sole supplier item, and there may be many new suppliers in the market offering similar commodities or services. Due to the good relationship between the agency and the supplier, the purchaser may not want to readily open up the item to competition, especially if the agency is very satisfied with the product. To knowingly maintain a proprietary status on the product could be considered unfair to the other suppliers, non-competitive and, thus, unethical.

Despite these concerns, there are times when, even with other available vendors, the purchasing agency may have a good reason to maintain the relationship with a specific vendor. Changing suppliers can sometimes lead to hidden costs to the purchasing agency, especially if the new supplier has slightly different specifications that may require modification to the existing arrangement in the agency. For instance, if the commodity in question is technological, it may do the same thing as the original product, but may require time to retrain technicians and users. Depending on how many people would be affected, the agency may choose to continue buying from the original vendor. Major software changes in some agencies could require the loss of valuable resources, which means lost manpower while users are trained, the delay of activities in the interim, and cost to do the actual training. The agency must, therefore, balance the need for equity and fairness for vendors and efficiency and effectiveness within the organization.

The actions of a public purchaser should not diminish a supplier's advantage or competitive "edge" in the procurement process. One of the instruments used by public purchasers in the procurement process is the RFP. In responding to such a document, the supplier will sometimes divulge unique and novel ideas. This quite often happens in presentations by the competing suppliers, where they offer innovative approaches to the problem facing the agency. It is the obligation of the public purchaser to protect and guard such ideas from that vendor's competitors until such time that the information is deemed public by law. Even then, the practice of actively directing other suppliers to the existence of such ideas may constitute a violation of the relationship with the affected supplier.

Additionally, even when the law prescribes public disclosure, there are times when statutory exemptions protect some information from public disclosure laws (e.g., Section 119.07, Florida Statute). Competing vendors should find competitive information on their own, even when the purchaser's organization can benefit immensely. It is not only ethical to protect such information, when possible, but it makes good business sense because suppliers who know that their ideas are protected will be more willing to participate in competitive bidding with the purchasing agency.

The obligation of treating all suppliers equitably means that information, explanations or clarifications, allowances for deviation in specifications, time allowances, and other conditions be afforded equally to all potential suppliers. In all business transactions, it is possible for either the vendor or purchaser to make honest mistakes that could be of great cost to the party committing the error. It is considered unethical to capitalize on an apparently honest mistake by the supplier. It is certainly not fair to the supplier for the purchaser to try to hold him or her to an erroneously quoted price, especially if the quoted price is obviously a small fraction of the fair market price. This does not mean, however, that the buyer should accept a correction that will make a purchase non-competitive and would exclude another supplier who is offering a better value. The purchaser's obligation to the supplier goes beyond the discussion here, and the main focus is on fairness. There must be the awareness that fairness should be both real and perceived, and it is important to convey the image of the purchaser doing what is ethical and, thus, right.

Obligations to the Profession

There are laws that govern the function of procurement, and the ones that will be mentioned here are the Uniform Commercial Code and the antitrust laws. The Uniform Commercial Code (U.C.C.) has been effective in all the states and consists of provisions that govern commercial transactions conducted by government agencies. Each state has enacted its own version of the Code, and may provide its own interpretation and discussion based on varying case law (NIGP, 1986). Due to the voluminous nature of the U.C.C., procurement officials need only acquaint themselves with the relevant concepts and provisions that affect the government as buyer. The antitrust laws include several laws aimed at curbing anticompetitive practices by both suppliers and public purchasers. They include The Sherman Act, The Clayton Act, The Federal Trade Commission Act, and other miscellaneous and related acts.

...antitrust laws include several laws aimed at curbing anticompetitive practices by both suppliers and public purchasers.

In addition to national laws that relate to procurement, there are international rules that have been established to regulate government procurement. The World Trade Organization (WTO), in noting that government procurement represents approximately 10% to 15% of Gross Domestic Product (GDP), addresses the issue of discriminatory procurement practices:

> A growing awareness of the trade-restrictive effects of discriminatory procurement policies and of the desirability of fulfilling these gaps in the trading system resulted in a first effort to bring government procurement under internationally agreed trade rules in the Tokyo Round of Trade Negotiations. As a result, the first Agreement on Government Procurement was signed in 1979 and entered into force in 1981. It was amended in 1987, with this amended version entering into force in 1988. In parallel with the Uruguay Round, Parties to the Agreement held negotiations to extend the scope and coverage of the Agreement. The Agreement on Government Procurement (1994) (GPA) was signed in Marrakesh on 15 April 1994—at the same time as the Agreement Establishing the WTO. The new Agreement entered into force on 1 January 1996. The GPA is one of the "plurilateral" Agreements included in Annex 4 to the Agreement Establishing the WTO, signifying that not all its members are bound by it.

It behooves professional purchasers to familiarize themselves with the relevant sections of these laws. In most instances, government procurement officials are exempt from legal actions brought against them for procurement violations involving their actions on behalf of a government agency. In cases where the question of the liability of government officials in actions violating antitrust laws have surfaced, the courts have indicated that state officials cannot be held personally liable if their actions were within the authorized parameters granted by their agencies (NIGP, 1986). However, they may not be protected if they acted beyond their scope of authority. This means that if a violation should occur and it is proven that the public purchaser acted without authority, then the purchaser may be held personally liable for the violation. This is sufficient reason for public purchasers to walk a straight line and try their utmost to operate within the laws and ethical standards that are established.

As mentioned earlier, professional procurement associations, like NIGP and the UPPCC, have established codes of ethics to guide purchasers in their capacity as procurement officers. (See NIGP and UPPCC Codes of Ethics, Appendices A and B, respectively.) These codes of ethics warn against public purchasers being engaged in the direct or indirect acceptance of gifts, gratuities, and other things of value from suppliers. Things of value can include excessive entertainment or private trips, promise of future employment, and personal favors to the purchasers or their families and friends. The American Bar Association (ABA) publishes a Model Procurement Code that addresses the issue of ethics in public contracting. Article 12 of *The 2000 Model Procurement Code for State and Local Governments* covers standards of conduct, remedies for breach of these ethical standards, and a discussion of ethics commission. Provisions from the Code have been adopted by states.

Perhaps one of the most overlooked aspects of ethical conduct in the profession involves the individual's behavior off the job. If a person is seen as lacking integrity in activities that are not job related, such a reputation may be extended to their position as a procurement representative for the public agency. If individuals cannot be trusted in their private lives, why should they be trusted in their public roles? In the same way that the private behavior of an elected official can ruin his or her reputation in the public realm, the same is true for procurement officers. Public purchasers have an obligation to project a favorable image of themselves to the general public and anyone who comes into contact with them. The public purchasing agent should be seen as someone truthful and honest in personal transactions. An individual who is seen as discriminatory in their personal life will have a hard time convincing others that such a reputation does not affect their work. Above all, purchasers should not portray the image of being opportunistic, avaricious, or corrupt in their personal endeavors.

The public purchaser also has an obligation to the user department. The user department must be assured that the purchaser handling its purchases is someone who will provide the department with the best quality at the best price. Some authors in the field of procurement (Flynn & Leenders, 1995) have summed up the basic elements of the procurement function as the "six rights." That is "ensuring that the right goods and services, of the right quality, arrive at the right time, in the right place, in the right quantities, at the right price" (p. 6). In public procurement, the term "quality" can be taken to mean "suitability." The goods or service does not necessarily have to be the highest overall quality but must be the right quality for the purpose intended. Going above the required quality may result in unnecessary elevated prices, which would not equate to the "right price." Although it may not ostensibly seem to be a matter of ethics, it is good business practice to try and meet the user department's needs as best possible. All of this must be accomplished within the confines of the legal limits and under the ethical standards of the organization and profession.

Obligations to the Field of Public Administration

In addition to their obligations to the employer, the supplier, and the profession, the public purchaser has an obligation to the field of public administration in general. There are ethical standards that are general to the field of public administration, and the public purchaser must abide by these standards. This means that the public procurement official must oppose any discrimination based on race, color, religion, sex, national origin, political affiliation, physical handicaps, age, or marital status in any and all aspects of public policy. Likewise, a person's private personal lifestyle should not give cause or excuse for discrimination if it is legal and does not impair or impede the ability to perform required tasks. No sexual, racial, or religious harassment should be allowed, and appropriate channels should be provided for harassed persons to seek redress. In the event of a proven offense, support should be given for appropriate action to take place.

Supervisors should be alert that no illegal action originates from, or is sponsored by their immediate office; and they should inform their subordinates, when necessary, that no illegalities will be tolerated within their offices. Public employees who reasonably suspect illegal action in any public agency should channel information regarding the matter to appropriate authorities. It is the ethical duty of all to help eliminate all forms of illegal discrimination, fraud, and mismanagement of public funds; and to give support to colleagues who experience any difficulty because of responsible efforts to correct such illegal discrimination, fraud, mismanagement, or abuse. All public servants should support authorized investigative agencies and should support, when appropriate, independent auditors reporting to committees independent of their management or agency.

Effective fiscal and management controls and inspections should be viewed as important protections for supervisors, staff, and the public interest. If a bid is advertised as being a formal sealed bid, then the bidding process should be treated in that manner. This means that if the rules for formal bidding stipulate that sealed bids must be opened in the presence of two or more procurement employees at a prearranged time, two or more procurement employees should always be present for such bid openings at the stated time, even if no one outside the division would know. Procurement officials should not deviate from these principles. Even under those conditions where no vendor was present, there was no need to ensure that the process was ostensibly conforming. Supervisors should assure their staff that constructive criticism can be aired without reprisal and that such criticism may be carried to an ombudsman or other designated official if the organization structure and protocol provides for such an arrangement.

One area of ethics that should not be overlooked is that which deals with information technology. In government, inadequate equipment, software, procedures, supervision, and poor security controls give rise to both intentional and inadvertent misconduct. The procurement division has an ethical obligation to seek adequate equipment and software, outline procedures, and establish controls to reduce the organization's vulnerability to inappropriate computer activities. Special care must be taken to secure access to confidential information stored on computers. Care must also be taken to ensure that information gathered electronically is protected and guarded from intrusion. Purchasers must remember that in some agencies, email correspondence is not confidential. One should be wary in asking for sensitive vendor information to be sent via email. This becomes even more important as agencies seek to expand their e-government, since it is unethical to render sensitive government information vulnerable to unauthorized access.

While there are disclosure laws, some information in public offices is privileged because of laws or ordinances. However, when other governmental agencies have a legitimate public service need for information possessed by the procurement division or department, purchasers should do all they can to facilitate them within the limits of statute law, administrative regulations, and promises made to those from whom the purchaser acquired the information. Still, when purchasers undertake discussions with colleagues about privileged information, they should be sure those colleagues need the information discussed; and the purchaser should seek assurances of confidentiality from them.

Obligations to the General Public

...Americans expect government to be compassionate, well organized, and operating within the law.

The procurement office's relationship with the public should not be overlooked, even though it sometimes seems that the public has no significant role to play in the procurement function. As a public servant, the purchaser must remember that part of servicing the public responsively is to encourage citizen cooperation when appropriate and to involve civic groups when possible. As pointed out by the American Society for Public Administration (ASPA) (ASPA, 1997), administrators have an ethical responsibility to bring citizens into contact with the government as far as practical, both to secure citizen support of government and for the economies or increased effectiveness that will result from such interaction. ASPA urges public servants to respect the right of the public to know what is going on in their agencies, even though certain interest groups may raise queries for partisan or other nonpublic purposes.

ASPA (1997) also notes that Americans expect government to be compassionate, well organized, and operating within the law. Citizens within a given jurisdiction should be assured that public servants are adhering to local ordinances and procedures. For instance, local jurisdictions have local ordinances and procedural rules that govern procurement. Conducting purchasing outside the purview of these rules constitutes unauthorized procurement. Some offenses may be as simple as conducting unauthorized procurement of goods or services from vendors when the same goods or services are available within the agency. Others may involve obtaining items under contract from suppliers other than those who hold agency contracts, adding unauthorized purchases to previously approved purchase orders without obtaining permission, or giving false information that informal quotes were obtained without actually contacting the vendors. Disregarding the rules that are established by the duly elected representatives of the citizenry is clearly unethical.

Public employees should understand the overall mission of their agency and the role they play in achieving that mission. As such, answers to questions on public policy should be complete, understandable, and true. The procurement staff must exhibit courteous conduct when dealing with citizens and should devise a system to ensure helpful and pleasant service to the public. Wherever possible, public purchasers should show citizens how to avoid mistakes and be effective in their relations with their government. It will do no harm to share information on the accomplishments of procurement activities with the citizenry, and avenues for public feedback should be opened. On the other hand, not every procurement blunder must be aired in public, but procurement officials must be willing to give accurate accounts of incidences if the public or media should launch an inquiry. In the final analysis, the tax paying public is best served when the individuals conducting the procurement processes are capable of effectively, efficiently, and ethically executing their duties.

Conclusion

The discussion on ethics was quite general in its approach, and no attempt was made to compile a list of ethical or unethical practices. This was intentional, since different agencies in different states have slightly different rules of operations. The offences and obligations discussed, and the examples used, were generic and typical of the kind of issues that purchasers face in their daily activities. Still, they may not apply in every public organization. The goal was to convey the idea that even when clear rules are absent, it is incumbent upon the purchaser to decipher what is right or wrong and what is acceptable and unacceptable behavior. Treating others the way you would want to be treated if you were in a similar situation may not always be good enough, and sometimes rules or laws require much more from the government employee conducting procurement for a government agency.

The discussion was not intended to discourage friendly relations with suppliers, and it does not mean that purchasers cannot go the extra mile to be helpful to suppliers who seek their help. It also does not mean that the procurement official cannot be firm in dealing with contractors who lapse in important stages of the procurement process. No one expects the public purchaser to operate in a vacuum, and no one says individuals cannot err. However, it must be remembered that purchasers may be asked to account for their actions; and, when that time comes, they would want to be on the right side. Remember that the actions of purchasers are their own, and they should be vigilant of what favors are asked of them by suppliers or by their fellow purchasing coworkers.

While they ensure that their actions are honorable, public procurement specialists should also encourage and help fellow workers also to be upright in their undertakings. This is good, not only for the organization, but for the profession and public administration in general. Procurement specialists should strive to know the ordinances that are established for procurement within their jurisdiction, and familiarize themselves with the relevant laws. NIGP's Code of Ethics (Appendix A) is a good place to start in understanding the environment of public procurement. Procurement supervisors and their staff should strive for personal professional excellence and should encourage the professional development of new recruits and those seeking to enter the field of public procurement.

Staff members, throughout their careers, should be encouraged to participate in professional activities and associations for purchasers at both the national and regional levels. These associations help to disseminate information and new direction important to the field, thus, perpetuating the "intrinsic culture" needed to fortify the profession. They should also be reminded of the importance of doing a good job and of their responsibility to improve the public service. When possible, procurement administrators should make time to meet with students and to help bridge the gap between classroom studies and the realities of public jobs. Administrators should also encourage and lend their support to internship programs that can help attract public administration students who have acquired a "body of knowledge" desirable for the profession. This would be helpful in the "regulation of entry" into the field, which is another important attribute of professionalism.

References

Aljian, G. W. (1974). *Purchasing handbook* (3rd ed.). New York: McGraw-Hill Book Company.

American Bar Association (2000). *The 2000 model procurement code for state and local governments.* Chicago: American Bar Association.

American Society for Public Administration (1997). *Code of ethics and implementation guidelines.* Available from http://www.aspanet.org/.

Barry, D. D., & Whitcomb, H. R. (1987). *The legal foundations of public administration* (2nd ed.). New York: West Publishing Co.

Bowman, J. S., & Elliston, F. A. (1988). *Ethics, government, and public policy: A reference guide.* Portsmouth, NH: Greenwood Publishing Group, Inc.

Brody, E. W. (1989). *Professional practice development: Meeting the competitive challenge.* New York: Praeger Publishers.

Buck, V. J. (1979). *Politics and professionalism in municipal planning.* Beverly Hills, CA: Sage.

Callahan, J. C. (1988). *Ethical issues in professional life.* New York: Oxford University Press.

Dobrin, A. (2002). *Ethics for everyone: How to increase your moral intelligence.* New York: John Wiley & Sons, Inc.

Dowst, S. R. (1972). *Basics for buyers.* Boston: Cahners Publishing Co., Inc.

Flynn, A. E., & Leenders, M. R. (1995). *Value-driven purchasing: Managing the key steps in the acquisition process.* New York: Irwin Professional Publishing.

Glickauf, J. S. (1971). *Footsteps toward professionalism.* Chicago: Arthur Anderson and Co.

Maister, D. H. (1997). *True professionalism: The courage to care about your people, your clients, and your career.* New York: The Free Press.

Massengale, E. W. (1991). *Fundamentals of contract law.* Connecticut: Greenwood Publishing Group, Inc.

National Institute of Governmental Purchasing, Inc. (NIGP) (1991). *Public purchasing and materials management.* Herndon, VA: NIGP.

Rabin, J. (Ed.). (1983, Spring). *Professionalism in public administration: Towards conceptual Clarity-A symposium. Public Personnel Administration,* 3(2), 1-14.

Rose-Ackerman, S. (1999). *Corruption and government: Causes, consequences, and reform.* Cambridge, UK: University Press.

Thai, K. V. (1983, Spring). Public administration: A professional education. *Public Personnel Administration,* 3(2), 1-14.

Woolf, H. B. (Ed.). (1976). *Webster's new collegiate dictionary.* Springfield, MA: G. & C. Merriam Company.

World Trade Organization (n. d.). *Government procurement: The plurilateral agreement.* Available from http://www.wto.org/english/tratop_e/gproc_e/over_e.htm.

Chapter 7

Legal Considerations for Software Licensing

As the use of technology to perform public sector management functions grows exponentially, the need to execute contracts for software licensing has also grown tremendously. Since most software packages are proprietary to a specific service provider, these arrangements are frequently processed as a sole-source procurement with little room for negotiation. While it is common for the software provider to draft its own unilateral terms and conditions of the agreement, a knowledgeable and savvy public procurement official can navigate through the legal maze of a software license agreement in an effort to maximize the protections of the public entity.

This chapter will explore the various components of a software contract and provide a list of issues that the official should consider when negotiating and executing software license agreements.

Negotiating Software Procurement Contracts

What are the most important terms of a software contract? Is it the cost of the software? Is it the payment terms? Is it the license rights or the maintenance provisions? It is critically important to any eCommerce or major software acquisition that the public procurement official address all of the key terms necessary to protect the entity's investment as well as to ensure a good, smooth ongoing relationship between the entity and the supplier. A well-drafted agreement will protect the entity's reputation and reduce the risk that the entity will be forced to litigate against a supplier.

Some of the more important areas to address in a major software acquisition are:

- Software Cost
- License/Use Rights
- Implementation Terms and Cost
- Source Code Escrow

- Payment Terms
- Maintenance Terms and Costs
- Warranty
- Indemnity in Connection with Intellectual Property Claims.

Software Cost

Clearly, the cost of the software is where most people want to focus all their attention, as it is initially the highest cost element of the total acquisition. The cost of the software should depend upon its functionality. With some research, the procurement official can obtain data (such as amounts others are paying for the same or similar software) in order to determine whether the supplier is offering the software at a fair price. Market research companies, such as Meta, Gartner Group, and IDC, may be helpful in this endeavor.

The procurement official should avoid acquisitions where the costs are tied to the number of users, number of employees, or the budget of the entity. The agreement should also be structured so that the supplier will break out the maintenance cost separate from the software cost in the first year, and the buyer should pay maintenance only on the software cost during subsequent years.

Payment Terms

Previously, most software companies operated under the accelerated basis of accounting, which means that they accounted for all of the revenue at the time of agreement. However, due to a number of changes in general accounting practices and encouragement from the Securities Exchange Commission (SEC), many software companies have transitioned to a contract basis method, which means that the revenue is recognized as it is received, or as certain aspects of the implementation are achieved. Most eCommerce software suppliers now operate under contract basis accounting, which makes it easier to negotiate payment terms. The public entity should inquire as to which accounting method the supplier uses. If the supplier is not forthcoming with information but is a publicly traded company, the type of accounting method used can be found in the supplier's SEC 10K report. Ideally, from the public entity's point of view, the payments would be spread over the period of time that the software is implemented. Payments to the supplier may be based on the supplier's achievement of defined milestones, with final payment due when the software is fully operational.

Deferred payment terms, such as the following, are common:

- 25% upon the signing;

- 25% upon installation;

- 25% upon full implementation and beta functionality; or

- 25% upon "go live" in a production environment with full functionality demonstrated and accepted.

License/Use Rights

This is one area that can lead to exorbitant additional costs if not structured properly. It is important in any software acquisition that the usage rights for the software be documented (i.e., subsidiaries, joint ventures, etc.) The agreement should also provide that the entity is entitled to use the software on a global basis. Moreover, the entity should ensure that there are no additional or hidden charges for moving the software, changing hardware or operating systems, etc. The license should allow for use by anyone in the organization; use should not be limited in terms of numbers of people or specific names or job titles.

Maintenance

Over time, maintenance can become the highest overall cost in the total life cycle cost of the software. Software maintenance costs are the key revenue and profit producer for most software suppliers. Suppliers may ask the public entity to agree to pay 20% of the "then current list price of the software," but this is excessive. A more reasonable cost would be between 10% and 25% of the net software purchase price, with a clause included to limit any increase in maintenance costs to a maximum of 5% over the previous year's fees.

Service levels defining what is included with the maintenance and remedies for non-performance should be included in all software acquisitions. Service levels should be written around updates as to what is provided and when it is provided. There should also be agreement provisions calling for receipt of enhancements and new releases at no extra charge. There should also be support for prior releases, error/bug corrections, problem priority level definitions (severe, critical, moderate, etc.), response and resolution times according to each priority level, and an escalation process so that the priority level becomes higher if the supplier has still not corrected the problem after a defined period of time.

In addition, the agreement should also provide the public entity with remedies in the event of non-performance by the supplier. These might include a prorated refund of the maintenance fees paid for a given portion of the maintenance period. For example, if a weighted value is assigned to each service level and if a supplier misses that level over a certain period of time, the maintenance cost would be multiplied by the value of that service level, and that portion is either refunded or credited to the public entity.

Implementation Costs

Some eCommerce and/or eProcurement suppliers may attempt to shift implementation to one of their integration partners and will attempt to segregate the purchase of the software license from the implementation of the software. By doing this, the software supplier has minimal or no stake in the implementation phase. For this reason, the procurement official should not agree to any arrangement where the supplier can readily decouple the software license from the implementation. A good way to keep the two intact is through payment terms for the software that are tied to various milestone completions of the implementation.

In any work order...

the procurement

official should

include warranties

for performance to

the agreed-upon

specifications.

The costs of implementation should be negotiated as a fixed fee transaction, with payments based on actual completion and progress towards a committed schedule. Most suppliers will push strongly for a "time and materials" pricing approach to implementation; this arrangement is like writing a blank check, since the costs can quickly escalate beyond the initial quoted and/or budgeted amount. The supplier should provide a quote and schedule for implementation based on its assessment of the work required to meet the desired objectives, and the supplier should be held accountable to meet that quote and schedule. However, the supplier can reasonably ask that it not be penalized if there are events beyond its control, e.g., a change in scope at the behest of the public entity. In those situations, the supplier should provide a revised quote and a revised work order.

In any work order or separate agreement for implementation services, the procurement official should include warranties for performance to the agreed-upon specifications. The official should also include service levels and penalties to be applied if the promised implementation schedule is not met. For example, for every day that the supplier is late on meeting a critical milestone, a reduction is made in the amount payable to the supplier. The agreement should also provide that delays in meeting any milestone will not give rise to an extension in meeting later milestone deadlines.

Warranties

The procurement official should demand warranties to cover software, services, and maintenance. Software warranties should include performance of the software to the specifications as published by the supplier, and there should be no time limitation on this. Suppliers may attempt to limit warranties to periods as short as 90 days, but the procurement official should not agree to such a short period of time. Moreover, the public entity should require the supplier to warrant that it either owns the software or has the legal right to license the software to the public entity. In addition, the supplier should warrant that the buyer is receiving the most current version of the software and that the use of the software will not infringe the rights of any third party. The resulting contract should include remedies for any breach of these warranties. Service warranties should provide for conformance of the services provided to the mutually agreed upon specifications in a statement of work.

Software Licenses: Watch the Small Print

C hanging or adding a few words in a contract can make a significant difference in contract protections and usage rights. The public entity should ensure that these issues are addressed in its software agreements. The assumption must be made that the software contract is written by suppliers to protect their rights and enables them to charge for any changes in the agency's environment.

Although it is easy to overlook some important software contract terms and conditions, doing so may have an impact on long-term usage rights and contractual protections, which can affect the total cost of ownership of these products over time. Agencies need to develop a checklist to ensure that these terms and conditions are included in all their contracts. When licensing new software or adding new software to an older agreement, public agencies can often get the software supplier to agree to these changes, including the following.

Perpetual License Agreement

Many suppliers do not include the word "perpetual" in their license agreement or grant but will usually add it when requested. This addition will clearly enable the public agency to continue to use the software for some period if the supplier stops supporting the software or goes out of business.

The public entity should also include the right to use the software in support of a parent, a subsidiary, or an affiliate. An affiliate should be clearly defined as it relates to a governmental entity, since new departments, offices, or bureaus may be created within the entity that may have a need for this software.

Transferable as Listed in Contract

The contract should provide the right to transfer the software at no cost to the "parent" agency, a subsidiary, or an affiliate of the public entity, or in case of creation of a new department, office, or bureau. The contract should also provide the right of the public entity to transfer the software to another hardware platform as long as the software supplier supports it. This may not be possible if the licensing cost is based on the size of the platform; but, if it is based on other business metrics, such as number of employees or "seats," there should be no cost to change to another supported platform. Finally, the contract should provide the right of the public entity to transfer the software operating system at no cost as long as the supplier supports that operating system.

Maintenance and Technical Support

Contractual terms addressing maintenance and technical support are not usually detailed in the contract; however, the following terms should be considered.

- *Hours of Support.* If the public entity requires 24/7 support, the entity should ensure that this extended support is provided because suppliers may only provide support from 8:00 AM to 5:00 PM.

- *Number of Contacts.* Software suppliers may limit the number of technical support personnel who can call in to the supplier's support line for assistance. The public entity should ensure that it could function with these reasonable restrictions.

- *Telephone or email.* Some suppliers are requiring that the initial request for support come via email. This is unreasonable for a production system that is not working. The public entity should ensure that its technical support personnel could place a call to the supplier when needed.

- *Cost.* The first year of maintenance costs needs to be included in the contract with a cap of increases per year. When possible, it is best to tie a supplier to a multi-year agreement that limits the increase each year, either through a flat rate or a rate that is tied to an index such as the CPI-All Urban Index.

Software Indemnification

Software agreements may reduce the contractual obligation of the software supplier in the event there is an infringement against the supplier. For example, the contract terms could state that the software supplier "may" do something. These terms should be changed to "shall," which increases the supplier's obligation to perform. Additionally, suppliers should be minimally required to refund the license fee based on a five-year, straight-line depreciation.

Definitions

Contractual definitions are critical in providing legal clarification. Some examples are:

- *User.* There could be a big difference between a named user, a logged-on user, and a concurrent user. The public entity should ensure that the definition of "user" meets its agency's requirements.

- *Employee.* Several software suppliers base their license cost for HR systems on the number of employees. Employees can include retirees, part-time employees, temporary employees, and seasonal employees. Additionally, if an entity has a large number of employees with a high turnover, it will not want this number to be based on the W-2 statements issued in a year. Entities that have a large number of part-time employees may want to consider the use of a definition based on full-time equivalents (FTEs).

- *Revenue.* Several software suppliers base their financial software on a revenue model. Financial experts for the government agency should provide a clear definition of revenue and how it is to be measured. This is especially important for enterprise funds as well as arrangements where a revenue model almost universally drives eProcurement models.

Software Licenses: The Key Points

Comparing a Sale/Assignment versus License

The sale or assignment of software permits a buyer to distribute, display, copy and resell the software in derogation of the owner of the software copyright. This arrangement is more expensive than a license that permits the licensee to use the software only in accord with the terms of the software agreement. Unlike shrink-wrap agreements (retail sales of software); commercial license agreements are not as likely to be subject to adhesion contract arguments.

The basic legal components of a license agreement should define who is an authorized user and where the CPUs on which the software will run are located. The hardware and actual operating system for the software must also be included. The Uniform Commercial Code (U.C.C.) will apply to most of these agreements if the software, and not service, is the primary good being purchased in the transaction.

Model Agreement Provisions for Licensees

Model agreement provisions for licensees should address the following:

- Who is the public entity/customer and who is the licensor? The public entity should ensure that not only the named licensor but also a successor or merged entity is covered by the agreement.

- Who are the affiliates, and will the license include only those affiliates existing at the time of the agreement or cover any additional affiliates such as new departments?

- How will the contract define a failure of the software? Many software licenses use the phrase "critical error that substantially impairs" the use of the software. This is a difficult burden for an agency, or any user, to prove. A material breach of the contract should be clearly defined as well as the criticality and number of allowable errors. The public entity should consider reductions in price for maintenance/support as options for failures.

- Who is writing the functional specifications, and who decides what and how it is written? To the using department, functional specifications may be one thing and mean something entirely different to the software engineer. Be as specific as possible, and avoid ambiguous phrases, such as "needs to be robust."

- What are the differences between the Object Code and Source Code? The Object Code is what the licensee obtains with the purchase to run the software. It is machine code; therefore, the vast majority of individuals would have no idea how to make it functional. The Source Code, on the other hand, is the human readable code that gets the computer to function. The Source Code is usually copyrighted and is what makes the software proprietary; licensees get the Object Code but not the Source Code. Therefore, it is recommended that the public entity negotiate the placement of the Source Code in an escrow account established by the licensee. This escrow should include everything that is needed for the computer to function and protects the public entity in those situations where the licensor becomes bankrupt or terminates the contract—get the Source Code in an escrow account established by the licensee.

- The software license is typically personal (customer only), non-exclusive (licensor can license or sell it to others), non-transferable, and non-assignable (licensee cannot sell it or rent or otherwise transfer it). This is why the definition of whom the customer is, and who the customer may become, is so important.

- All intellectual property rights remain with the licensor.

- The licensee cannot modify or otherwise tamper in any way with the software. If the licensee does reengineer and produce a very useful modification or reconfiguration, the licensor still owns all rights to the modification and any future benefits or profits that may arise from the modification.

- No third party can access or use a license without the copyright owner's permission.

- Termination rights should be bilateral. If the licensee does not pay or violates a term of agreement, the licensor must have termination rights. On the other hand, public entities should be careful to adequately protect themselves from a default on the part of the licensor in case the licensor ceases to provide the support as prescribed or fails to provide upgrades on a timely basis. Further, it should be noted that trade secret protection survives any termination.

- The original price of the license should relate directly to the cost of support/ maintenance. The public entity should negotiate a fixed-price cost for support and cover an extended period. If this is not possible, the public entity should attempt to tie the increase for support to some type of index. The contract should also specify how often the price might be raised. Most software licenses provide increases on a yearly basis, but attempts should be made to negotiate a less frequent period. Paying slightly more for the license and fewer dollars for support over the life of the agreement may result in lower total costs. The public entity should negotiate payment terms and retention, especially if the purchase includes installation and implementation.

- The public entity should define its exact needs for support services in terms of level criticality and frequency. Some support agreements restrict the first notice of incident to email notification. If the incident is a critical failure, the customer cannot rely on waiting for an electronic response to an email that may not be delivered. If there is a need for 24/7 response, this level of support must be defined. Since greater support means greater cost, up-front user training may be more economical.

- If the public entity needs the software, the entity must realize some limitations and indemnity concerns. The key is to negotiate a favorable contract. As a public entity, the supplier is assured of payment, and this should be used as a negotiating advantage. Some issues include limiting and disclaiming U.C.C. warranty provisions, such as merchantability and fitness for a particular purpose; liquidated damages; limitation of consequential damages; limitation of third party damages; and payment of defense for a claim arising out of possible copyright or trademark infringement.

- The public entity is obligated to pay for the license upon acceptance of the software, usually after a defined testing period. If any error is found during the testing of the software, the testing period should start over. Since the licensor will strive for payment upon delivery, and sometimes upon shipment of software from the supplier, the public entity should attempt to negotiate payment terms that allow this testing period.

- The public entity should consider the risk of loss, especially since the risk usually passes to the entity upon delivery to the licensee.

- The public entity should attach specifications and/or a Statement of Work and a statement of deliverables to the contract. The schedule of payments should be tied to defined deliverables and benchmarks.

- The public entity should consider all risk management issues, including professional liability, errors, and omissions.

- The public entity should make every attempt to separate maintenance/support agreements from the original license agreement.

Substantive Terms of the Transaction

Any form of technology transaction includes some very basic substantive components, whether a license agreement relating to the manufacture and sale of new products or a research arrangement for the development of new applications for an existing package of technology assets. First, the parties must agree upon the scope of the intellectual property assets to be included in the relationship. Second, the consideration to be paid by the parties with respect to the use of the intellectual property assets should be defined. Finally, an effort must be made to allocate the responsibilities of the parties with respect to the protection of the intellectual property assets and the risks associated with any third-party claims that might be made as a result of the use of the assets in the relationship.

The parties should enter the negotiation stage with a basic understanding of the technical strengths and requirements of each, and the due diligence investigation should identify each of the specific intellectual property assets potentially useful in achieving the overall objectives of the relationship. Accordingly, it should be easy to define the specific technology assets to be assigned or licensed between the parties, as well as the scope of any limitations or restrictions to be placed upon the uses of such technology.

Once the parties have identified the technology to be licensed, procedures should be established to protect the technology against the adverse claims and actions of third parties. For example, if patent rights are involved in the transaction, the parties must reach an agreement as to the rights and duties of each party to bring actions against any third party. This would include actions against a third party who might infringe upon the transferred patents. It may also include actions to defend the transferred patents against any claims of third parties with regard to the ownership of the patented inventions or the validity of the patents themselves. Similarly, if trade secrets are involved, it is essential for the parties to agree upon the steps to be taken to maintain the confidentiality of the information.

In order to make any technology license more effective, it may be necessary to include provisions for technical and management assistance, as well as training, from the provider to the recipient. While technical assistance arrangements are an important part of any transaction, training and consultation will be required even when the recipient is a large and sophisticated technology enterprise. Cooperation of this type may lead to a further level of involvement between the parties, especially when the assistance relates to research and engineering efforts aimed at adapting the technology for use in a specified application.

Technical assistance might include equipment procurement and engineering assistance, as well as basic training in the use of the transferred technology. Finally, when the recipient is to assume some obligation for servicing the products of the transfer, the transferor should provide ongoing technical support.

The due diligence investigation may uncover one or more specific risks to which an allocation of potential damages must be made at the outset of the relationship. For example, if analysis discloses potential problems, such as any substantial risk of a future infringement action being brought by a third party, it may be appropriate to consider escrowing part of the consideration being paid in the transaction. This could include a provision that the escrowed funds will be returned to the purchasing party (i.e., the licensee in a licensing arrangement or the public entity when technology rights are being purchased in their entirety) if the value of the technology is ultimately reduced by subsequent litigation. If an escrow is not practical, indemnification against any losses that might be suffered by the public entity from a future infringement action might be built into the agreement.

Legal Opinions

A legal opinion is usually an important part of any transaction in which intellectual property assets are involved. The scope of the opinion will depend upon the specific structure of the transaction, as well as the form of intellectual property at issue. For example, an opinion might be required in order to assure prospective investors that a specified product is eligible for patent protection. In a licensing arrangement, the importance of the standard indemnification provisions relating to infringement may turn upon counsel's opinion regarding the risk that a claim can successfully be raised. In an acquisition, directors and officers of the acquiring company might be concerned about the possibility of personal liability for infringement damages associated with the products of the acquired business.

Types of Intellectual Property Opinions

Intellectual property opinions must be carefully tailored to the facts and circumstances of a particular transaction. In many cases, the opinion will cover fundamental questions regarding the ownership of a particular technology asset and the ability of the agency to expect legal protection for the asset under specified laws and regulations. Other matters that may be addressed in the opinion include the validity of any assignment or other purported transfer of an intellectual property right (whether or not a specific invention, product, or work infringes upon the existing legal rights of a third party) and the possible outcome of intellectual property litigation.

Trade secret opinions might address the question of whether or not the information actually is a trade secret. Counsel will need to examine documents and other information published in the relevant area, as well as the procedures that are being used to protect the information. Another area of concern is the risk that information has been misappropriated from others. In this case, counsel will be reviewing the activities of employees with former employers, as well as any agreements regarding the use of third-party trade secrets.

...a careful review should be made of any agreements assigning ownership of inventions, copyrighted works, or proprietary information to the hiring party.

Patent opinions generally involve a search of prior submissions in order to determine whether a product not yet fully developed will satisfy the novelty standard required for patent protection. It may also ascertain whether a completed product will infringe upon the existing patent rights of others. An opinion may allow the developer to alter design plans to avoid infringement and serves as a means for monitoring the technology activities of competitors. In addition, in those cases where the product is found to be infringing, the existence of a prior patent opinion may be useful in rebutting a claim of willful infringement.

A trademark "clearance" opinion can be used to determine whether the trademark can, in fact, be registered. In addition, trademark opinions can be obtained regarding the possibility that a mark may infringe upon the existing rights of a third party.

Copyright opinions often focus on procedural matters, such as whether or not the copyright remains in force, whether or not the copyright as well as prior transfers have been properly registered, and the existence of any adverse claims relating to the use of the copyrighted work.

An assignment of statutory intellectual property rights usually requires compliance with a number of formal requirements. As such, it is usually good practice to ensure that counsel has reviewed, and opined upon, the instruments of transfer in order that they be adequate for recording and filing.

In almost every transaction, some form of opinion will be requested regarding any third-party consents or approvals required in order for the transaction to be effective. In the context of a technology transfer involving licensed rights, which generally cannot be assigned without the consent of the licensor, an opinion should be obtained regarding the need for, and adequacy of, any consents or approvals. It should be noted that even when the transfer occurs by operation of law, such as in a merger, it may still be necessary to obtain a consent from the licensor if the licensed rights are considered personal rights and, therefore, not assignable by operation of law.

When employees and consultants are involved in developing intellectual property assets, a careful review should be made of any agreements assigning ownership of inventions, copyrighted works, or proprietary information to the hiring party. If appropriate, an opinion might be requested regarding the sufficiency of any such agreements, perhaps in the context of a broader opinion covering ownership of the intellectual property assets. Other opinions may be rendered regarding the validity and enforceability of employment and consulting agreements, including the hiring party's ability to terminate such agreements and the consequences of termination.

Counsel is often asked to provide some sort of opinion regarding the possible outcome of pending or threatened litigation matters, including the damages and costs to be incurred if the agency ultimately loses. Clearly, this type of opinion may be very difficult for counsel to render, since the outcome will be a function of the disposition of a variety of issues of fact and law, many of which may have yet to be determined as of the date of the opinion. Moreover, the amount of any potential loss may vary substantially at any given point in the litigation process. As such, it is generally not good practice for counsel to assign any sort of probability to the agency's chances of prevailing in the litigation.

Keeping Software Prices in Check: Lock in Prices and Terms

Negotiating advantage is greatest just before a new software license agreement is signed. The public entity should ensure that price protections are included in its contract terms and conditions for future product licenses and software maintenance. According to the Gartner Report, organizations that lock in their future prices and terms for licenses and their maintenance during the initial acquisition will save a minimum of 8% per year (Disbrow, 2001).

Once new software is deployed, the cost of changing to a different product can range from five to more than ten times the cost of the initial license. Suppliers view this customer exposure as a significant revenue opportunity, because the agency is "locked in" to the technology. When appropriate terms and conditions are included in the initial contract, the supplier's capability to leverage its investment in the sale of the original software is limited.

Since the public entity benefits from contractually negotiated fees, it is recommended that agencies include price protections in every negotiation for a new software license prior to signaling the supplier that the licensing decision is made. This is somewhat difficult in the public arena due to sunshine laws, but care should still be taken to not "telegraph" any decision to the supplier that is not necessary or required by public records laws. Periodically, the supplier may need to be reminded that although its product may have been ranked number one, there are other choices available if the agreement is not beneficial to both parties in the end. Negotiators should always try for a "win/win" agreement so that each party achieves what is best. In most cases, once the agreement is signed, it signals the start of a long partnership, where both parties must work at being successful.

Software Maintenance Agreements

Steep discounts are often conceded to an organization to win a new contract. After the competitive bids are completed, if maintenance is not negotiated as part of the agreement, the supplier can, and often will, price maintenance to "make up" the difference. This can be accomplished in several ways.

- The first year's maintenance may be priced at 22% of the list price of the original license. Industry standards for software maintenance are typically between 18% and 22% of the software license fee, but can range from 10% to 50%. Therefore, if the software license fee was discounted to 50% of the list price and if the maintenance invoice is billed at 22% of the list price, the cost of maintenance is twice what would have been charged if maintenance had been negotiated based on the discounted licensed fee.

- Yearly maintenance increases billed can be significantly higher than the Consumer Price Index (CPI). Caps on maintenance increases are usually in the 5% to 8% range in the industry. It is common to see maintenance capped for only the first three to five years. Without appropriate terms, once the cap period is over, the supplier can significantly increase year-to-year fees. For example, if the initial year is discounted at 50% (consistent with the discount on the licenses), maintenance in the second year could approach undiscounted maintenance fees.

- The supplier can change its options for maintenance and how maintenance is priced. One supplier recently eliminated its 8 to 5 maintenance support, forcing its customers from 18% of the license fee to a 24/7 support at 22% of the license fee. This change resulted in a 22.2% price increase in a single year. For non-mission critical applications, this is an incredibly high increase over a one-year period.

- Maintenance is often billed based on the date the contract is signed, rather than the date the software is deployed or accepted. Because of the notoriously long lead times for receipt, installation, testing, and deployment of enterprise software, this time should be reasonably estimated, or an "acceptance date" should be used at the start of maintenance billing.

A Checklist for Public Agencies

- Build into the contract for the first year's dollar cost maintenance based on a percentage of the discounted price paid. On average, approximately 50% of the price is attributed to the right-to-new versions/releases and 50% for technical support. Therefore, rights to new versions (license rights) should carry the same discount as the original licenses. As the number of licenses increases, the number of calls to the supplier's technical support center decreases as a percentage of total number of licenses, because of the restrictions on the number of people who can call the supplier directly (e.g., the supplier typically requires a first-line help desk call only from the customer).

- The clock on maintenance billing should be negotiated to start on a reasonable date so that the agency will be able to have the software installed before maintenance begins.

- Increases should be contractually limited to a percentage, "not to increase" more than a set percentage per year. In addition, the supplier must be contractually not capable of charging more than what it is charging other customers for the same product. This keeps the "percentage" increase from becoming an entitlement to charge increases each year.

- Negotiate terms that obligate the supplier to provide its current price list and the business practices that could affect the terms in the original contract, as well as updates that occur during the contract period. Business practices define how the terms of the contract are interpreted and implemented. Examples include: conversion formulas for bundled products and license models, license minimums, migration rules, detailed definition and interpretation of terms defined in the contract, product-specific terms that have not been contractually defined, license support policies, and licensing requirements for backup servers.

- Extend price caps for maintenance for as long as maintenance is continuously purchased, not just for a three-to-five-year period.

- Build in rights to add software back to maintenance if it is dropped for some period. Ideally, this should be at a cost of 50% of what back maintenance would have cost to compensate for new versions of software. At worst case, eliminate any "reinstatement fee," and only agree to what the back payments would have totaled. Agency's should be capable of resuming software support and maintenance for lapsed periods of less than three years by paying the supplier an amount no greater than one year's back-support fee that would have been due if support and maintenance had been continued during the lapsed period. If the lapsed period is less than one year, the amount to be paid should be prorated on the number of months the support fee was not paid. It will be difficult to get the supplier to agree to only one-year's payment of maintenance. However, agency's can agree to not pay more than the entire back-support payment (thereby eliminating the reinstatement fee). The second sentence provides the capability to contractually restart maintenance that may have been canceled in error with no penalty.

- Conservatively estimate software deployments to minimize the costs of "shelf ware." Through 2005, 60% of organizations will fail to accurately forecast deployment of complex applications and will incur at least 50% higher software and maintenance costs for products that have become shelf ware. In addition, once a product is deployed in production, licenses for additional software products may be required. Organizations may be surprised to find software that was positioned, as a basic product during the selling cycle is actually an option or a complementary product that must be licensed separately.

- Estimate any new license that may be needed to roll out the purchase system. Negotiate "not to exceed" prices for those additional licenses for at least a two-to-three-year period.

- Evaluate the different software products that are available from a supplier and research to determine if there is any interest in adding those products later. In some cases, additional modules or separately licensed products may work in conjunction with the products that have already been licensed by the agency and may enhance functionality. The contract should include the rights to license these products at some discount off list price or a "not to exceed" price. Attach a copy of the current price schedule and any discount to the contract with a guarantee that the attached price schedule will remain in effect for one year after the acceptance date of the software and that it can only be amended on the anniversary date of the term of the agreement. Any increase in the prices set forth in the price schedule should be limited to the CPI — not to exceed 5% per year — but in no case should the price exceed the supplier's current standard pricing.

- Build in cost protections for additional software licenses and software maintenance. Additional license purchases and ongoing maintained cost can significantly affect the total cost of ownership of software. Best-in-class contracts will build in price protections that ensure the benefit of any reductions in software prices.

Reference

Disbrow, J. (2001). *Research note: The basic steps to getting a good deal* (SPA-13-4495).

Chapter 8

Relevant Procurement Case Law

This chapter will present selected court decisions that may affect decisions made by a procurement agent. Many of the cases have been decided at either a trial court or appellate court level and are, therefore, only applicable to the specific district or circuit in which the case was decided. As always, before making a final decision based on a certain case, advice of the public agency's legal counsel should be sought. Decisions and rulings discussed in this chapter are only binding on the jurisdiction in which they were decided, but they offer sources of legal thought and interpretation of contract law.

Cases Involving Acceptance and Rejection of Goods

When purchased items arrive at the plant damaged, the procurement official must act quickly because a number of issues may be at stake. These issues include rejection, withholding payment, making the decision on repairs, and determining how much time is allowable to respond. The following cases illustrate practical points that will guide procurement managers in handling these difficult breach-of-contract situations.

Where there is an installment contract and one of the delivered installments contains defective goods, what are the Buyer's rights?

The court dealt with this question in *Midwest Mobile Diagnostic Imaging v. Dynamics Corp of America*, 965 F. Supp. 1003 (W.D. Mich. 1997). The contract involved the purchase of four trailers designed to hold Magnetic Resonance Imaging (MRI) equipment. The trailers had to be specially designed and built because of the technical nature of MRI equipment. The purchaser received the first of the trailers but found it to be defective. As a result, the buyer was forced to cancel appointments that had been made with prospective patients.

Eight days later, the seller presented to the buyer a redesigned trailer that purportedly solved the problem. However, the buyer still claimed that defects existed, rented a substitute trailer from another supplier, and notified the seller of its intent to cancel the contract. In deciding the lawsuit, the first question for the court was whether to treat the contract as being an installment contract.

As is frequently the case, the parties did not specifically use the words "installment contract." However, since the contract authorized separate deliveries of the four trailers and the payment schedule called for payment of the balance due for each trailer upon shipment, the court concluded that this was an installment contract. The court then explained that the buyer's right to reject goods under an installment contract differed from the right to reject goods under other types of contracts. In the non-installment type of case, U.C.C. Section 2-601 allows the buyer to reject the goods by reason of *any* defect, whether it is in the quality of the goods, the timing of performance, or the manner of delivery. In other words, Michigan, like many other states, follows the "perfect tender" rule. However, under U.C.C. Section 2-612, which covers installment contracts, the buyer may not reject a non-conforming tender unless the defect substantially impairs the value of the installment.

Moreover, if the non-conformity is curable and the seller gives adequate assurances of cure, the buyer must accept the installment. Furthermore, even if the buyer properly rejects the goods, it may not cancel the contract unless the defect substantially impairs the value of the whole contract. Here, the buyer had no choice but to permit the seller the opportunity to fix a defect that both parties thought could be cured. Since the amount of time the seller was allowed for cure was not fixed in the contract, the seller had a "reasonable" time to cure under U.C.C. Section 2-508. Thus, when the seller provided a purportedly conforming trailer eight days later, it was considered timely.

However, the court found that the second trailer was, nevertheless, also non-conforming and not suited to accommodate the effective use of the MRI machine. The court stated that even under an installment contract, the seller's right to cure was limited. When the seller's re-design attempts failed on the second try and the buyer faced the loss of patients unless it obtained suitable equipment elsewhere, the buyer had a valid basis for canceling the contract. The seller's breach had now substantially impaired the entire contract, the court said. The court then held that the buyer could recover the amount it had paid for the first installment plus the cost of rental of a substitute trailer. Although the rental of a trailer, as opposed to purchase, technically did not constitute "cover" within the meaning of the U.C.C., the rental costs were recoverable as incidental damages.

Where the equipment purchased proves to be defective, can the Buyer recover as incidental damages the cost to have the equipment repaired by a third party?

The purchaser should proceed with caution before having the equipment repaired. In *Magnum Press Automation, Inc. v. Thomas & Betts Corp.*, 758 NE2d 507 (Ill. App. 2001), the buyer of industrial presses brought a claim against the seller for the costs of unsuccessful attempts to repair the machinery prior to the buyer's revocation of acceptance. The equipment was valued at approximately $46,000 and the repairs cost approximately $11,000. Although the trial court awarded the buyer the cost of repairs as incidental damages, the appellate court reversed and remanded the question for retrial.

The appellate court questioned whether it was proper for the buyer to go through with such a major repair without previously warning the seller of its intention to do so if the seller did not promptly fix the problem. The message for buyers is that, at the very least, it should issue a written warning to the seller before undertaking a major repair.

What is the risk of reselling goods when the Buyer has not had sufficient time to determine whether the goods conform to the contract?

The court dealt with this question in *Riddle v. Heartland Nursery*, 2001 WL 1346261 (Tenn. Ct. App.). In the seller's action to collect the purchase price for the sale of nursery stock, the buyer alleged that the goods did not conform to the contract. In deciding the case, the court analyzed the effect of U.C.C. Section 2-606. This section of the Code states that the buyer has accepted the goods if he has done any of the following after a reasonable opportunity to inspect the goods: (1) signifies to the seller that the goods are conforming; or (2) indicates that he will take or retain them in spite of their non-conformity; or (3) fails to make an effective rejection (even though such acceptance does not occur until after the buyer has had a reasonable opportunity to inspect them); or (4) does any act inconsistent with the seller's ownership.

Some U.C.C. experts, such as White and Summers, say that U.C.C. Section 2-606 should be applied only where the buyer does something, such as sells the non-conforming goods, which is inconsistent with the seller's rights. This court, however, held that even though the non-conformity became apparent later (when the buyer's own customers complained that trees had died); the buyer had already accepted the goods and it was too late to reject them. This did not leave the buyer without remedies, but the buyer now had the burden of proving that the trees were non-conforming. Since the buyer was unable to prove why the trees died, the seller prevailed.

When the Buyer has paid for the goods on a C.O.D. basis, is there still time to reject goods if they turn out to be non-conforming?

In *Gragg Farms & Nursery v. Kelly Green Landscaping*, 674 NE2d 785, 32 UCC.Rep.Serv.2d 1119 (Ohio Mun. Ct. 1996), the court held that even though the buyer had already paid the freight charges for delivery of the goods; it still had a reasonable time to inspect them. When the buyer notified the seller the following day that the goods were "junk" and were being rejected, the buyer was not required to pay for the goods.

What must a Buyer do to revoke acceptance under the U.C.C.?

U.C.C. Section 2-608 does not specify the manner in which revocation is done. The Official Comment says that the content of the notice is to be determined by considerations of good faith, prevention of surprise, and reasonable adjustment. In *Cissell Manufacturing Co. v. Park*, 36 P. 2d 85 (Colo. App. 2001), the court said that for the notice of revocation to be sufficient, it should fairly apprise the seller that the buyer wants to give back the goods and receive a substitute or money in return. The court found that Park's letter, which described in detail the alleged non-conformity in the good (a dryer), was sufficient to constitute revocation of acceptance because it attempted to "reject acceptance," demanded that Cissell remove the machine from the premises, and requested that damages be paid.

Do industry standards have any effect upon the time in which the Buyer must reject non-conforming goods?

The answer is, yes. In *B/R Sales Co., Inc. v. Krantor Corp.*, 226 AD2d 328, the seller's representative testified, without contradiction by the buyer, that the custom and practice in the industry is that all claims had to be made upon delivery or within a "reasonable" time frame, normally 48 hours after acceptance of the first shipment or any additional shipments. Since the buyer did not reject the goods until four weeks after delivery, the court held that the rejection was untimely.

Bid Award Cases

Does a Bidder have a standing to sue when it is the apparent low bidder but is not awarded a contract?

In *Ardmare Construction Company, Inc., v. Freedman* (Commissioner of Administrative Services, Connecticut [467 A. 2d, 674]), Ardmare was the lowest bidder on a project but was not awarded the bid due to his failure to meet the signature requirements on the bid form. A suit was filed as an action for mandamus (command) to require the named defendant (Freedman) to award the plaintiff (Ardmare) a contract for labor and materials on a certain state project.

The case involves whether Ardmare had standing to sue.

Standing to sue is the legal right to set judicial machinery in motion. One cannot rightfully invoke the jurisdiction of the court unless he has, in an individual or representative capacity, some real interest in the cause of action, or a legal or equitable right, title, or interest in the subject matter of the controversy.

Originally, the district court ruled that the plaintiff had standing to sue. However, the Supreme Court disagreed with the basis of the court's decision and remanded the case back to the district court, with instructions to dismiss the lawsuit. The Supreme Court found that the plaintiff did not have standing to sue because he had no enforceable legal or equitable right in contract; therefore, not unlike any other person whose offer has been rejected, a disappointed bidder has no right to judicial intervention. This court declared, "[a] bid, even the lowest responsible one, submitted in response to an invitation for bids is only an offer which, until accepted by the municipality, does not give rise to a contract between the parties." The announcement that the plaintiff had submitted the lowest bid did not amount to acceptance. Acceptance occurs only after it is determined that the bid conforms to the statutory requirements and the bidder is "competent to perform the work."

The Supreme Court further ruled that the competitive bidding statute does not provide the disappointed bidder with standing to sue. The court stated: "municipal competitive bidding laws are enacted to guard against such evils as favoritism, fraud, or corruption in the award of contracts, to secure the best product at the lowest price, and to benefit the taxpayers, not the bidders."

It should be noted that there is no uniformity of decisions among the states on this issue of standing to sue. The competitive bidding statute in each state will control the outcome of this question. For example, some state courts have held that an unsuccessful bidder has absolute standing to sue under the competitive bidding statute. Other state courts have found that unsuccessful bidders have limited standing pursuant to a particular state statute. Still other state courts have found standing to sue only if the unsuccessful bidder was a taxpayer.

Can a public entity award a contract to the apparent low bidder if this bidder fails to acknowledge an addendum as required in the bid specifications?

Martel Construction, Inc., a Montana corporation, is a regularly licensed contractor with its office in Bozeman, Montana. William Martel is an officer of Martel. Volk Construction, Inc., a Montana corporation, is also a regularly licensed contractor with its office in Great Falls, Montana.

In late 1982, Montana issued a solicitation for competitive bids for the construction of the Montana Children's Treatment Unit to be built in Billings, Montana. The bid opening was to be held on February 9, 1983. Prior to the bid opening date, the state officers amended the solicitation for bids by addendum 1, dated January 18, 1983; addendum 2, dated February 2, 1983; and addendum 3, dated February 4, 1983.

The solicitation for bids contained a section entitled "Instructions to Bidders," which provided in paragraph 2, Section E, Proposals, "Proposals shall be in a sealed envelope and addressed to... and [bidders] shall acknowledge receipt of all addenda issued."

The bid form had on it a place for the acknowledgment of each addendum, with the date of each addendum. The bid submitted by Volk failed to acknowledge, on the envelope or on the bid form, receipt of addenda two and three as required by the "Instructions to Bidders."

When bids were opened on February 9, 1983, Volk had the low general contractor's bid of $1,698,000. The next bid submitted by Martel for the same options, was $174,600 higher. Martel protested Volk's bid. The architect contacted Volk to inquire whether the company received addenda 2 and 3 and reported, "I was assured that Volk received and considered all addenda."

The Montana Board of Examiners received a memorandum from its legal counsel advising them not to accept Volk's bid and to set out the project for re-bidding. Nevertheless, the Board met for a fourth time on April 7, 1983. They concluded that Volk was aware of addenda 2 and 3 and could be bound to a contract, including all the addenda. The Board then proceeded to award the contract to Volk as the lowest bidder.

Martel commenced legal action in the case of *Martel Construction, Inc., v. Montana State Board of Examiners* (668 P. 2d, 222). In its ruling, the trial court emphasized the importance of protecting the competitive bidding process for the construction of public works. The court further stated that in this case Volk, after the bid opening, knew that it had the lowest bid, because he could disclaim knowledge of the addenda, and could accept or reject the contract. The court wrote:

> There is a fear that the integrity of the bidding process is endangered by recognition of oral acknowledgments of addenda because (1) there is then no assurance that there is a clear meeting-of-the-minds between the public body calling for the bids and the low bidder; (2) there is then no assurance that all bidders are bidding on the same thing; and (3) that the action of the State Board of Examiners opens the door to the nightmare of oral acceptances if it gives Volk the benefit of its bid under its oral acknowledgment of addenda 2 and 3.

The Board, in opposition, contended that Volk was bound to perform all of the addenda under its bid because Volk was aware of and considered the addenda in making its bid. The Board pointed to the fact that Volk had obtained a supplier's written price bid for material required only on addenda 2 and that the architect had called Volk on February 8, 1983, to discuss the addenda. The state officers relied on previous case law (*Boger Contracting Corp. v. Board of Commissioners of Stark County*, 60 Ohio App. 2d 195), for authority that it could separately determine whether Volk could be bound and whether Volk had actual knowledge of the addenda.

The State Board of Examiners appealed to the Montana Supreme Court, which wrote:

> We regard the concerns in this with a good deal of respect. We agree that the bidding process for public contracts should be impartial, with equal opportunity given to all those participating in the public bidding, to avoid corruption, and that the process should at the same time procure for the State quality materials and workmanship for the most reasonable cost. We, therefore, look to the facts of this case to determine (1) whether there was a meeting of minds between the State and Volk under its bid and (2) whether Volk could be held by the State to perform all of the addenda under its bid.

The evidence that Volk was contacted by telephone regarding the last two addenda and that Volk had begun preparation for fulfilling the obligations of addenda 2 and 3 is adequate to show that Volk had actual knowledge of the addenda. It also established that there was a meeting of the minds as to the existence and the respective requirements for fulfillment of the terms of those addenda.

Pertinent to the examination of whether Volk could be held by the State to perform the addenda is in other language in the solicitation for bids. Paragraph H.5 of the solicitation provided:

> All written addenda issued by the Architect/Engineer will become part of the Contract Documents and all Bidders shall be bound by such addenda, whether received or not by the Bidder. No oral or telephonic modifications of the Contract Documents will be considered.

Again, Paragraph I.2 of the solicitation for bids provided: "2. The Owner reserves the right to reject all bids and to waive any informality or irregularity in any bid received."

The language of this solicitation binds the bidder to full performance of the contract documents, including all of the addenda, whether received or not. In making its bid, Volk agreed to that provision. All bidders, including Martel and Volk, agreed that the State had the right to reject all bids or to waive any informality or irregularity in any bid received.

Thus, Volk, in submitting the bid, bound itself to the full performance of the contract documents, including the addenda. Deviations in bid submissions which do not go to the substance of the bid (here, Volk acknowledges his full responsibility for the addenda as well as the contract) and irregularities which do not give one bidder a substantial advantage over other bidders are types of irregularities that can be waived by public officers in awarding contracts.

The Supreme Court, therefore, determined that, in this case, mandamus interfered with the discretion of the State officers in awarding the contract to the qualified bidder. The Court reversed the ruling of the trial Court, finding that:

1. State officers in determining whether bidders are qualified and whether they will perform a contract in conformity with specifications and terms are acting in a discretionary manner

2. There was a meeting of the minds between the state and the successful bidder under its bid.

3. Successful bidder, in submitting a bid, bound itself to full performance of contract documents, including addenda to solicitation.

4. Failure of a successful bidder to make written acknowledgment of receipt of addenda was an immaterial irregularity that could be waived by state officers.

If a public entity rejects all bids due to the fact that the lowest bid was non-responsive and re-bids the project, can the second low bidder on the first bid claim rights to the contract?

In the 1981 case of *Dickinson Company, Inc. v. City of Des Moines*, IA (347 NW, 2d, 436), the City of Des Moines solicited bids on the "Fleur Drive Signal System Project." The plaintiff, Dickinson Company, Inc., and the two other firms, M. Peterson Construction Company and Iowa Signal and Electric Company, as joint ventures, were among the construction companies submitting bids. According to rules set by the Iowa Department of Transportation (DOT), any bid made by a contractor was to be accompanied by a bid bond as a proposal guarantee. In the case of a joint venture bid, all contractors were required to sign a bid bond. In this case, only one contractor of the joint venture, M. Peterson Construction Company, submitted a bid bond with the bid. According to DOT rules, if a bid bond failed to meet the requirements, the bid bond was to be declared invalid, and the respective bid proposal was not to be considered. Nevertheless, their bid was opened and considered with the other contractors' bids.

The joint venture's bid of $397,210 was the lowest bid received. Dickinson's bid of $455,991.50 was second lowest. The city council met and accepted the bid of Peterson and Iowa Signal, subject to approval by the DOT, which was supplying 95% of the funding for the project. At the same meeting, the city also received an additional bid bond to cure the defect in the original bid.

The Iowa Attorney General's office, on behalf of the DOT, informed the city that the subject bid did not conform to the bid proposal requirements; therefore, the contract could not be awarded to the firm. The Attorney General's office further informed the city:

> We find your bid document forms acceptable and could concur in the award of the contract to Dickinson Co., Inc., as the lowest responsible bidder. You should also be aware that were the City of Des Moines to relet the project by rejecting all bids, our participation would be limited to $455,991.56; the amount of the lowest acceptable bid.

The city, thus, had a choice of accepting Dickinson's next lowest bid or rejecting all bids and opening up the project for bidding again. The city chose to reject all bids and re-advertise. In the re-bidding, Dickinson's bid was $451,991.50, and Peterson's bid was $394,210. Peterson's bid was the lowest, and the contract was awarded to them.

Dickinson filed suit in District Court claiming the contract should have been awarded to him, after the low bidder, Peterson, was found to be non-responsive after the first bidding.

Without deciding whether the city's action in opening and considering Peterson/Iowa Signal bid was illegal, the District Court found that those actions did not give Dickinson a cause of action for damages. The city was alerted to the invalidity of the Peterson/Iowa Signal bid after it had conditionally awarded the contract to Peterson/Iowa Signal. By statute, it had the choice of rejecting all bids or of accepting the lowest responsible bid, which would have been Dickinson's bid.

Dickinson claimed the city would not have reopened the bidding if it had not known that the Peterson/Iowa Signal bid was lower and that a new bid by Peterson/Iowa Signal would be similarly low. Dickinson argued that the city's decision to reopen the bidding was, therefore, unreasonable, arbitrary, capricious, illegal, and an abuse of discretion. However, the court did not find evidence to support Dickinson's charges. The city opened the second bidding to everyone. No company was favored. Dickinson joined in the new bidding process and had the opportunity to submit a lower bid. In the first bidding process, Dickinson's bid was $58,781.50 higher than Peterson/Iowa Signal bid. In the second bidding, Dickinson lowered its bid by $4,000; Peterson/Iowa Signal's second bid was $3,000 less than their first one. The bids met all technical requirements in the second bidding. The city awarded the bid to the lowest responsible bidder, Peterson/Iowa Signal.

On appeal, the State Supreme Court wrote:

> Competitive bidding in the granting of municipal contracts "is employed for the protection of the public to secure by competition among bidders, the best results at the lowest price, and to forestall fraud, favoritism and corruption in the making of contracts."... In this regard, municipal authorities possess a discretionary power in the awarding of contracts.... As a general rule, we are reluctant to interfere with a local government's determination of who is the lowest responsible bidder, absent proof that the determination is fraudulent, arbitrary, in bad faith, or an abuse of discretion.

> Furthermore, merely because the city may have been mistaken in considering Peterson/Iowa Signal's first bid, Dickinson may not receive damages from the city for any such mistake. Because of the large discretion conferred upon the city in awarding a public contract, "in the absence of fraud or conspiracy, an action by an unsuccessful bidder for public work will fail"... and the trial court will not substitute its own judgment for a discretionary action of a public body.

As a mere bidder, Dickinson had no legally enforceable contract right, property interest or entitlement that was harmed by the city's mistaken consideration of Peterson/Iowa Signal's first bid. Therefore, Dickinson had no legitimate claim for damages. Accordingly, the court ruled:

1. In the absence of fraud or conspiracy, an unsuccessful bidder, although he may be low bidder, has no remedy.

2. Under statues providing that contract for public improvement must be awarded to lowest responsible bidder, discretion is wide in scope

3. City has authority to reject all bids and fix a date for soliciting new ones, even without declaring, with respect to bids already received, that lowest bidder is not the lowest, responsible bidder.

4. Contractor who submitted second lowest bid in initial bidding and re-bidding has no legally enforceable contract right, property interest or entitlement that was harmed by the City's actions.

Can a public entity decide to reject a bid if the bidder was encouraged to submit a bid by the project architect but failed to attend a mandatory pre-bid conference?

In the case of *Gibbs Construction Co., Inc. v. Board of Supervisors of Louisiana State University* (447 So. 2d, 90), the University of New Orleans advertised for public bids to construct certain alterations to the University's graduate school building. The contract documents included a date, time and location for a pre-bid conference and provided that "no bid shall be accepted from any contractor who does not have a responsible representative attend this meeting." Only one contractor attended the pre-bid conference and subsequently submitted a bid. This contractor was then awarded the contract. Gibbs Construction Co., Inc. did not have a representative at the pre-bid conference.

Subsequent to the pre-bid conference and without the knowledge or consent of the University, the project architect contacted Gibbs Construction Co. and requested that the company submit a bid. The architect represented to the company that it could submit a bid, although it did not have a representative at the pre-bid conference. The architect even drew a line through that portion of the documents requiring attendance at the conference.

In reliance upon the architect's representations, but without communicating with anyone at the University, Gibbs Construction Company, Inc., submitted a bid. The University did not accept Gibbs' bid, although it would have been the lowest, because Gibbs had not had a representative at the pre-bid conference. The contract was awarded to the lowest responsible bidder with a representative in attendance at the pre-bid conference, although this bid was higher than Gibbs' bid would have been.

Gibbs filed suit on the theory that Gibbs was the lowest responsible bidder and should have been awarded the contract.

The courts ruled that Gibbs Construction Co., Inc. was the only contractor alleged to have bid lower than the bidder to whom the contract was awarded. However, Gibbs did not qualify as a bidder because it failed to comply with the pre-bid procedures mandated by the bid advertisement, thus, preventing them from submitting a bid that could be considered by the University.

Gibbs argued that its bid was acceptable and should have been considered by the University, because the architect had requested the bid and had represented that the bid would be acceptable. The plaintiffs also argued that the architect was the agent of the University and that the University should be bound by his representations. Further, the plaintiffs argued that the University has the power to waive the requirement of attendance at the pre-bid conference.

The facts as alleged by plaintiffs do not indicate the existence of any type of agency relationship between the University and the project architect concerning the advertising and letting of the contract. Further, even assuming the University had the power to waive attendance at the pre-bid conference, the University was not obligated to make this waiver and apparently did not waive the requirement as indicated by the non-acceptance of Gibbs' "bid." This action by the University was not arbitrary but was in accord with the advertisement.

Having concluded that the petition fails to state a cause of action and that the deficiency cannot be cured by amendment, the court ruled that Gibbs' lawsuit should be dismissed on the premise that the University properly refused to consider the bid submitted by Gibbs because the company was not represented at the pre-bid conference, even though the project architect had requested the bid.

If a public entity's governing board awards a contract to a bidder, can it subsequently rescind the award if a contract has not yet been executed?

Pursuant to advertisements, Dedmond submitted his bid on or before March 3, 1970, for a lease to operate concessions at County-owned Rosemond Johnson Beach. On March 6, 1970, the County board voted four to one to award the subject lease to Dedmond. The minutes of the commission meeting reflected that three bids were received and each was subjected to close scrutiny and analysis resulting in a report that Dedmond's bid was best and most beneficial to the County on the basis of both anticipated income and service to the public. The other two bidders were willing to be open only on a more limited service basis. On March 9, 1970, the clerk of the circuit court and ex-officio county auditor addressed a letter to Dedmond on behalf of the county board that stated:

> This is to advise you that the Board of County Commissioners accepted your bid on Rosemond Johnson Beach Concession as being the most favorable to the County and voted to award you the lease for a period of five (5) years, beginning May 1, 1970. Please contact County Attorney Jack Greenhut by March 16, 1970, to execute the lease agreement with the county.

The March 16th date referred to in the clerk's letter was consistent with that portion of the instructions to bidders providing that "the person to whom the lease has been awarded shall execute and file with the county the lease agreement within ten (10) days from the date of the award."

On March 13, 1970, the County voted to rescind its action of March 6th awarding the lease to Dedmond and voted to re-bid the contract. This action on March 13th took place three days before the due date of March 16th given to the appellant to execute a written lease agreement pursuant to the instructions to bidders. A review of the minutes of the board's meeting of March 13th reflects that the underlying reason for rescinding the award to Dedmond was a change of mind by the members as to whether Dedmond's bid was in fact, the best.

In the case of *Dedmond v. Escambia County* (244 So.2d. 758), the trial court held that there was no binding contract created between the parties until a written lease is executed and that the County was authorized to rescind its earlier award to Dedmond prior to the execution of a lease agreement.

Trial court decision was appealed. Dedmond contended that the lower court's ruling dismissing the complaint with prejudice was erroneous, and the appeals court agreed. The principle governing the question raised is correctly stated as follows: "Until that time (acceptance of bid) the bidder is free to withdraw his bid. On the other hand, acceptance of a bid results in a contract even though a formal contract has not been executed."

The appellate court found that the trial court's ruling was erroneous and reversed the lower court's decision, finding in favor of Dedmond.

Does a city have the legal authority to accept a bid, which, at the time of bid opening, was nonconforming as to acceptable materials and components but was subsequently amended, prior to acceptance, to conform to the specifications as stated in the original proposal?

The City of Cape Coral desired to build a water treatment plant and, in March 1976, published the necessary advertisement for bids. The advertisement for bids contained the following provision:

> Prior submittal by manufacturers whose equipment has not been specified is required. The City Engineer's written approval of that equipment must be obtained for that equipment to be authorized for inclusion in the Bid Documents' Equipment Schedule or project work.

The instructions to bidders contained the following condition:

> (1) The Contract will be awarded to the lowest responsible bidder complying with the conditions of the Advertisement, Instructions to Bidders, General and Special Conditions, Drawings and Specifications provided such bid is reasonable and provided it be to the interest of the Owner to accept it.

Since a major component of the water plant required the use of expensive and powerful pumps, the specifications for the bids said the following about the various types of pumps to be used: "As a point of information, this project has been designed based on the use of [pumps]... as manufactured by Johnson Pump Company; FMC Corporation, Peerless Pump Division; or equal." Each bid required the bidder to specify the manufacturer of the pumps that he proposed to supply under his bid.

At the time of bid opening, the Gulf Corporation submitted the name of a pump manufacturer that was not acceptable to the City or the project engineers; however, Gulf was the low, apparent bidder. Subsequently, the city engineer contacted Gulf and asked them to indicate whether they would use an acceptable pump manufacturer. Gulf agreed to use an acceptable pump manufacturer and made no other changes. At the next City Council meeting, a contract was awarded to Gulf, as the low, responsible, responsive bidder.

The Pepper Company, the number two bidder, filed for injunction, contending that the award was unlawful because of the change allowed to the bid. The City contended that this was a minor change and was in the best interests of the City. The trial court held that the City had such authority. Pepper appealed the case.

In its ruling, the appellate court, ruling in favor of Pepper, stated that the purpose of the bidding process is:

> To protect the public against collusive contracts; to secure fair competition upon equal terms to all bidders; to remove not only collusion but temptation for collusion and opportunity for gain at public expense; to close all avenues to favoritism and fraud in its various forms; to secure the best values for the county at the lowest possible expense; and to afford an equal advantage to all desiring to do business with the county, by affording an opportunity for an exact comparison of bids. It is apparent that the entire scheme of bidding on public projects is to insure the sanctity of the competitive atmosphere prior to and after the actual letting of the contract. In order to insure this desired competitiveness, a bidder cannot be permitted to change his bid after the bids have been opened, except to cure minor irregularities.

In this case, it was clear that prior to the awarding of the contract on June 3rd, the City was aware of the nonconforming nature of Gulf's bid. The test for measuring whether a deviation in a bid is sufficiently material to destroy its competitive character is whether the variation affects the amount of the bid by giving the bidder an advantage or benefit not enjoyed by the other bidders. Here, there is no doubt that the difference between the conforming and nonconforming pumps was material, yet Gulf was permitted to modify its bid. Further, the inclusion of the non-conforming pumps was an advantage not enjoyed by other bidders, who were required to specify only approved equipment.

Gulf had everything to gain and nothing to lose. After everyone else's bids were opened, Gulf was in a position to decide whether it wanted the job badly enough to incur the additional expense of supplying a conforming pump.

The Supreme Court of Minnesota put the applicable proposition well in *Coller v. City of Saint Paul*, 223 Minn. 376, 26 N.W.2d 835, 842 (1947):

> If officials charged with the letting of public contracts should be permitted in their discretion to permit bids to be changed after they have been received and opened, it would open the door to the abuses which it is the purpose of the requirements of competitive bidding to prevent and suppress.

Faced with Gulf's substantially nonconforming bid, the City had but two proper alternatives: to award the contract to the next lowest bidder who met the specifications or to reject all bids and re-advertise for new ones. The City exceeded its authority by allowing Gulf to bring its bid into conformity with the specifications and then accepting it.

Can a public entity waive the requirement for the agent's signature on the bid as informality?

In the case of *Michael Menefee v. County of Fresno* (163 Cal. App. 3d 1175), Menefee Construction Co. is a general partnership and licensed contractor under California law.

Brewer-Kalar is a joint venture also engaged in the construction business. Both Menefee Construction Co. and Brewer-Kalar submitted bid forms to Fresno County for a contract to construct water, sewer, drainage, and street improvements in a county service area. The bids were opened April 29, 1982. Brewer-Kalar's bid was the lowest at $699,998, and Menefee Construction Co. was next lowest at $725,946; however, Brewer-Kalar failed to sign the appropriate line on the proposal sheet (page 4) of its bid's form. The bond accompanying the bid was properly signed.

The deputy county counsel who reviewed the documents for the board of supervisors concluded that Brewer-Kalar's failure to sign the bid's proposal sheet was a material irregularity that rendered the bid "non-responsive" and invalid. The county counsel advised the board not to accept the bid.

The board met June 1, 1982, and heard arguments by counsel for both Brewer-Kalar and Menefee. It then voted to accept the Brewer-Kalar bid and waive any irregularity caused by the absent signature on page 4 of the bid form.

Menefee filed a petition for writ of mandate with the Superior Court to enjoin construction and compel the county to contract with Menefee. Because relief was denied at trial, and the construction project was now complete, the issues became moot; nevertheless, Menefee still wished to obtain a reversal of the denial of their petition for writ of mandate and the adverse judgment in their action for declaratory relief.

Appellants and the county agree on the basic rules governing public works contracts. The contract requires competitive bidding. The general rules of contract law apply to the competitive bidding process. Bids are irrevocable offers or options given to the public agency involved. A contract is complete and binding when a valid bid is accepted.

The real issue is whether the contractor (here Brewer-Kalar) would have been liable on the bond if they had attempted to back out of their bid after the board had accepted it. If the contractor would be able to avoid forfeiture of the bond after their bid is accepted, then the deficiency of the bid would have given them an unfair advantage over other bidders and would render the bid invalid.

The county adopted regulations controlling the bidding process (Fresno County Ord. Code, Section 4.8030), but none of them specifically requires a signature. The specifications for this project adopted some of California Department of Transportation's regulations as part of the specifications, and these regulations require an authorized signature. The court ruled that the board does have discretion to waive details of the bid specifications if it determines that such a waiver will not make the bidding process unfair, i.e., if the deviation from the specifications is inconsequential.

Under California's statutes for relief of bidders on public contracts, the only mistakes that could release Brewer-Kalar from its bid are typographical or arithmetical errors. Relief is only allowed if the bidder can establish that "the mistake was made in filling out the bid and not due to error in judgment or to carelessness in inspecting the site of the work, or in reading the plans or specifications." This statute clearly does not contemplate relief from the mistaken submission of a bid. The court rules that if such relief is not available, Brewer-Kalar did not have an unfair advantage because its bid was unsigned, so the county should be able to waive the signature requirement.

In those cases where the bid solicitation requires a bid bond, can a public entity accept a bid that is accompanied by a form of security that is different than the form required by the entity?

The Dade County Board of County Commissioners' Advertisement for Bid in connection with a contract to renovate the James E. Scott Homes provided:

> A Certified Check or bank draft, payable to the Dade County Department of Housing and Urban Development, Housing Division, U.S. Government Bonds, or a satisfactory Bid Bond executed by the bidder and acceptable sureties in an amount equal to five percent (5%) of the bid shall be submitted with each bid. The successful bidder will be required to furnish and pay for satisfactory Performance and Payment of Bond or Bonds... The Dade County Department of Housing and Urban Development reserves the right to reject any or all bids and to waive any informality in the bidding.

Subsequent addenda required that a bid bond for 5% of a portion of the cost be submitted with the bid.

Robinson submitted the lowest bid of $10,368,515 along with a cashier's check for 5% of the designated cost as security. The second lowest bidder, a company not a party to this appeal, also submitted a cashier's check. Marvin Markowitz, Inc., submitted the highest bid, $10,700,000; its bid included a bid bond in the correct amount. When the Director of Dade County Housing and Urban Development opened the bids and learned that the two lowest bidders had submitted cashier's checks instead of bid bonds, he asked the County Attorney for his opinion. Upon receiving a recommendation that Robinson's bid be approved, the Board of County Commissioners awarded the contract to Robinson. Markowitz sued the Board, requesting injunctive relief. Robinson intervened in the lawsuit. Upon hearing testimony, the trial court found Robinson's bid to be non-responsive because it lacked the required form of security. The court vacated the award of the contract to Robinson and ordered the County to reissue an Invitation for Bids (IFB).

The trial court agreed with Markowitz, finding Robinson's bid was non-responsive because it lacked the required form of security. The court ordered the county to reissue the IFB.

In the case of *Robinson Electric, Co. v. Dade County* (417 So.2d. 1032), Robinson appealed the decision of the trial court. Robinson contended that the court erred in vacating an administrative decision that was not shown to be arbitrary or unreasonable. The Board, it contended, correctly waived the immaterial variance in the form of the security; the difference in the security did not affect the nature or purpose of competitive bidding. Furthermore, argued Robinson, the County reserved the right to waive formalities. Markowitz, on the other hand, argued that since its bid met the qualifications, it should have been awarded the contract without re-issuance of the IFB.

At this point, the County reversed itself and supported the trial court's ruling vacating the contract and requiring re-bidding and agreed with the finding that the documents were ambiguous. This argument represented a change in the County's position; the County was aware of the variance in the security when it awarded the contract to Robinson.

Although a bid containing a material variance was unacceptable (*Glatstein v. City of Miami*, 399 So.2d 1005), not every deviation from the invitation is material. In determining whether a specific noncompliance constitutes a substantial and, hence, non-waivable irregularity, the courts have applied two criteria: (1) whether the effect of a waiver would be to deprive the municipality of its assurance that the contract will be entered into, performed, and guaranteed according to its specified requirements and (2) whether it is of such a nature that its waiver would adversely affect competitive bidding by placing a bidder in a position of advantage over other bidders or by otherwise undermining the necessary common standard of competition.

In application of the general above principles, it is sometimes said that a bid may be rejected or disregarded if there is a material variance between the bid and the advertisement. A minor variance, however, will not invalidate the bid. In this context, a variance is material if it gives the bidder a substantial advantage over the other bidders and, thereby, restricts or stifles competition.

The appeals court reversed the trial court and ordered the award be reinstated to Robinson.

Is the second low bidder entitled to a contract award based on a 'lowest and best' bid if the first low bidder is deemed non-responsive—or can the public entity reject all bids?

In the case of *Intercontinental Properties, Inc. v. State of Florida, Department of Health and Rehabilitative Services* (606 So. 2d 380), the Florida Department of Health and Rehabilitative Services (HRS) was in need of 29,600 square feet of office space. It issued an IFB for a nine-year lease with options to renew. When the bids were opened, Coliseum Lanes, Inc. was the low bidder and was awarded the contract. The high bidder, Intercontinental Properties, Inc., filed a protest, saying that the low bidder's bid was unresponsive. An administrative hearing officer conducted an evidentiary proceeding and concluded that both bids were unresponsive. The hearing officer recommended that both bids be rejected and HRS did so. The high bidder has appealed.

Shortly after HRS rejected both bids, the low bidder (Coliseum) dropped out and rented its building to other tenants. The practical issue now remaining is whether the Department erred in rejecting the Intercontinental bid.

In this case, it is essential to understand the difference between a "responsive" bid and a "lowest and best" bid.

- Under the IFB, "responsive" refers only to matters of form. A responsive bid means that a bid is submitted on the correct forms and contains all required information, signatures, and notarizations. Upon opening, each bid was reviewed for responsiveness. Each responsive (technically complete) bid was then forwarded to a bid evaluation committee in order to obtain a recommendation for which bid should be accepted.

- Under the IFB, the award was to be made to the "Lowest and Best Bid," i.e., the lowest cost and best quality. "'Lowest' refers to least present value cost over term of the lease and options, while 'best' refers to results of total evaluation score." The evaluation score was obtained from a numerical scale set forth in the IFB. Thus, both cost and quality of the facility were to be rated in deciding which would be the successful bid.

In this case, Coliseum was much better on both criteria. Coliseum's bid was $1,200,000 lower than that of Intercontinental. When rated on the numerical scale, Coliseum received 923 points out of a possible 1,000, while Intercontinental received 653. The evaluative comments about Intercontinental were uniformly negative: (1) not conducive for ES business; (2) not safe for client and staff; (3) history of poor maintenance; (4) not recommended as a Service Center; (5) owner will charge clients for parking; and (6) office space offered on multiple floors.

By contrast, the comments on the low bidder, Coliseum, were all positive and did not have the drawbacks identified for the Intercontinental building. The only negative factor was a need to negotiate priority on move-in because the building was undergoing renovation.

Because Coliseum was the low bidder and offered the much better facility, HRS awarded the bid to Coliseum. HRS treated both the Coliseum bid and the Intercontinental bid as being "technically responsive," as defined in the IFB, but found Coliseum to have submitted the "lowest and best bid."

The protest by Intercontinental contended that Coliseum's low bid was unresponsive, because it was signed by an agent without attaching proof of the agent's authority to act on behalf of the property owner. Intercontinental affirmatively asserted that its own bid was responsive and it pled, "Intercontinental Properties, Inc., was the lowest and best responsive bidder and was entitled to the award of the bid pursuant to applicable law."

Coliseum intervened, contending that its low bid was responsive and that if the bid was not responsive, any deviation was a minor irregularity that would not eliminate it from consideration for the contract award. Additionally, Coliseum also raised the question whether the Intercontinental bid "contains irregularities which are not minor so as to render the bid ineligible for contract award consideration." The matter proceeded to hearing with Coliseum, Intercontinental, and HRS as parties.

The hearing officer found that Coliseum's low bid had been signed by Pamela Stewart, who used the title, "Property Coordinator, Coliseum Lanes, Inc." No documentation was attached to the bid that identified Ms. Stewart as an agent and set forth her authority to act for Coliseum Lanes.

After the bids were opened, HRS requested a letter from Ms. Stewart clarifying her relationship with Coliseum, and Ms. Stewart provided a letter that HRS considered sufficient, even though not signed by an officer of Coliseum. At the evidentiary hearing, the president of Coliseum Lanes testified that Ms. Stewart had a longstanding agency relationship with Coliseum and that Ms. Stewart had full authority to act on behalf of Coliseum in submitting the bid to HRS.

The hearing officer ruled that the Coliseum bid was unresponsive. The hearing officer reasoned that since Ms. Stewart was an agent and the bid had not included the necessary statement regarding her authority to act for Coliseum, the Coliseum bid was in technical noncompliance with the IFB and, therefore, was unresponsive.

The court in ruling differently, stated:

> There is a very strong public interest in favor of saving tax dollars in awarding public contracts. There is no public interest, much less a substantial public interest, in disqualifying low bidders for technical deficiencies in form, where the low bidder did not derive any unfair competitive advantage by reason of the technical omission.

In this case, there was no sound reason for the hearing officer to override the judgment of the department in awarding this contract to Coliseum. The evidentiary record was developed before the hearing officer revealed that both bids were submitted with the full authority of the owner. While the failure to attach proof of the agent's authority rendered each of the two bids technically nonconforming, both deficiencies were easily remedied. "This is plainly the sort of deficiency that a public agency can, in its discretion, allow a bidder to cure after the fact."

If at the time of the proceedings there had still been an active contest between Coliseum and Intercontinental, then the correct result would have been to reverse the department's order on the theory that the original award to Coliseum was correct. However, once the department disqualified both bids, Coliseum had dropped out and had rented its premises to other tenants. The only remaining contestant was Intercontinental, whose building was rated unsatisfactory and whose rental was $1,200,000 higher than the low bid. Because Intercontinental has failed the objective performance criteria and because Coliseum has dropped out, the department's order rejecting both bids now stands as being right for the wrong reason.

The district court found that the administrative hearing officer was incorrect in finding Coliseum had bid non-responsively. Coliseum should have been allowed to demonstrate as they attempted to at the hearing that the agent did in fact have full authority to act for the owner. However, because of Coliseum's withdrawal and because the high bidder did not pass the objective criteria of the bid, the order to reject all bids was found to be correct.

Can a public entity waive, as informality, the failure of a bidder to submit two alternative products as required in the bid specifications?

In March 1980, the Board of County Commissioners of Liberty County (Liberty County) advertised for bids on a road-resurfacing project. Bids were requested for two mutually exclusive types of asphalt, Alternate A (asphaltic concrete) and Alternate B (a sand asphalt hot mix). Either alternative was acceptable for the roads to be resurfaced.

Seven companies bid on the project. Since the County Engineer inadvertently failed to forward to Gulf Asphalt Corporation (Gulf) the last page of an information sheet requiring bids on both Alternates A and B, Gulf bid only on Alternate B. (The industry practice is to bid only on one alternate.) Gulf's Alternate B bid was the low bid at $906,895. The next lowest bid on Alternate B was $1,055,201 submitted by Baxter's Asphalt & Concrete (Baxter's). For Alternate A, the lowest bid was Baxter's at $1,094,226.

At an April 1980 Commission meeting, the County Engineer recommended that Gulf's bid on Alternate B be accepted because it was $148,000 less than the bid by Baxter's on the same Alternate. Gulf's bid on Alternate B was likewise less than Baxter's Alternate A. The Board unanimously waived the irregularity of Gulf's failure to submit a bid on Alternate A and awarded the contract to Gulf.

Baxter's has immediately filed suit and obtained a temporary injunction preventing Liberty County from entering into a contract with Gulf. At trial in May 1980, the court ruled in favor of Liberty County and Gulf, and the injunction was dissolved. Baxter's appealed and the district court in March 1981 found that Gulf's failure to bid on Alternate A violated Florida Statutes. The court directed Liberty County to re-advertise for bids. However, because there was no restraining order during the time of appeal and the district court had denied a motion for a stay pending appeal, Liberty County had already entered into a contract with Gulf for the resurfacing project and Gulf had completed the project. All parties moved for a rehearing and the district court filed a second opinion in November 1981, holding that Liberty County was liable to Baxter's for damages, including reasonable costs and attorney's fees, based upon Liberty County's implied promise to comply with the competitive bid statute.

In the case of *Liberty County v. Baxter's Asphalt and Concrete, Inc.* (421 So. 2d 505), Liberty County then sought discretionary jurisdiction in the Supreme Court (Florida), which ruled as follows:

The Florida Supreme Court has previously said that public bids statutes

> . . . serve the object of protecting the public against collusive contracts and prevent favoritism toward contractors by public officials and tend to secure fair competition upon equal terms to all bidders, [and] they remove temptation on the part of public officers to seek private gain at the taxpayers' expense, are of highly remedial character, and should receive a construction always which will fully effectuate and advance their true intent and purpose and which will avoid the likelihood of same being circumvented, evaded, or defeated.

Nothing in the above is subverted by the trial court's actions. That court found that there was no connection between Gulf and any of the county commissioners that may have affected the county's decision-making. More importantly, the court found no illegality, fraud, oppression, or misconduct on the part of either Liberty County or Gulf and that Liberty County acted in good faith in the awarding of the subject bid. With no fraud or misconduct on Liberty County's part, it was clearly within the commission's discretion to award the subject bid to Gulf.

Baxter's further argued and the district court agreed that the waiving of the bid irregularity was unlawful because Gulf's failure to comply with the specifications was material.

The Supreme Court disagreed. They found this case was a situation of a relatively minor irregularity in the technical bidding requirements. Liberty County in the Advertisement for Bids reserved the right to waive irregularities in any bid and the court found under the facts of this case (with trial court findings of no fraud or misconduct on Liberty County's part and with no competitive advantage accruing to Gulf), that there was substantial compliance with the bidding statute.

Lastly, Baxter's argued that the district court was correct in awarding it damages based upon the doctrine of promissory estoppel in that "the public entity by soliciting bids promised that the contract would be awarded to the lowest possible bidder, and that the rejected bidder reasonably and detrimentally relied on that promise."

The Supreme Court stated, "We need not address this issue since it has been found that the lowest responsible bidder was in fact Gulf and not Baxter's. The opinion of the district court of appeal was quashed and the final judgment of the trial court was reinstated."

Applying Legal Situations to the U.C.C.

What happens when actual damages exceed the allowances specified for liquidated damages?

Under the contract signed by the two firms, Owens Enterprises agreed to buy all of the citrus fruit of merchantable quality produced in the groves of Davis Fruit on or before February

19th. The price specified was $1.25 a box, and the groves were expected to produce in excess of 20,000 boxes.

The contract also contained the following clause:

> The Buyer has this day advanced to the Seller the sum of $11,000, the receipt of which is hereby acknowledged by the Seller and which sum is an advance and part payment for said fruit at the price above stated. Should the Buyer fail to comply with the terms and conditions herein enumerated, this contract shall therefore become null and void, and the advance made to the Seller shall be retained by the Seller in full payment of liquidated damages.

Owens did fail to comply with the terms and conditions. After accepting 12,000 boxes of fruit, and paying an additional $5,000 over and above the $11,000 advance, Owens lost a major customer and had no use for the remainder of Davis' production. Davis was unable to find another buyer and watched the equivalent of 9,500 boxes rot on the trees.

Does a buyer's unforeseen risk leave a citrus grower without payment for damages? The U.C.C. generally follows the common law rules governing liquidated damage provisions. Under U.C.C. (2)-718 (1), damages for the breach of a contract for the sale of goods by either party may be liquidated in the agreement, but only by an amount that is reasonable in the light of (1) the anticipated or actual harm caused by the breach; (2) the difficulties of proof of loss; and (3) the inconvenience or non-feasibility of otherwise obtaining an adequate remedy.

This provision concludes by stating that a term fixing unreasonably large liquidated damages is void as a penalty. An unreasonably small amount would be subject to similar criticism and might be stricken under the section as unconscionable.

Simply stated, the law, as a matter of public policy, opposes the use of liquidated damage provisions to set damages that are viewed as "penal" in character. This includes agreements for damages unreasonably disproportionate to the anticipated losses. The probable reason for the courts' opposition to penalty clauses stems from the belief that one should be free to breach one's contract upon payment of the actual damages the breach causes and that certain breaches maximize economic resources.

Further, penalty clauses contradict the basic rule of contractual damages, which is based on the notion that the non-breaching party should only recover damages that cover the "benefit of the bargain" and no more. Whatever the reasons, the rule is well accepted that liquidated damage clauses are valid and enforceable, while penalty clauses are not.

In this case, Owens, the buyer, contends that the grower/seller should be limited to the recovery of the $11,000 liquidated damages specified in the contractual provision and that the grower/seller has already collected a sum in excess of that amount. Davis, the grower/seller, argues that the parties contracted for the sale of all of the fruit of merchantable quality from the seller's orchards. Although the buyer has paid the seller a total of $16,000 on the contract, he has left 9,500 boxes of merchantable fruit un-purchased, which would have earned the grower/seller an additional amount of approximately $12,000 if the buyer had fully complied with his agreement. The grower/seller contends that to enforce the liquidated damage provision would constitute a penalty against him because it is an unreasonably small amount and, therefore, would be unconscionable.

If the court as a matter of law finds the contract or any clause of the contract to have been unconscionable at the time it was made, the court may refuse to enforce the contract. Alternatively, it may enforce the remainder of the contract without the unconscionable clause, or it may so limit the application of any unconscionable clause as to avoid any unconscionable result.

While most cases on liquidated damages occur when the stipulated sum is unreasonably high, there are some decisions in which the complaining party demonstrated that the liquidated figure was so inadequate as to justify the court permitting him to recover his actual damages. Here then, the grower/seller would be entitled to a further recovery if he can prove that the amount is too small and, therefore, unconscionable.

Absent a finding of unconscionability, the grower/seller may still find relief in U.C.C. Section 2-719(2), which provides: "Where circumstances because an exclusive or limited remedy to fail of its essential purpose, remedy may be had as provided in this code."

There may have been good reason to enforce the liquidated damages provision in this case had the buyer utterly failed to perform the contract. However, the buyer had already taken delivery of enough fruit to use up the deposit. If the grower/seller's recovery is limited to the amount of the deposit, he will be entitled to no damages whatsoever for the buyer's failure to pick the remaining 9,500 boxes. This could easily be a case in which the circumstances have caused an exclusive remedy, the liquidated damage provision, to fail its essential purpose of permitting the grower/seller to pursue other remedies provided by the Code.

When does the "indefiniteness" of a contract still constitute an enforceable contract?

Company President Steve Janelle claims that the loose ends of a contract will nullify the agreement to purchase computer chips from a supplier named MicroChips. The contract did not specify when or where delivery will take place, and the price was whatever the market would bear when the chips were delivered. Although Janelle's company had accepted delivery on that premise, the market changed within the next two months, and Steve Janelle had found another supplier willing to confirm time and place of delivery as well as a good price. When MicroChips attempted to perform under the first contract a week later, Janelle refused, arguing that he "didn't have a contract because the important terms had been left open."

Janelle Computers argues that the alleged contract with MicroChips, Inc., failed for indefiniteness due to its numerous "open terms," such as time and place of delivery. In addition, Janelle argues that the price term for the memory chips (i.e., "market price at time of delivery") is too indefinite to allow enforcement of the contract. Although Janelle's argument might have had some merit under common law/pre-U.C.C. cases, when all essential terms to a contract had to be included or the contract would fail, this argument has no chance of success on the facts under the provisions of the U.C.C.

The controlling section in this regard is U.C.C. Section 2-204(3), which provides as follows: "Even though one or more terms are left open, a contract for sale does not fail for indefiniteness if the parties have intended to make a contract and there is a reasonably certain basis for giving an appropriate remedy." It appears from the facts that at least the following terms were agreed upon by the two parties:

- The type of memory chips ordered;
- The quantity ordered;
- The price to be paid for the quantity ordered (market price at time of delivery); and
- The approximate delivery date.

The facts as presented put to rest any argument as to whether, under the first prong of the test in Section 2-204(3), the parties intended to make a contract. Similarly, these terms, if in fact entered into, would also provide a reasonably certain basis for giving an appropriate remedy.

Thus, the legal question posed by the second prong of Section 2-204(3) must also be answered in the affirmative. The alleged contract clearly delineates a promise to sell identifiable goods of a specified type and quantity at a specified or reasonably determinable price and time.

Accordingly, even though the contract contains several open terms, the contract does not fail for indefiniteness, because the U.C.C.'s "gap filler" provisions may supplement such open terms. For instance, time and place of delivery are dealt with in Sections 2-308 and 2-309, which provide that in the absence of a specified place and time in the contract for delivery, the place for delivery is the seller's place of business and the specific time for delivery shall be a reasonable time.

Moreover, the traditionally more difficult issue of a market-based open price term is expressly recognized by the Code as an acceptable contract under Section 2-305(1)(c): "(1) The parties if they so intend can conclude a contract for sale even though the price is not settled. In such a case the price is a reasonable price at the time of delivery if... (c) the price is to be fixed in terms of some agreed market or other standard. . . ." Accordingly, Janelle's argument that the terms of this contract are indefinite is without merit.

When do additional terms on a Purchase Order represent an unenforceable, material change to the contractual relationship between buyer and seller?

When the Simpson School complex was destroyed by fire, the cause was identified immediately. Children playing under the building had ignited exposed polystyrene insulation. School Officials launched a suit against the manufacturer, Dominion Insulfoam.

Dominion explained in court that it formed Insulfoam by expanding and molding polystyrene beads supplied to it by SWANCO. The company argued that if it was to be held liable for fire damage to the school and its contents, it was entitled to indemnification from SWANCO as the negligent manufacturer of the polystyrene beads. SWANCO, however, pointed to the indemnity provision on the reverse side of purchase order confirmations it routinely sent to Dominion after Dominion had placed an order but before the beads were shipped. The indemnity provision states:

> INDEMNIFICATION—Buyer (Dominion) agrees to defend, indemnify, and save harmless Seller (SWANCO) from any and all claims of whatsoever nature, including but not limited to injuries to Buyer's or Seller's employees or to third parties (including death), or for damages to the property of Seller, or to the property of Buyer, or of third parties, caused by, arising directly or indirectly from, or occurring on a) any handling of said materials, including but not limited to unloading railroad cars, tank cars, trucks, tank trucks, or barges, or in handling containers of materials sold, and b) any use of said materials.

Arguably, this express indemnity provision shielded SWANCO from Dominion's implied indemnity claim. Nevertheless, Dominion claimed that the hold-harmless indemnification provision was a "material alteration" of the parties' agreement and, thus, is not a term of the contract under the U.C.C.

The key issue here is whether the indemnification clause contained in SWANCO's confirmation form was incorporated into the parties' purchase agreement under U.C.C. Section 2-207 and whether the indemnity provision constituted a "material alteration" of the parties' agreement and, as such, did not become a term of the parties' contract.

Section 2-207 of the U.C.C. states:

> (1) A definite and reasonable expression of acceptance or a written confirmation, which is sent within a reasonable time, operates as an acceptance even though it states terms additional to or different from those offered or agreed upon, unless acceptance is expressly made conditional on assent to the additional or different terms.

> (2) The additional terms are to be construed as proposals for addition to the contract. Between merchants such terms become part of the contract unless (a) the offer expressly limits acceptance to the terms of the offer; (b) they materially alter it; or (c) notification of objection to them has already been given or is given within a reasonable time after notice of them is received.

One must first determine whether the small proviso contained on the front side of SWANCO's confirmation form converts an otherwise valid acceptance into a de facto rejection and counteroffer. That is, if SWANCO's purchase order confirmation form operates as an acceptance, then the indemnification clause becomes incorporated only if it is not a "material alteration" of the parties' contract under Section 2-207(2)(b). Confirmations such as SWANCO's are routinely held by a majority of the courts to operate as acceptances, rather than counteroffers, and contested clauses thus incorporated only if deemed immaterial under 2-2007(2)(b).

Consequently, the express indemnity clause contained on SWANCO's purchase order confirmation form is enforceable only if it does not constitute a material alteration of the parties' purchase contract. Generally, materiality is a question of fact. U.C.C. Section 2-207 provides that the test for materiality is whether the newly introduced clause would result in surprise or hardship to the non-assenting party.

Generally, warranty disclaimers are routinely deemed material as a matter of law. Similarly, courts commonly hold that indemnification clauses like SWANCO's are "material" as a matter of law. These factors lead us to predict that courts would hold that SWANCO's indemnity clause was a material alteration of the parties' purchase contract under Section 2-207(2) (b) of the U.C.C.; and, therefore, the clause is unenforceable as a matter of law.

When can a Buyer rely on skill and judgment of the Supplier to invoke a warranty of fitness for a particular purpose under the U.C.C.?

Tropic Construction contracted to install multiple pipelines between several Caribbean islands for their local governments. Tropic decided that it needed a certain type of pipe that did not alter the delicate underwater ecosystem of the Caribbean.

Tropic contacted a leading pipe supplier, Coated Pipe Company, and spoke to a materials representative regarding the Coated Pipe Company's expertise with the type of pipe that will support the coral reefs and the underwater ecology. Tropic discussed its project needs, requirements, and objectives with Coated Pipe and subsequently executed and sent a purchase order to Coated Pipe. In the purchase order, the quantity, price and shipping terms were listed. In addition, the purchase order specified that the pipe was to be "coal tar enamel-lined." Coated Pipe accepted the order and shipped the goods according to specifications.

Upon installation, Tropic discovered that the lining was not compatible with the coral reef environment and that the pipeline had to be replaced. Tropic sued Coated Pipe for breach of contract arguing that Tropic had relied on Coated Pipe's expertise in pipes when they ordered the specified pipes for this job. Coated Pipe contended that it did nothing wrong.

The U.C.C. provides for several types of implied warranties, warranties included in the sales contract even though not specifically agreed to by the parties. Tropic is seeking recovery under the 'breach of an implied warranty of fitness for a particular purpose."

The circumstances under which an implied warranty of fitness for a particular purpose will arise are specified in U.C.C. Section 2-315:

Where the seller at the time of contracting has reason to know any particular purpose for which the goods are required and that the buyer is relying on the seller's skill or judgment to select or furnish suitable goods there is, unless excluded or modified under the next section, an implied warranty that the goods shall be fit for such purpose.

By the terms of U.C.C. Section 2-315, an implied warranty of fitness will not arise unless the buyer "is relying on the seller's skill or judgment to select or furnish suitable goods." It is essential, therefore, that the buyer proves that his or her organization relied upon the judgment and skill of the seller for the actual selection of the goods purchased. Courts recognize that buyers may rely upon a seller to "furnish" goods suitable for a particular purpose, even though the individual unit purchased is selected by the buyer.

The seller must have reason to know two things: (1) the particular purpose for which the buyer requires the goods and (2) the buyer is relying on the seller's skill of judgment to select or furnish suitable goods.

Both these requirements must exist before the warranty will be implied. It is not enough that the seller has reason to know the use to which the buyer intends to put the goods unless the seller also has reason to know that the buyer is relying on the seller's skill or judgment to select or furnish suitable goods.

The reliance factors, however, are in the disjunctive; the second requirement is satisfied based on the seller's skill or judgment to select or furnish suitable goods. The seller need not both select and furnish; either will suffice. Accordingly, the fact that the buyer selected the goods he or she wanted does not preclude reliance on the seller to furnish pipe suitable for the known application.

In this case, Tropic chose the pipe but informed Coated Pipe of the pipe's intended application. One can presume that Tropic wanted Coated Pipe's expertise in the selection of the requisite pipe or at least the benefit of Coated Pipe's experience regarding the specified application. Arguably, Tropic did not expect Coated Pipe to stand silent as to any possible problems and merely ship the pipe. Consequently, Tropic has a good case against Coated Pipe. Tropic advised for what the pipe was to be used and arguably relied on Coated Pipe's expertise even though Tropic picked the specific pipe.

Under Law of Agency provisions, when does "implied authority" constitute real authority in a contract for the purchase of goods under the U.C.C.?

In this situation, the Vice President of Contracts and Purchasing for the largest furniture wholesaler in the Southeast summons a new agent to his office and verbally instructs him to get the best value from the fabric wholesalers. The new agent began networking with other agents to research this commodity and discovered that it is the custom in the industry for such agents to commit their companies for periods of six months or longer. The new agent contracted with Jamie Ltd. for six months' worth of woven fabric. The day after the contract was executed, the Vice President informed the new agent that he was ordering a substantially upgraded fabric that would bankrupt the company. The Vice President also informed the agent that he did not have the authority to contract for more than three months.

When the Vice President attempted to cancel the contract with Jaime Ltd., the company sued, alleging they had a valid contract for six months. The Vice President contended that the agent did not have the authority to enter into a six-month contract.

Will the Vice President's company have to honor the six-month contract? Yes. If the principal tells an agent, either orally or in writing, to perform certain acts, the agent has express authority to carry out those acts. If the act that has been authorized is entering into a contract on the principal's behalf, the principal will be bound by the terms of the contract entered into by his agent.

Sometimes, however, principals do not explain in detail all of the authority that they wish an agent to have. In such situations, the law implies that the agent has:

- incidental authority: the authority to perform the acts necessary to accomplish the principal's objective; and

- customary authority: authority that agents in this company or in similar businesses in the community customarily have.

Both express authority and these two types of implied authority are varieties of actual authority that agents may possess.

A principal is the master of the relationship and may expressly deny an agent the authority that is normally implied in a similar agency relationship. For example, sales representatives in a particular industry may customarily have the authority not only to offer products but also to enter into contracts on their principal's behalf.

The three basic components of apparent authority are that:

- the principal holds the agent out as an agent;

- the third party reasonably relies on that holding out; and

- the third party changes position or relies (e.g., enters into a contract) to his or her legal detriment.

If these three elements are present, the law permits a third party to hold a principal responsible on a contract negotiated by an agent lacking any actual authority.

Clearly, implied authority is real authority. It includes the authority to perform acts reasonably necessary to achieve an authorized act and arises from custom and usage. According to the analysis presented, the furniture wholesaler is liable, despite the limitation they had placed on the new agent's procurement authority.

The Vice President and the new agent were engaged in a master/servant agency relationship. The agent possessed apparent authority to bind the company when he entered into the six-month contract with Jamie Ltd. The agent had implied authority because the Vice President had placed him in a position of dealing with suppliers and allowed him to make orders. These facts, together with the custom of the industry, allowed Jamie Ltd., the innocent third party, to develop a reasonable belief that the agent was acting within his authority. Hence, there was implied authority on the agent's part and the furniture wholesaler was liable for the breach of contract.

Does a buyer have to comply with volume purchase commitments and low-cost supplier provisions?

In July of 1996, Freemen, Inc., entered into a purchase agreement with Justin Foundry. This agreement incorporated two key provisions. The first was a "volume purchase commitment" under which Freeman "committed to purchase yearly an amount of 300,000 pounds of aluminum castings and 990,000 pounds of brass castings" from Justin.

This commitment was "predicated upon a continuation of a business sales level of Freeman products that requires the amount of aluminum and brass castings specified above on a yearly basis." No fixed period or termination date for this commitment was specified.

The other provision was what the parties termed the "low-cost supplier clause." The purchase agreement states:

> In situations where the cost per pound does not permit Justin to be the low-cost supplier of castings, Freeman will provide Justin with the opportunity to make every attempt to become the low-cost supplier of castings for Freeman. This opportunity to discuss individual price requirements that differ from competitive cost schedules is intended to be a mutually beneficial agreement to allow Justin the opportunity to compete to be the low-cost supplier in all situations and to also maximize Freeman's ability to remain cost-competitive in the marketplace.

Freeman never met the annual purchase commitments for brass and aluminum castings and a year after signing the agreements was not even soliciting bids from Justin on additional work. By fall of 1997, Freeman had completely terminated Justin as a vendor.

Because Freeman was Justin's major customer, this termination had dire consequences on the Foundry. In December of 1997, Justin ceased operations and filed a petition for bankruptcy. Justin also filed an adversary proceeding in the bankruptcy court, alleging that Freeman breached its contract by failing to comply with the volume purchase commitment and low-cost supplier clause.

Does Justin have a case? Yes, Freeman may have some liability under the volume purchase commitment but not under the low-cost supplier clause. Article 2 of the U.C.C. governs the resolution of Justin's claims under the "volume purchase commitment" concept.

As noted, Freeman committed to purchase 300,000 pounds of brass castings from Justin, predicated "upon a continuation of a business sales level of Freeman products that require the amount of aluminum and brass castings specified above on a yearly basis." The volume purchase commitment is a "requirements contract." Such contracts are governed by U.C.C. Section 2-306, which states that "(a) term which measures the quantity by the... requirements of the buyer means such actual... requirements as may occur in good faith, except that no quantity unreasonably disproportionate to any such estimate... may be tendered or demanded." The volume purchase commitment expressly conditioned the quantities of aluminum and brass castings to be purchased on Freeman's requirements.

Thus, although Freeman never purchased the stated amount of brass castings in the years 1996-1997 and also failed to purchase the stated amount of aluminum castings in 1997, these failures constitute a breach only to the extent that Freeman, in good faith, had a requirement for such castings but refused to purchase them from Justin.

Accordingly, the bankruptcy court should determine whether in the years 1996-1997 Freeman had a good-faith requirement for up to 990,000 pounds of brass castings and whether in the year 1998 Freeman had a good-faith requirement for up to 300,000 pounds of aluminum castings. To the extent that Freeman may have had good-faith requirements for castings up to the quantities set forth in the contract but failed to purchase them from Justin, Freeman would have breached its purchase commitment and would be responsible to Justin for damages, including but not limited to lost profits.

As previously mentioned, the agreement also included the low-cost supplier clause. According to the agreement, Justin would provide castings "should (Freeman) desire" that it do so. The agreement then states that Freeman will provide Justin "the opportunity to make every attempt to become the low-cost supplier of castings," the "opportunity to compete" for all casting orders, and the "opportunity to discuss individual price requirements."

This is not a language of obligation and does not create a contractual duty on the part of Freeman to purchase castings from Justin; it merely sets forth a willingness to consider bids to fill additional orders by Justin. Clearly, this clause did not obligate Freeman to purchase any additional castings from Justin, and any failure by Freeman to purchase such additional castings was not a breach of contract.

References

American Bar Association (1982). *The model procurement ordinance for local governments.* Louisville, KY: American Bar Association.

American Bar Association (1993). *The model procurement code for state and local governments* (5th ed.). Louisville, KY: American Bar Association.

Black, H. C. (1979). *Black's law dictionary* (5th ed.). St. Paul, MN: West Publishing Co.

Canadian Federal Government (1993). *Glossary of materiel information management terms for the Canadian government.* Ottawa Ontario, Canada: Assets Information Management Project.

Canadian Public Works and Government Services (1994). *Supply policy manual* (Chapter 12, Glossary of Procurement Terms, Amendment #94-1. Gatineau Quebec, Canada: Supply Policy & Management Directorate.

Lallatin, C. S., CPPO, C.P.M. (1995). *Public purchasing and materials management.* Reston, VA: National Institute of Governmental Purchasing, Inc.

Merriam-Webster (2003). *Merriam-Webster's collegiate dictionary* (11th ed.). Available from www.merriam-webster.com/info/faq.htm.

National Association of State Procurement Officials (NASPO) (1994). *State and local government purchasing* (4th ed.). Lexington, KY: NASPO.

National Contract Management Association (1989). *Desktop guide to basic contracting terms* (2nd ed.). Vienna, VA: National Contract Management Association.

National Institute of Governmental Purchasing, Inc. (NIGP) (1999). *General public purchasing.* Reston, VA: NIGP.

National Institute of Governmental Purchasing, Inc. (NIGP) (2000). *Public procurement management* (Parts 1 and 2). Reston, VA: NIGP.

Smith, L. Y., & Roberson, G. G. (1977). *Business law: Uniform commercial code* (4th ed.). St. Paul, MN: West Publishing Co.

U.S. Department of Defense (1987). *Armed services pricing manual.* Chicago, IL: Commerce Clearing House, Inc.

U.S. FAR Secretariat (1994). *Federal acquisition regulation.* Washington, DC: Office of Federal Acquisition Policy, Government Services Administration

Appendix A

NIGP Code of Ethics

The Institute believes, and it is a condition of membership, that the following ethical principles should govern the conduct of every person employed by a public sector procurement or materials management organization.

- Seeks or accepts a position as head or employee only when fully in accord with the professional principles applicable thereto, and when confident of possessing the qualifications to serve under those principles to the advantage of the employing organization.

- Believes in the dignity and worth of the services rendered by the organization and the societal responsibilities assumed as a trusted public servant.

- Is governed by the highest ideals of honor and integrity in all public and personal relationships in order to merit the respect and inspire the confidence of the organization and the public being served.

- Believes that personal aggrandizement or personal profit obtained through misuse of public or personal relationships is dishonest and not tolerable.

- Identifies and eliminates participation of any individual in operational situations where a conflict of interest may be involved.

- Believes that members of the Institute and its staff should at no time or under any circumstances accept directly or indirectly, gifts, gratuities, or other things of value from suppliers which might influence or appear to influence purchasing decisions.

- Keeps the governmental organization informed, through appropriate channels, on problems and progress of applicable operations by emphasizing the importance of the facts.

- Resists encroachment on control of personnel in order to preserve integrity as a professional manager. Handles all personnel matters on a merit basis. Politics, religion, ethnicity, gender and age carry no weight in personnel administration in the agency being directed or served.

- Seeks or dispenses no personal favors. Handles each administrative problem objectively and emphatically without discrimination.

- Subscribes to and supports the professional aims and objectives of the National Institute of Governmental Purchasing, Inc.

Appendix B

UPPCC Code Of Ethics

All applicants for UPPCC certification must subscribe to the following ethical principles.

Breaching this Code of Ethics will be just reason for revocation of UPPCC certification.

- I will seek or accept a position of employment only when fully in accord with the professional principles applicable thereto, and when confident of possessing the qualifications to serve under those principles to the advantage of my employer.

- I believe in the dignity and worth of the services rendered by my employment and the societal responsibilities assumed as a trusted public servant.

- I shall be governed by the highest ideals of honor and integrity in all public and personal relationships in order to merit the respect and inspire the confidence of my employer and the public served.

- I believe that personal aggrandizement or personal profit obtained through misuse of public or personal relationships is dishonest and intolerable.

- I will identify and eliminate participation of any individual in operational situations where a conflict of interest may be involved.

- I believe that individuals that possess UPPCC certification should at no time or under any circumstances accept directly or indirectly, gifts, gratuities or other things of value from suppliers, which might influence or appear to influence purchasing decisions.

- I will keep my governmental organization informed, through appropriate channels, on problems and progress of applicable operations by emphasizing the importance of the facts.

- I will handle all personnel matters on a merit basis. Politics, religion, ethnicity, gender and age carry no weight in personnel administration in the agency being directed or served.

- I shall not seek or dispense personal favors that are in conflict with my profession.

- I will handle each administrative problem objectively and empathetically without discrimination.

- I subscribe to and support the professional aims and objectives of the Universal Public Procurement Certification Council.

Appendix C

Glossary of Selected Legal Terms

A

ABA: American Bar Association.

ABA Model Procurement Code for State and Local Governments: a code developed by the American Bar Association, initially adopted in 1979 and revised in 2000; serves as a model of statutory principles and policy guidance for managing and controlling public procurement; may be adapted by state and local governments to their own organizational and political constraints.

ABA Model Procurement Ordinance for Local Governments: a code similar to the **ABA Model Procurement Code**, but is intended for use by small or local jurisdictions.

Accept: (1) to receive as approved, adequate, or satisfactory (2) to receive willingly with the intent of retaining.

Acceptance: (1) Approval of specified services, supplies, or construction delivered as partial or complete fulfillment of a contract: (2) the act of receiving by an authorized representative with intention of retaining; (3) an indication of a willingness to act in accordance with; (4) the assumption of a legal obligation by a party to a contract to the terms and conditions of that contract; (5) the act in which the person to whom the offer is made exchanges his or her own promise or performance for the promise made in the offer; approval of specified services, supplies, or construction delivered as partial or complete fulfillment of a contract. It is one of the elements in forming an express contract.

Acceptance of offer: the agreement of the vendor to deliver the goods ordered for the price offered.

Acceptance of order: the agreement of the purchaser to an offer submitted by a vendor.

Acknowledgment: a form used by a vendor to advise a purchaser that an order has been received; usually implies acceptance. Also, receipt acknowledged.

Act of God: an extraordinary interruption of the usual course of events by a natural cause (such as a flood or earthquake), or by a force majeure that cannot be reasonably foreseen or prevented.

Addendum: an addition or supplement to a document, for example, items or information added to a procurement document.

Adjustment: the amount of variation permitted by an adjustment clause in the contract generally permitting a change upward or downward in the price or obligations in case certain events transpire. See price adjustment clause.

Administrative change: a unilateral change to a contract, in writing that does not affect the substantive rights of the parties, such as changes in addresses or funding accounts.

Administrative law: rules and regulations promulgated by governmental administrative or regulatory agencies; has the force and effect of law.

ADR: see **Alternative Dispute Resolution**.

Advantageous: in the jurisdiction's best interest; beneficial.

Advertise: to make a public announcement, or legal notice, of forthcoming solicitation with the aim of increasing the response and enlarging the competition; often required by law.

Advertising: the act of preparing and distributing advertisements which call attention to a contemplated public purchase or sale.

Affidavit: a written statement of facts made under oath before a notary public or other officer authorized to administer such an oath.

Affiliate: (1): a branch or unit of a larger organization (2) a company effectively controlled by another or associated with others under common ownership or control.

Agency: (1) an administrative division of a government (2) a legal relationship that exists between two parties by which one (the agent) is authorized to perform or transact specified business activities for the other (the principal). See law of agency.

Agent: one who is empowered to act for or in place of another. See broker.

Agreement: (1) a duly executed and legally binding

contract (2) the act of agreeing (3) a consensus of two or more minds in respect of anything done or to be done.

All or none: a bid submitted in response to an invitation for bids (IFB), in which the bidder states the bidder will not accept a partial award, but will only accept an award for all the items or services included in the IFB. Compare with non-responsive bid and non-responsible bid.

Alternate bid: (1) a substitute bid (2) a bid submitted with an intentional substantive variation to a basic provision, specification, term, or condition of the solicitation.

Alternative Dispute Resolution (ADR): any procedure used voluntarily to resolve issues in controversy without the need to resort to litigation. These procedures include, but are not limited to, mediation, fact-finding, and arbitration.

Amendment: (1) a revision or change to a document; often used to correct a solicitation. Compare with modification, a term generally used with respect to changes to an existing contract (2) an agreed addition to, deletion from, correction or modification of a document or contract.

Amendment previous value: value of the document as last amended.

Amendment status: identifies the number and description of amendments issued to a bid solicitation or contract document, and gives a description of the previous wording.

Anti-trust legislation: laws and regulations for the protection of trade and commerce from monopolies that eliminate or preclude noncompetitive business practices.

Apparent Agency (a.k.a. "estoppel agency"): an agency relationship whereby the Principal's conduct implies that an Agent has authority to act on the Principal's behalf and thereby the Principal becomes bound to and responsible for what the Agent signed or did.

Approval: official permission, consent, sanction.

Approval date: the date on which a procurement document was approved by the appropriate authority.

Arbitrary, capricious or fraudulent action: action by whim or caprice, with irrational disregard of facts or circumstances; can provide grounds for courts to overrule or remand an administrative decision or ministerial action by a public purchaser.

Arbitration: (1) a process by which a dispute between two contending parties is presented to one or more disinterested parties (arbitrators) for a decision (2) the resolution of a disagreement by such a process.

As is: term describing goods offered without guarantee or warranty, in present condition, with all risk assumed by purchaser without recourse to the vendor.

Assignment: legal transfer of a claim, right, interest, or property.

Assignment of payment: payment made to other than the vendor of the goods or services, for example, payment made to a vendor's creditor.

Attach: take legal possession.

Authority: the right to perform certain acts or prescribe rules governing the conduct of others. See delegation of authority.

Authorization to release: permission to release requested goods to the using agency against existing supply agreements.

Authorized deviation: deviations specifically permitted by contracting authority.

Award: the presentation, after careful consideration, of a purchase agreement or contract to the selected bidder or offeror. Also used as a verb.

B

BAFO: Best and final offer. In competitive negotiation, the final proposal submitted after negotiations are completed that contains the vendor's most favorable terms for price and services or products to be delivered.

Best interest of the (state, county, city, etc.): in the absence of specific authority, law, regulation, or instruction, provides the rationale for an official to use discretion in taking the action deemed to be most advantageous to the jurisdiction.

Bid: an offer submitted by a prospective vendor in response to an invitation for bid (IFB) issued by a procurement authority; becomes a contract upon acceptance by the buyer.

Bidder: one who submits a response to an invitation for bid (IFB).

Bid documentation: file containing all information

relating to the bid, including requirements, purchase request, invitation for bid (IFB), all bids in response to the IFB, bid evaluation, and award information.

Bid protest: a formal complaint made against the methods employed or decisions made by a procurement authority in the process leading to the award of a contract.

Bid rigging: the agreement among potential competitors to manipulate the competitive bidding process, for example, by agreeing not to bid, to bid specific prices, to rotate bidding, or to give kickbacks to purchasers.

Blanket Order: a contract under which a contractor or vendor agrees to provide goods or services to a purchaser on a demand basis; the contract generally establishes prices, terms, conditions, and the period covered, although no quantities are specified; shipments are to be made when and as required by the purchaser.

Boilerplate: a colloquialism, used in procurement to identify standard terms and conditions incorporated in solicitations, contracts, or purchase orders which are often preprinted or incorporated by reference. See terms and conditions.

Bona fide: in good faith.

Breach of contract: failure to fulfill a contract, wholly or in part, without legal excuse.

Breach of warranty: the failure to meet an express or implied agreement as to the title, quality, content, or condition of something sold. See express warranty, full warranty, implied warranty, limited warranty.

Broker: a person or agent acting as an independent manufacturer's or distributor's representative who, for a fee or commission, negotiates contracts of purchase and sale without personally taking title to or possession of the goods being sold.

Buyer's option: the right, established in a purchase document, to buy an item or service at a fixed price within a specified time.

C

Capacity: the legal capacity to understand and appreciate the nature of consent or agreement and the consequences of doing so.

Caveat emptor: Latin maxim for "let the buyer beware." A common warning indicating responsibility for defects or deficiencies in goods or services lies with the purchaser.

Caveat venditor: Latin maxim for "let the seller beware." A common warning indicating the responsibility for defects or deficiencies in goods or services sold lies with the vendor.

Certificate of compliance: a document with vendor's or manufacturer's written assurance that the goods or services delivered fulfill contractual requirements.

Certificate of damage: a document, issued by the receiving office, establishing merchandise received was damaged; includes a precise description of the damage and the number of damaged items.

Certificate of non-collusion: a document signed by a bidder affirming that the bid is made freely, without collusion or consultation with another vendor.

Certificate of origin: a document issued by an authority in the exporting country to certify the point of origin of goods, materials, or labor; used to obtain preferential tariff rates, or, in some states, to obtain title to a vehicle.

Certification of cost and pricing data: contractor certification that to the best of its knowledge and belief, the cost or pricing data submitted was accurate, complete, and current as of a mutually determined date prior to the date of the pricing of any contract, change order or modification.

CFR: Code of Federal Regulations.

Change order: a written alteration to a contract or purchase order, signed by the purchasing authority, in accordance with the terms of the contract, unilaterally directing the contractor to make changes. Compare with modification.

Civil law: refers to that body of law affecting the relationships among individuals. Contract law is an example of civil law.

Clarification: a communication with an offeror for the sole purpose of eliminating minor irregularities or apparent clerical mistakes in a proposal; may be initiated by either offeror or purchaser; does not give offeror an opportunity to revise or modify its proposal, except to the extent the correction of apparent clerical mistakes result in revision.

Clayton Anti-Trust Act (1914): a supplement to the Sherman Anti-Trust Act. Prohibits price discrimination between different buyers, tying arrangements, and certain mergers and acquisitions, where the effect is to substantially lessen competition.

Code of Federal Regulations (CFR): the codification of the general and permanent rules published in the Federal Register by the Executive departments and agencies of the United States Federal Government.

Collusion: a secret agreement, whether expressed or implied, to commit a fraudulent, deceitful, unlawful, or wrongful act. See collusive bidding.

Collusive bidding: the response to invitation to bid by two or more vendors who have secretly agreed to circumvent laws and regulations regarding competitive bidding.

Commercial law: (1) principles and rules by which rights and obligations in commercial transactions are determined, found in the Uniform Commercial Code (2) business law.

Common law: law based on custom and usage, or confirmed by court decisions, rather than law created by the enactment of legislative bodies.

Competitive Negotiation: a method for acquiring goods, services, and construction for public use in which discussions or negotiations may be conducted with responsible offerors who submit proposals in the competitive range.

Conditions of purchase: terms or provisions of a purchase order.

Conflict of interest: an actual or potential situation in which the personal interests of a vendor, employee, or public official are, or appear to be, in conflict with the best interests of the jurisdiction.

Consideration: (1) something of value which is exchanged by two parties and which serves to form or bind a contract; (2) in a contract, an interest, right, profit or benefit accruing to one party while some loss, detriment or responsibility is suffered or undertaken by the other party; (3) that which is given or promised in order to bring a binding contract into existence; (4) a type of mutual commitment that must exist to form an express contract. It means that the person making an offer intends that the person to whom it is made does or promises to do something he or she is not legally obligated to do; and that the person accepting the offer actually does or promises to do something not legally required.

Consignee: a person or company, usually the buyer, to whom goods are to be delivered by the consignor.

Consignment: the goods or property sent via a common carrier from one person to another.

Consignor: a person or company that ships goods to another.

Contract: (1) a legally binding promise, enforceable by law (2) an agreement between parties, with binding legal and moral force, usually exchanging goods or services for money or other consideration (3) all types of agreements, regardless of what they may be called, for the procurement or disposal of supplies, services, or construction.

Contract administration: the management of all actions that must be taken to assure compliance with the terms of the contract after the award of the contract.

Contract carrier: a person or company that is under contract to transport people or goods for individual contract customers only.

Contract ceiling: maximum amount available for payment of cost and fee, which the contractor cannot exceed without approval of the purchasing authority.

Contract date: the date on which all parties accept a contract thereto; the date of award.

Contract file: see contract record.

Contracting officer: a person with the authority to enter into, administer, and/or terminate contracts, and make related determinations and findings.

Contractor: any individual or business having a contract with the governmental body to furnish goods, services, or construction for a certain price.

Contract record: a report providing particulars regarding the orders or releases placed for delivery of goods against a contract so the volume of contract purchases can be determined. Also, contract file.

Conveyance: (1) a formal written instrument, usually called a deed, by which the title or other interest in real property is transferred from one person to another (2) a means of transporting goods or people; a carrier such as a railroad, car, truck, vessel, barge, or airplane.

Cost-Plus Contract: a contract to sell a product or perform work for the price plus a fixed fee or percentage.

Counter-offer: a statement by the person to whom an offer has been made rejecting the offer and creating a new offer.

Covenant: an agreement or promise of two or more parties, in writing, stipulating that something is done, or shall be done, or as to the truth of certain facts. Compare with contract.

Crime: an act for which the law imposes punishment, such as imprisonment or a fine.

D

Damages: compensation for injury or damage to goods, person or property.

Davis-Bacon Act (1931): a federal law requiring all contractors performing federally funded public works construction projects to pay their workers, at a minimum, the prevailing wage rate paid in the area for similar work, as set by the Secretary of Labor.

Debarment: the exclusion of a person or company from participating in a procurement activity for an extended period of time, as specified by law, because of previous illegal or irresponsible action. See suspension.

Default: failure by a party to a contract to comply with contractual requirements.

Delegation of authority: the conferring of authority, by someone who has it, to another person, in order to accomplish a task.

Determination and findings: a legal document prepared by a purchasing agent justifying the decision to take a certain action; includes conclusion, or determination, and the reason, or findings of fact.

Dispute: disagreement between parties to a contract over performance or other contract term requiring administrative action to resolve. See protest, alternative dispute resolution.

E

Electronic commerce (EC): the integration of electronic data interchange, electronic funds transfer, and similar techniques into a comprehensive electronic-based system of procurement functions; could include the posting of IFBs and RFPs on electronic bulletin boards, the receipt of bids via electronic data interchange, notification of award by e-mail, and payment via electronic funds transfer, for example. Also called paperless procurement.

Electronic data interchange (EDI): the electronic transfer and exchange of business documents, such as bid requests, quotations, purchase orders, invoices and payments, from one computer directly to another computer, using established technical standards.

Ethics: (1) the study of right and wrong; (2) the principles of conduct governing the behavior of an individual or a profession. See purchasing ethics.

Evaluation Team: a team established to conduct interviews and negotiations during proposal evaluation for a specific product or service.

Express authority: that authority that is explicitly given in direct language, rather than inferred from conduct. Compare with implied authority.

Express contract: those contracts, either written or oral, in which all of the formal elements for contract creation exist.

Express warranty: an explicit guarantee as to certain facts given by a vendor in direct and appropriate language, rather than left to inference or implication (when one contracting party promises or asserts the existence of certain facts and those promises and assertions become a reason that the other party enters into the contract.)

F

Fair and reasonable: a subjective evaluation of what each party sees as equitable consideration in such areas as terms and conditions, cost or price, assured quality, timeliness, and any other area subject to negotiation.

Fair trade statute: a law, in some states, which allows a manufacturer to set a minimum retail price on his products. Such a law is a violation of federal anti-trust law if it affects interstate commerce.

Federal Acquisition Regulation (FAR): the primary regulation for executive agencies of the federal government regulating their acquisition of goods and services with appropriated funds; issued as Title 48, CFR (Code of Federal Regulations).

Firm: a partnership or business unit of two or more persons not recognized as a corporation.

Firm bid: a bid that binds a bidder until a specified time of expiration.

Force majeure: acts beyond the control of the party in question; acts of God or disruptive conditions for which a vendor or carrier cannot be held responsible.

Full warranty: a warranty as to full performance covering both labor and material; the warrantor must remedy the product within a reasonable time and without charge after notice of a defect or malfunction. See breach of warranty, express warranty, implied warranty, limited warranty.

G

General provisions: the portion of a contract that incorporates the standard clauses and requirements common to all contracts. See terms and conditions. Also called boilerplate.

I

Implied authority: authority that is not defined expressly, but is only determined by inferences and reasonable deductions arising out of the conduct of the principal toward the agent and the agent's actions. Compare with express authority.

Implied-in-fact contract: those contracts in which some of the formal elements of contract formation occur through conduct rather than words.

Implied-in-law contract: certain instances in which the law imposes an obligation on a person to achieve justice even though no true contract exists.

Implied warranty: a warranty or promise arising by operation of law that something which is sold shall be merchantable and fit for the purpose for which the seller has reason to know it is required. A contract to do certain work, such as a building contract, contains within itself an implied warranty that the work shall be done in a professional manner. See breach of warranty, express warranty, full warranty, limited warranty.

Indemnify: (1) to protect against hurt or loss; to exempt from incurred penalties or liabilities; (2) to compensate or pay for damage.

Informality: a minor or immaterial defect in a bid that is a matter of form rather than of substance; a variation of a bid or proposal from the exact requirements of the IFB or RFP, which can be corrected or waived without being prejudicial to other bidders, and has no material affect on the price, quality, quantity or delivery schedule for the goods,

services or construction being procured. See waiver of mistake or informality.

L

Labor-hour contract: a variation of the **time-and-materials contract** differing only in that materials are not supplied by the contractor. Provides for the acquisition of services on the basis of **direct labor hours** at specified fixed **hourly rates**; is generally used when it is not possible to estimate the extent or duration of required work.

Law of agency: provides that a **principal** can appoint an **agent** to act on its behalf, and when the agent acts, it is the principal, and not the agent, that is bound.

Latent defect: an unknown deficiency or imperfection that impairs worth or utility that cannot be readily detected from initial or visual examination of a product, such as the use of materials in manufacturing that do not meet specifications or missing internal parts, or a bug found in software after acceptance.

Legal notice: a public notice required by law. For example, the legal notice required to announce an intent to purchase can be posted in a public place, sent to potential bidders, and/or placed as a formal advertisement in a newspaper or newspapers, depending on the specific legal requirements.

Letter contract: a written, preliminary, contractual instrument that authorizes a contractor to begin the immediate performance of services, or manufacture of supplies; usually followed by a definitive contract document.

Limited warranty: a written warranty which fails to meet one or more of the minimum standards for a full warranty. See breach of warranty, express warranty, implied warranty.

Liquidated damages: a specific sum stated in the contract to be paid by the party who is in default, or who breaches the contract, to the other party in settlement for damages.

Long term contract: a decision to contract with a specified vendor over an extended period of time.

Lowest responsible bidder: the bidder that submitted a responsive bid at the lowest price of all the responsive bids submitted, and whose past performance, reputation, and financial capability is deemed acceptable. See responsive bidder.

M

May: denotes the permissive in a contract clause or specification. Compare with shall.

Mechanic's lien: a lien in favor of those who have performed work or furnished materials for the construction of a building; is attached to the land as well as to the building in order to secure payment.

Merchantable: of commercially acceptable quality; the quality and condition of the item to be sold fulfill the requirements of the purchaser.

Merchantable Quality: a requirement of the Sale of Goods Act that goods must be fit for at least one ordinary purpose; adequate for ordinary use.

Misrepresentation: a false statement of fact made with the intent to deceive or mislead; the failure to present something correctly or adequately.

Mistake in bid: an error in the preparation of a bid which results in an incorrect price or other condition and which might affect the eligibility for the award of a contract.

Mistake of Law: an error, not in the actual facts but in their legal significance, relevance or consequence, for which there is no relief from the Courts.

Mistake of Fact: a misunderstanding of the facts or flawed perception of the real state of affairs, which may be remedied by the Court.

Modification: any written alteration to a provision of any contract accomplished by mutual agreement of the parties to the contract. See supplemental agreement. Compare with amendment, change order.

Monopoly: (1) a situation where there is one seller and many buyers of a product that has no close substitute and where the seller has considerable control over price because of the lack of competition; (2) the exclusive right to carry on a particular activity.

Mutual assent: in contracts, the agreement of each party to all the terms and conditions in the same sense and with the same meaning.

Mutual mistake: where the parties misunderstand each other and each makes a mistake.

N

Negotiate: to communicate or confer with another to reach an agreement or compromise to settle some matter.

Negotiated award: see competitive negotiation.

Negotiation: (1) bargaining process between two or more parties, each with its own view points and objectives, seeking to reach a mutually satisfactory agreement on, or settlement of, a matter of common concern 2: contracting through the use of proposals and discussions, or any contract awarded without the use of sealed bidding.

Negotiation team: see evaluation team.

No bid: a response to an invitation for bid stating that respondent does not wish to submit an offer; functions to prevent suspension from the bidders list for failure to show active interest or submit bids.

Non-competitive negotiations: the process of arriving at an agreement through discussion and compromise when only one source is available to meet the requirement.

Non-conformance: the failure of material or services to meet specified requirements for any characteristic or quality.

Non-responsible bid: a bid from a vendor who does not have the capability to perform fully the contract requirements, or who does not have the integrity and reliability to assure performance. See **responsible bid**.

Non-responsive bid: a bid that does not conform to the mandatory or essential requirements of the invitation for bid. See non-conformance, all or none.

Novation agreement: a legal document executed by the original parties to a contract and a successor to whom interest in the contract has been transferred by one of the parties, which transfers all obligations and rights under the contract to the successor.

O

Offer: a response to a solicitation that, if accepted, would bind the offeror to perform the resulting contract. See bid or sealed bid for the response to an IFB in competitive sealed bidding.

Offeree: the person to whom an offer is made.

Offeror: (1) one who submits a proposal in response to an RFP in competitive negotiation; (2) one who makes an offer in response to a solicitation.

Oligopoly: a market situation in which a few companies control or dominate the market for a product or service. Compare with monopoly.

Open end contract: a contract which sets forth the general provision of supplies and services that may be delivered or performed within a given period of time, but in which quantity and/or duration is not specified. The quantity and delivery are specified with the placement of orders. See blanket order, requirements contract, term contract.

Option: a unilateral right in a contract which the jurisdiction may choose to exercise to purchase additional supplies or services called for in the contract, or to extend the period of performance.

Option to extend: an option in a contract that allows a continuance of the contract for an additional period of time, in accordance with contract terms. Compare with option to renew.

Option to renew: an option in a contract that allows a party to reinstate the contract for an additional term, beyond that stated in original contract, in accordance with contract terms. Compare with option to extend.

Ordinances: generally refer to laws that county and municipal legislative bodies, such as boards of supervisors and city councils, pass applicable to those jurisdictions.

Outsourcing: a version of the make-or-buy decision in which an organization elects to contract for an item or service that was previously provided by in-house resources. Compare with privatization.

P

Parol Evidence Rule: (1) a common law principle that prevents one party to a contract from presenting evidence of agreements occurring before or contemporaneously with creation of a contract to explain that contract. The rule applies if the court determines from the language of the contract that the parties intended the written document to be a final and complete reflection of their agreement; (2) verbal commitments cannot be used to modify or contradict a written contract, although it may be used to clarify an issue.

Past Consideration: consideration for a service already performed, which does not support a promise or create a contract that can be enforced.

Partnership: an agreement under which two or more persons agree to carry on a business, sharing in the profit or losses, but each liable for losses to the extent of his or her personal assets.

Patent: a governmental grant of exclusive rights to the inventor to produce and sell the patented article for a given term.

Payment bond: a bond, which assures payments, as required by law, to all persons supplying labor or material for the completion of work under the contract. Also called labor and material bond.

Performance bond: a bond, executed subsequent to award by a successful bidder, to protect the buyer from loss due to the bidder's inability to complete the contract as agreed; secures the fulfillment of all contract requirements.

Person: any business, individual, union, committee, club, other organization, or group of individuals, other than a governmental unit.

Personal property: (1) tangible or intangible property, other than real property; (2) movable property subject to ownership, with exchangeable value.

Political subdivision: a subdivision of a state, which has been, delegated certain functions of local government. Can include counties, cities, towns, villages, hamlets, boroughs, or parishes.

Pre-award contract review: an audit or survey performed before a contract is awarded to determine the vendor's or contractor's technical, managerial and financial ability to perform under the proposed contract, as well as the establishment of and compliance with appropriate procurement system procedures.

Price adjustment clause: (1) a clause in a contract allowing for adjustment in price in accordance with circumstances arising during the term of the contract. (2) a provision that must be included in contracts requiring contractor certification of cost and pricing data stating that price, including profit or fee, shall be adjusted to exclude any significant sums by which the jurisdiction finds the price was increased because the contractor-furnished cost or pricing data was inaccurate, incomplete, or not current.

Price agreement: a contractual agreement in which a purchaser contracts with a vendor to provide the purchaser's requirements at a predetermined price. See blanket order, open end contract, requirements contract, and term contract.

Prime contract: a contract entered into by the jurisdiction with a business entity for the purpose of obtaining supplies, services or construction items of any kind. Compare with subcontract.

Prime contractor: the business entity that has entered into a contract with the jurisdiction. Compare with subcontractor.

Principal: (1) one who employs an agent; (2) a person who has authorized another to act for him/her.

Privatization: the divestiture of both management and assets of a public function to the private sector in order to change the status of a function formerly performed by the government to one that is privately controlled and owned, including the transfer of real and personal property. Compare with outsourcing.

Privity of contract: the direct contractual relationship existing between parties that allows either party to enforce contractual rights against the other and seek remedy directly from the other party with whom the relationship exists.

Procurement method: method by which goods, services, or material may be acquired, such as blanket orders, call-ups, emergency purchases, standing offers, purchase orders, transfers, competitive bidding, competitive negotiation, inter-governmental loans or cannibalization.

Promissory note: an unconditional written promise to pay a certain sum in money, on demand or at a fixed or determinable future date, either to the bearer or to the order of a designated per

Proposal: in competitive negotiations, the document submitted by the offeror in response to the RFP to be used as the basis for negotiations for entering into a contract.

Proprietary article: an item produced and marketed by a person or persons having the exclusive right to manufacture and sell it. See trade secret, patent.

Protest: a written objection by an interested party to an IFB or RFP solicitation, or to a proposed award or award of a contract, with the intention of receiving a remedial result. See dispute.

Public contract law: that body of law addressing the manner by which governments buy goods, services and construction and administer the resulting contracts.

Public law: that body of law, such as criminal, administrative and constitutional law, that is not civil law. It also is the name given a law that Congress or a state legislature has passed, and that the President or a governor of a state has signed. Public laws are in the form of the bills that the legislative body passed with a specific "public law" number assigned them, such as "Public Law 95-235." Public laws become statutes when they are integrated into existing statutes.

Purchaser: one who acquires goods and services on behalf of an organization.

Purchasing: the act and the function of responsibility for the acquisition of equipment, materials, supplies, and services. In a narrow sense, the term describes the process of buying. In a broader sense, the term describes determining the need, selecting the vendor or contractor, arriving at fair and reasonable price and terms, preparing the contract or purchase order, and following up to ensure timely delivery.

Purchasing Authorities:

Delegated Authority: authority granted through legislation or by an organization's governing body to specific individuals to exercise certain rights within specific terms of reference of guidelines. These individuals may be granted rights to delegate within policy limitations.

Spending Authority: permission granted by an organization to an individual who permits such person to spend funds up to a pre-established limit against an operating or program account or budget. Often spending authority may have restrictions based on certain types of expenditures, such as automobiles, technology over a stated dollar figure, dangerous goods or the like. Spending authority levels, like delegated authority, may vary by position within the organization and by the skill or expertise of the individual holding the respective position. Spending Authority may also be known as Expenditure Authority.

Commitment Authority: permission granted to an individual, usually with "Agent" authority, to commit funds to an external third party. This kind of authority is usually granted to a purchasing agent within the procurement organization who is acting as an agent on behalf of internal users.

Receiving, Certification and Acceptance Authority: permission granted to an individual within an organization who is specifically tasked with the role and responsibility to receive, inspect, test and validate delivery of goods or services and to insure that the goods or services comply with the terms of a contract. Usually, the individual with spending or commitment authority over a transaction does not also hold receiving, certification and acceptance authority over the same transaction.

Payment Authority: permission granted to an individual to disburse funds and make payments (issue checks) against a contract or purchase order when certification and acceptance of the work has been granted. This function is usually performed within the Finance Department of an organization. It is incumbent on the grantor of such authority to review the legality of any disbursements or payments and to exert appropriate financial controls.

Approval in Principle: is applicable to an individual, operation or business unit that proposes a certain program or operation through a business case or other document. The approving authority, usually a Board, Cabinet, Council, Executive Committee or the like, provides authorization in principle to proceed to the next stage of an implementation plan. Additional approval is required before any formal action may be taken. When "Approval in Principle" is granted, usually definite conditions are placed on the program or operations managers that must be met prior to proceeding. In some instances, specific information or policy or procedural amendments or funding allocations must be obtained. Approval in Principle may be granted for a number of reasons and the parties to the transaction must fully comply with each condition. Approval in Principle is sometimes linked to a supplier's ability to meet conditions and requirements imposed by an organization's operational requirements. For example, Approval in Principle to award a long term contract might be contingent upon the supplier providing some pre-determined benefit to the organization. If the supplier meets this obligation, then the contract is advanced; if not, then the contract does not proceed without the approving body being consulted for further directions.

Purchasing agency: any governmental body, other than the chief procurement officer, which is authorized to enter into contracts.

Purchasing ethics: moral principles or code to be respected and followed by procurement personnel. Prohibits breach of the public trust by any attempt to realize personal gain by a public employee through conduct inconsistent with the proper discharge of the employee's duties.

Purchasing officer: an official in charge of the procurement operation, from the determination of needs to follow up, to ensure timely delivery.

Q

Qualified bidder: a bidder determined by the procurement organization to meet the minimum set standards of business competence, reputation, financial ability, and product quality for placement on the bidders list. See responsible bidder.

R

Real estate: see real property.

Real property: (1) land and its permanently affixed buildings or structures; (2) any property which is not personal property. Also, real estate.

Regulation: a statement by a governmental body to implement, interpret, or prescribe law or policy, or to describe organization, procedure, or practice, often promulgated in accordance with an administrative procedures act. See rules and regulations.

Renegotiation: deliberation, discussion, or conference to change or amend the terms of an existing agreement.

Request for proposal (RFP): all documents, whether attached or incorporated by reference, utilized for soliciting competitive proposals

Request for quotation (RFQ): an informal solicitation or request for information, where oral or written quotes are obtained from vendors, without formal advertising or receipt of sealed bids. Used only where statutes do not require formal sealed bids, such as small or emergency purchases, but price competition is desired.

Requirements contract: a form of indefinite delivery/indefinite quantity contract where all actual purchase requirements for specific supplies or services during the contract period are filled by the selected vendor, with deliveries to be scheduled by placing orders with the vendor.

Responsible bidder or offeror: a bidder or offeror who has the capability in all respects to perform fully the contract requirements, and the experience, integrity, perseverance, reliability, capacity, facilities, equipment, and credit which will assure good faith performance. Also, responsible offeror.

Responsive bidder: a vendor who has submitted a bid which conforms in all material respects to the requirements stated in the IFB. See informality.

Robinson-Patman Act: a 1936 amendment to the Clayton Anti-Trust Act. Intended to eliminate discriminatory and predatory pricing practices; states a vendor can only offer differing prices to customers if the price is cost justified or to meet competition.

Rules and regulations: governing precepts and procedures, made by an administrative body or agency under legislative authority, that sometimes have the force and effect of law.

Rules of Interpretation: refers to a set of well-established principles in common law that courts use to interpret the meaning of contracts.

S

Schedule contract: a contract that consolidates agency requirements by pre-establishing a bid opening date and requiring using agencies to submit requirements by a specified time. Also called scheduled purchase. Compare with blanket order, systems contract, term contract.

Sealed bid: a bid submitted in response to an invitation for bid. Bid is submitted in a sealed envelope to prevent dissemination of its contents before the deadline for the submission of all bids. Compare with proposal.

Service contract: (1) an agreement calling for a contractor's time and effort rather than for a product; (2) an agreement to provide either professional services or general services such as landscaping and back hoeing.

Shall: denotes the imperative in contract clauses or specifications. Compare with may.

Sherman Anti-Trust Act (1890): primary federal anti-trust law. Prohibits contracts, conspiracies, or combinations which act in restraint of trade, or attempt to monopolize.

Single source procurement: a contract for the purchase of goods and services entered into after soliciting and negotiating only with one source, usually because of the technology required or uniqueness of the service provided. See sole source procurement.

Sole source procurement: only one vendor possesses the unique and singularly available capability to meet the requirement of the solicitation, such as technical qualifications, ability to deliver at a particular time, or services from a public utility

Solicitation: a request for bids to provide supplies, services, or construction items. See invitation for bids, request for proposals.

Sovereign immunity: the principle which absolves the country, state, county, city from responding in damages for past injuries to another party.

Standard contract: a contract in a pre-established format containing certain pre-determined terms and conditions.

Statutes: laws passed by Congress or a state legislature and signed by the President or the governor of a state, respectively, that are codified in volumes called "codes" according to subject matter.

Subcontract: a contract with another business entity entered into by a prime contractor or another subcontractor to obtain supplies, services, or construction items of any kind under a prime contract.

Subcontractor: a business entity holding a subcontract with a prime contractor.

Subrogation: the substitution of one person in place of another, whether as a creditor or as the possessor of any lawful right, so the substituted person may succeed to the rights, remedies, or procedures of the original person.

Supplemental agreement: any contract addendum or modification accomplished by the mutual action of both parties.

Surety: an individual or corporation legally liable for the debt, default, or failure of a principal to satisfy the obligations of a contract.

Suspension: the temporary exclusion of a person or company from participating in a procurement activity because of previous illegal or irresponsible action. Compare with debarment.

Systems contract: a contract that establishes a source of supply for a specified period for a large group or related family of materials, a method of procurement designed to improve reordering of materials used repeatedly. Contract usually includes a catalog with a list and description of items that can be purchased. Compare with blanket order, schedule contract, term contract.

T

Tender: In Canada, an offer (written/verbal/electronic) that is submitted in response to an invitation from a prospective client. A tender is considered to be valid if it meets all of the requirements stipulated in the invitation to tender.

Term contract: a **contract** in which a source of supply is established for a specified period of time for specified services or supplies; usually characterized by an estimated or definite minimum quantity, with the possibility of additional requirements beyond the minimum, all at a predetermined unit price. See requirements contract. Compare with schedule contract, systems contract, blanket order, open-end contract.

Termination for convenience: action by which the procurement entity, in accordance with contract provisions, unilaterally cancels all or part of the contract work for the best interest of the jurisdiction, and with no reflection on the contractor's performance.

Termination for default: action by which the procurement entity, in accordance with contract provisions, unilaterally cancels all or part of the contract work due to the contractor's failure to perform in accordance with the terms of the contract.

Terms and conditions (Ts and Cs): (US)(CN) all language in a contract, including applicable standard clauses and special provisions; the rules under which all bids must be submitted, and the stipulations, applicable to most contracts, often published by procurement authorities for the information of all potential bidders. See boilerplate, trade terms.

Terms of contract: stipulations made in contracts.

Terms of payment: the methods of payment under a sales contract, such as cash payment or open account purchase.

Time-and-materials contract (T&M): a contract which provides for the acquisition of supplies or services on the basis of direct labor hours at specified, fixed, hourly rates that include wages, overhead, profit, and general and administrative expenses, and materials at cost. See labor-hour contract.

Title: the instrument or document whereby ownership of property is established.

Tort: a wrong, other than a breach of contract, such that the law permits compensation for damages.

Trade secret: any aspect of a business or its operations which is known only to the manufacturer. See proprietary article.

Trade terms: the broadest classification applicable to purchase transactions with reference to understandings between buyer and vendor, either as to the meanings of certain abbreviations, words, or phrases, or to customs applicable to transactions as established by agreement between the parties, or as established by general usage. See terms and conditions.

Truth in Negotiations Act (TINA): established the requirement that for certain Federal contracts, contractors must submit cost or pricing data and must certify that, to the best of the contractor's knowledge and belief, the cost or pricing data submitted is current, accurate and complete.

Ts and Cs: see terms and conditions.

U

U.C.C: see **Uniform Commercial Code.**

Uniform Commercial Code (U.C.C): one of the uniform laws drafted by the National Conference of Commissioners on Uniform State Laws to simplify, clarify and modernize the law governing commercial transactions, and to make uniform the laws among the various jurisdictions; defines the rights and duties of parties in commercial situations and conforms the rules to modern commercial usages.

Unilateral: one-sided.

V

Vendor: one who sells goods or services; a supplier.

Vendor's lien: a seller's right to retain possession of property until payment for the property is received.

Void: without legal effect, unenforceable.

W - X - Y - Z

Waiver of bids: a process, usually statutory, whereby a government procurement office may procure items without formal bidding procedures because of uniqueness of circumstances related to that procurement action.

Waiver of mistake or informality: the act of disregarding minor informalities, errors, or technical nonconformities in the bid which will not adversely affect the competition or prejudice one bidder in favor of another.

Warranty: the representation, either expressed or implied, that a certain fact regarding the subject matter of a contract is presently true or will be true; a promise that certain facts are truly as they are represented to be and that they will remain so, subject to any specified limitation.

Index

About the Authors

Michael Flynn, Esq. is a professor of law at the Nova Southeastern University Shepard Broad Law Center in Fort Lauderdale, FL. Professor Flynn received his undergraduate, magna cum laude, and his law degree, cum laude, from Gonzaga University in Washington. He was a trial lawyer and litigator in private practice and the Assistant Attorney General in the Washington State Attorney General's Office. He served as the Chief of the Consumer Protection and Antitrust Division of the Washington State Attorney General's Office in Eastern Washington. He has taught at the University of Washington, the University of Miami, and Stanford University; has authored over 35 articles and has conducted or presented at seminars and conferences for various professional groups.

Kirk W. Buffington, CPPO, C.P.M., is the Director, Procurement Services for the City of Fort Lauderdale, Florida. Prior to public service, he was employed in the private sector. Mr. Buffington holds a Bachelors Degree from Florida State University and earned his Masters of Business Administration Degree from Webster University. A strong supporter of the profession, Mr. Buffington has served numerous positions of leadership in procurement associations on the local and National level. He sits on the NIGP Board of Directors. By invitation, Mr. Buffington presented a paper at the first International Symposium on Supply and Public Procurement in Budapest, Hungary in 2003. Mr. Buffington is a well-known speaker on government eProcurement topics.

Other books published by the
National Institute of Governmental Purchasing, Inc. (NIGP):

INTRODUCTION TO PUBLIC PROCUREMENT

CONTRACT ADMINISTRATION

DEVELOPING AND MANAGING REQUESTS FOR PROPOSALS IN THE PUBLIC SECTOR

SOURCING IN THE PUBLIC SECTOR

STRATEGIC PROCUREMENT PLANNING IN THE PUBLIC SECTOR

FUNDAMENTALS OF LEADERSHIP AND MANAGEMENT IN PUBLIC PROCUREMENT

ALTERNATIVE DISPUTE RESOLUTION

CONTRACTING FOR PUBLIC SECTOR SERVICES

CAPITAL ACQUISITIONS

LOGISTICS AND TRANSPORTATION

RISK MANAGEMENT IN PUBLIC CONTRACTING

WAREHOUSING AND INVENTORY CONTROL

CONTRACTING FOR CONSTRUCTION SERVICES